MINNESOTA/WISCONSIN
TRAVEL+SMART™ TRIP PLANNER

MINNESOTA WISCONSIN

TRAVEL◆SMART™ TRIP PLANNER

Alice M. Vollmar

John Muir Publications
Santa Fe, New Mexico

John Muir Publications, P.O. Box 613, Santa Fe, New Mexico 87504
Copyright © 1996 by John Muir Pulications
Cover and maps © 1996 by John Muir Publications
All rights reserved.

Printed in the United States of America.
First printing November 1996.

ISSN 1088-0720
⁏ ISBN 1-56261-298-0

Cover photo: Leo de Wys, Inc./Grace Schaub
Back cover photos: © Minnesota Office of Tourism,
Unicorn Stock Photos/Phyllis Kedl
Maps: American Custom Maps—Albuquerque, NM USA
Editors: Dianna Delling, Peggy Schaefer, Chris Hayhurst, Krista Lyons-Gould
Design: Linda Braun and Janine Lehmann
Typesetting: John Ericksen
Production: Marie Vigil, Nikki Rooker
Graphics Coordination: Joanne Jakub
Printing: Publishers Press

Distributed to the book trade by
Publishers Group West
Emeryville, California

HOW TO USE THIS BOOK

This *Minnesota/Wisconsin Travel+Smart Trip Planner* is organized in 16 destination chapters, each covering the best sights and activities, restaurants, and lodging available in that specific destination. Thanks to thorough research and experience, the author is able to bring you only the best options, saving you time and money in your travels. The chapters are presented in geographic sequence so you can plan and follow an easy route from one destination to the next. If you were to visit each destination in chapter order, you'd enjoy a complete tour of the best of Minnesota and Wisconsin.

Each chapter contains:
• User-friendly maps of the area, showing all recommended sights, restaurants, and accommodations.

• "A Perfect Day" description—how the author would spend her time if she had just one day in that destination.

• Sightseeing highlights, each rated by degree of importance: ✪✪✪ Don't miss; ✪✪ Try hard to see; ✪ See if you have time; and No stars—Worth knowing about.

• Selected restaurant, lodging, and camping recommendations to suit a variety of budgets.

• Helpful hints, fitness and recreation ideas, insights, and helpful tidbits of information to enhance your trip.

The Importance of Planning. Developing an itinerary is the best way to get the most satisfaction from your travels, and this guidebook makes it easy. First, read through the book and choose the places you'd most like to visit. Then, study the color map on the inside cover flap and the mileage chart (page 12) to determine which ones you can realistically see in the time you have available and at the travel pace you prefer. Using the Planning Map (pages 10–11), map out your route. Finally, use the lodging recommendations to select your accommodations.

Some Suggested Itineraries. To get you started, six itineraries of varying lengths and based on specific interests follow. *Happy travels!*

SUGGESTED ITINERARIES

With the *Minnesota/Wisconsin Travel✦Smart Trip Planner* you can plan a trip of any length—a one-day excursion, a getaway weekend, or a three-week vacation—around any special interest. To get you started, the following pages contain six suggested itineraries geared toward a variety of interests. For more information, refer to the chapters listed—chapter names are bolded and chapter numbers appear inside black bullets. You can follow a suggested itinerary in its entirety, or shorten, lengthen, or combine parts of each, depending on your starting and ending points.

Discuss alternative routes and schedules with your travel companions—it's a great way to have fun, even before you leave home. And remember: don't hesitate to change your itinerary once you're on the road. Careful study and planning ahead of time will help you make informed decisions as you go, but spontaneity is the extra ingredient that will make your trip memorable.

© Minnesota Office of Tourism

Best of the Region in One to Three Weeks

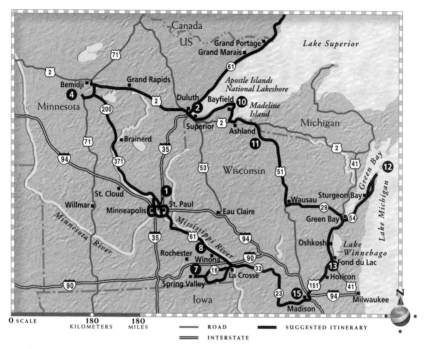

Following this "best of the region" itinerary will introduce you to the diversity of destinations within Minnesota and Wisconsin, including cities, wilderness areas, and lakes.

Week One:
- ❶ **Twin Cities** (historic sites, museums, parks)
- ❹ **The North Woods Lakes Region** (Mississippi River Headwaters, resorts)
- ❷ **Duluth and Minnesota's North Shore** (BWCA wilderness, Gunflint Trail, museums, scenic drives)

Week Two:
- ❿ **Bayfield and Madeline Island** (explore by water or by foot, Madeline Island Historical Museum)
- ⓫ **Wisconsin's North Woods** (hiking trails)
- ⓬ **Wisconsin's Door Peninsula** (bed and breakfasts, hiking, state parks)

Week Three:
- ⓭ **Lake Winnebago, Horicon Marsh, and the Kettle Moraine** (glacial moraine country, waterfowl habitat)
- ⓯ **Madison** (state capitol, University of Wisconsin arboretum)
- ❼ **Minnesota's Bluff County** (scenic drives, hiking and biking)
- ❽ **Great River Road** (historic hotels)

Nature Lover's Tour

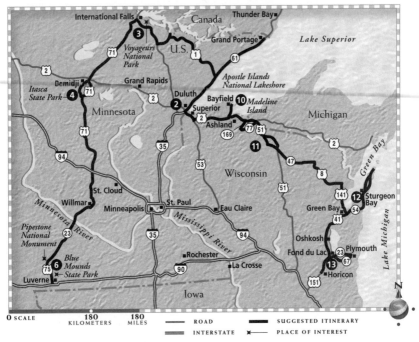

Nature and the outdoors take priority on this five- to 14-day route, which includes wilderness areas and lots of state parks.

❻ The Prairie Lands of Minnesota (Blue Mounds State Park, hiking, Pipestone National Monument)

❹ The North Woods Lakes of Minnesota (hiking, Itasca State Park, Wilderness Drive)

❸ Minnesota's Northern Wilderness Region (Voyageurs National Park)

❷ Duluth and Minnesota's North Shore (state parks, Gunflint Trail, Superior National Hiking Trail)

❿ Bayfield and Madeline Island (Big Bay State Park, Long Island)

⓫ Wisconsin's North Woods (Northern Highland-American Legion State Forest)

⓬ Wisconsin's Door Peninsula (Newport and Whitefish Dunes State Parks)

⓭ Lake Winnebago, Horicon Marsh, and the Kettle Moraine (hiking trails, Ice Age Visitor Center, Horicon Marsh Wildlife Area, Horicon National Wildlife Refuge)

Time needed: 2 weeks

The Water Lover's Tour

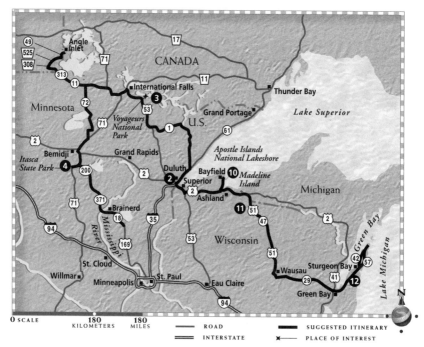

This five- to 14-day itinerary takes you to some of the best woods-and-water playgrounds that the Northern Heartland has to offer. The region's watery bounty includes the Mississippi River, nearly 37,000 lakes, two Great Lakes, and clear trout streams.

❹ The North Woods Lakes of Minnesota (Mississippi Headwaters, sand beaches)

❸ Minnesota's Northern Wilderness Region (BWCA, Lake of the Woods, Voyageurs National Park)

❷ Duluth and Minnesota's North Shore (Canal Park's Marine Museum, Lake Superior)

❿ Bayfield and Madeline Island (Apostle Islands-hopping, canoeing, kayaking, sailing, sea caves)

⓫ Wisconsin's North Woods (lakes of the Northern Highland-American Legion State Forest)

⓬ Wisconsin's Door Peninsula (fishing, maritime museums)

Time needed: 2 weeks

Country Backroads Tour

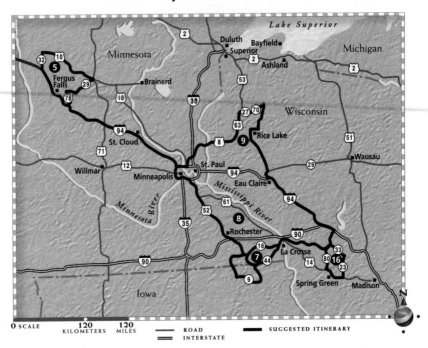

Follow this five- to 14-day itinerary to explore the lesser-known attractions in Minnesota and Wisconsin, wandering unmarked roads and making your own discoveries as you go.

❺ Minnesota's Otter Tail Country (lakes, lush hardwood forests, small towns)

❼ Minnesota's Bluff Country (County Road 4)

❽ The Great River Road (Apple Blossom Drive)

⑯ Wisconsin's Hidden Valleys Region (Highway 33—Reedsburg to La Crosse)

❾ Indianhead Country (Rice Lake, Birchwood, Stone Lake, Spooner, Shell Lake, Barronett, Cumberland—country potteries, farms selling honey and produce, wood carvers' shops/studios, and antique shops)

Time needed: 2 weeks

The Arts and Culture Tour

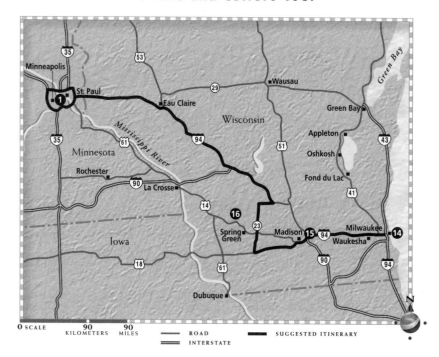

0 SCALE   90 KILOMETERS   90 MILES   ■■■■ ROAD   ■■■■ SUGGESTED ITINERARY
                                         ══ INTERSTATE

This five- to 14-day itinerary features artistic and cultural destinations in the
Twin Cities, legendary for their support of the arts, as well as in Milwaukee, a
city with a rich ethnic cultural heritage.

❶ **The Twin Cities** (Guthrie Theater, Institute of Art, Mixed Blood
Theater, Walker Art Center, Weisman Museum; Minnesota Orchestra,
Saint Paul Chamber Orchestra; Broadway productions, gallery shows,
dance, literary readings, opera; Saint Paul's Summit Avenue Victorian
architecture)

⓰ **The Hidden Valleys of Southwestern Wisconsin** (American Players
Theatre, Frank Lloyd Wright's Taliesin and Hillside School, Little
Norway)

⓯ **Madison** (Canterbury Bookstore and Coffee House, Elvehjem Museum of
Art, Frank Lloyd Wright's First Unitarian Society Meeting House,
Madison Art Center, Madison Repertory Theatre, Wisconsin State
Historical Museum)

⓮ **Milwaukee** (Charles Allis Art Museum, churches, ethnic festivals, ma
sions, Milwaukee Art Museum/War Memorial Building, walking tours)

Time needed: 2 weeks

The Family Fun Tour

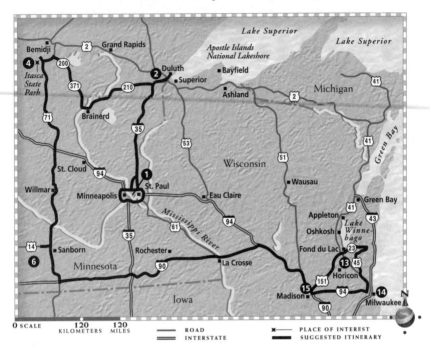

The family fun tour focuses on family-style activities, children's museums, a circus museum, and train rides—with separate trips in each state.

Minnesota

❶ Twin Cities (Children's Theatre Company, Como Park Zoo and Conservatory, Historic Fort Snelling, Minnesota Children's Museum, Minnesota Zoo, Science Museum of Minnesota, Valleyfair Amusement Park)

❷ Duluth (Canal Park, Lake Superior Museum of Transportation and Children's Museum, scenic train rides)

❹ North Woods Lakes of Minnesota (family activities, Itasca State Park, water sports)

❻ Prairie Lands (Laura Ingalls Wilder Dugout Site and Museum, sod houses)

Wisconsin

❶❺ Madison (Henry Vilas Park Zoo, Madison Children's Museum, Baraboo Circus Museum, North Freedom's train rides, Wisconsin Dells)

❶❹ Milwaukee (Milwaukee County Zoo, Milwaukee Public Museum, Old World Wisconsin)

❶❸ Lake Winnebago, Horicon Marsh, and the Kettle Moraine (Fond du Lac's, Galloway House and Village, marsh tours, walking trails)

Time needed: 2 weeks

USING THE PLANNING MAP

An important aspect of itinerary planning is determining your mode of transportation and the route you will follow as you travel from destination to destination. The Planning Map on the following pages will allow you to do just that.

First, read through the destination chapters carefully and note the sights that interest you. Then photocopy the Planning Map so you can try out several different routes that will take you to these destinations. (The mileage chart that follows will allow you to calculate your travel distances.) Decide where you will be starting your tour of Minnesota and Wisconsin. Will you fly into the Twin Cities, Milwaukee, or Madison, or will you start from somewhere in between? Will you be driving from place to place or flying into major transportation hubs and renting a car for day trips? The answers to these questions will form the basis for your travel route design.

Once you have a firm idea of where your travels will take you, copy your route onto one of the additional Planning Maps in the Appendix. You won't have to worry about where your map is, and the information you need on each destination will always be close at hand.

Planning Map: Minnesota/Wisconsin

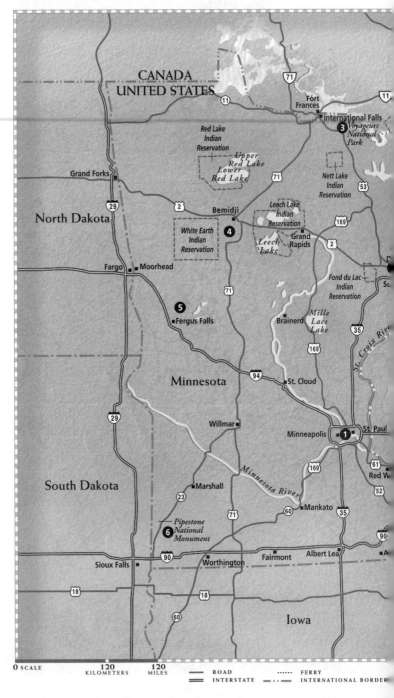

CANADA
UNITED STATES

Fort Frances

International Falls ❸ Voyageurs National Park

Red Lake Indian Reservation

Upper Red Lake
Lower Red Lake

Nett Lake Indian Reservation

Grand Forks

Bemidji

Leech Lake Indian Reservation

North Dakota

White Earth Indian Reservation ❹

Leech Lake

Grand Rapids

Fargo Moorhead

Fond du Lac Indian Reservation

❺ Fergus Falls

Brainerd

Mille Lacs Lake

Minnesota

St. Cloud

Willmar

Minneapolis ❶ St. Paul

Red W

South Dakota

Marshall

Minnesota River

Mankato

❻ Pipestone National Monument

Sioux Falls

Worthington

Fairmont

Albert Lea

Iowa

St. Croix River

0 SCALE | 120 KILOMETERS | 120 MILES

ROAD   FERRY
INTERSTATE   INTERNATIONAL BORDER

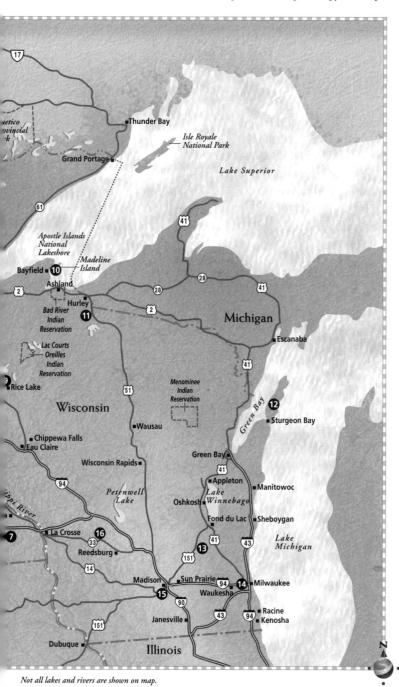

Not all lakes and rivers are shown on map.

MINNESOTA/WISCONSIN MILEAGE CHART

	Minneapolis	Saint Paul	Luverne	Fergus Falls	Bemidji	Ely	Duluth	Red Wing	Lanesboro	Bayfield	Rice Lake	Minocqua	Spring Green	Madison	Milwaukee	Fond du Lac	Oshkosh
Saint Paul	10																
Luverne	211	212															
Fergus Falls	186	186	216														
Bemidji	220	230	353	137													
Ely	242	238	453	292	173												
Duluth	151	147	310	212	145	108											
Red Wing	56	46	255	242	276	285	194										
Lanesboro	124	116	219	310	344	354	263	93									
Bayfield	217	207	397	299	232	195	87	222	309								
Rice Lake	111	101	322	297	239	202	94	101	188	121							
Minocqua	237	227	448	437	308	271	163	233	320	119	140						
Spring Green	258	248	363	428	460	423	315	180	144	360	221	241					
Madison	257	247	408	473	461	424	316	225	189	324	222	205	45				
Milwaukee	324	314	475	540	528	491	383	292	256	391	289	272	112	67			
Fond du Lac	300	290	439	496	500	463	368	270	220	324	261	205	114	69	73		
Oshkosh	284	274	423	480	484	447	352	254	204	308	245	189	130	85	89	16	
Sturgeon Bay	317	307	513	503	515	478	370	307	294	326	275	207	220	175	141	106	90

WHY VISIT MINNESOTA AND WISCONSIN?

Sailboats and fishing vessels ride the waves of two Great Lakes; river-boat paddle wheels churn on the Mississippi River. Bright blue and orange *dalahast* horses decorate doors and mailboxes in a Swedish town, while not far away, onion domes and steeples punctuate a city skyline. Native American culture and music in one region give way to foaming beer steins and apple orchards in another. In the North Woods, black bears look for blueberries and red-eyed loons dive in pristine lakes.

This is the Midwest's Northern Heartland: Minnesota and Wisconsin. Although similar in settlement and geological history, the states are distinct in what they offer visitors and residents. Each resists stereotype with unexpectedly diverse terrain and ethnicity. I encourage travelers to come and be surprised.

This guide highlights several dozen state parks, a handful of national parks and monuments, two state capitals, a wealth of historic sites, art museums both venerable and avant-garde, and a renowned repertory theater. It will take you to popular attractions and those little known. You can hike a solitary North Shore wilderness trail, sip champagne with the Twin Cities' glitterati before an Ordway Theatre musical, and eat blueberry or wild-rice pancakes in a cozy small-town café. Travelers can use the guide to immerse themselves in several destinations or to spend a few days here, a few days there.

Whichever approach you take, prepare to be welcomed by friendly and warm-hearted people, clean air, and an inspiring landscape that will keep you coming back.

HISTORY AND CULTURES

With the melting of glaciers that covered most of this region some 10,000 years ago came the first travelers. These nomadic bands of Asiatic hunters and gatherers crossed the Bering Strait on a land bridge, following herds of tusked mammoths and other big game. Subsequently, a series of cultures arose and declined in what are now Minnesota and Wisconsin. Among them were a copper culture and a culture of mound-builders who built various burial and ceremonial mounds into this landscape—from round, conical, and linear mounds to effigy mounds shaped like birds, bears, snakes, and other animals. Some of these mounds remain today. Grand Mound, on Rainy Lake in northern Minnesota, is the Upper Mississippi region's largest; other mounds can be seen at Saint Paul's Indian Mounds Park and Lizard Mound State Park in Wisconsin.

By the 1600s, Wisconsin's Native American tribes included the Winnebago, eastern Dakota (Sioux), Ojibwa (Chippewa), Fox, Sauk, and Menominee. The Dakota tribe occupied all of Minnesota, with a cultural center near Mille Lacs Lake, until they were forced out of the North Woods and onto the plains by the Ojibwa. French explorers, among them Jean Nicolet, and French fur traders established trade relations with the Native American tribes and set up trading posts. After lively competition, the French eventually capitulated to rival British fur traders, whose posts dominated the region until the War of 1812.

Growing United States government interest in the region's resources—particularly the lumber—changed Native American life forever. Treaties in the region relinquished vast tracts of land to the government. Lieutenant Zebulon Pike came upriver from St. Louis in 1805 and made a down payment to the Dakota tribe—$200 and 60 gallons of whiskey—to buy the land that is now Minneapolis and Saint Paul, with the promise of a "fair amount" of payment in the future. (The fair amount was $2,000, paid 14 years later.) Here, on the bluffs overlooking the Minnesota and Mississippi Rivers' confluence, Fort Snelling was established in 1819. This outpost of civilization in the wilderness remained active until 1849, nine years before Minnesota became a state. Wisconsin's statehood came earlier, in 1848. Native American peoples were relegated to reservations, and the Dakota were exiled from Minnesota for a number of years following the U.S.-Dakota Conflict of 1862, a futile attempt by the desperate and ill-treated Dakota to reclaim their land.

Logging boomed in the region, creating wealthy lumber barons. Discovery of iron in Minnesota and lead in Wisconsin spawned mining operations and even more wealth. By 1830, 5,000 Wisconsin miners had dug out close to 14 million tons of lead, which was used primarily to make ammunition and lead-based paint. In the 1890s, immigrant laborers by the thousands worked in Minnesota's Mesabi, Cayuna, and Vermilion iron ranges.

The first settlers in the region were New England businessmen and entrepreneurs, followed by European immigrants, predominantly Germans, Swedes, and Norwegians. Soon plows turned prairies and logged-out lands into farms, while land unsuited for growing crops gave way to Wisconsin's dairy industry.

These first settlers arrived by water and overland routes. When railroads reached the region, settlement exploded. Adding diversity to the dominant German-Scandinavian culture were immigrants of varying nationalities—Irish, French Canadians, Czechs, Dutch, Flemish, Polish, Danish, Welsh, Swiss, and Luxembourgers. Between 1890 and 1920, Finns, Ukrainians, Yugoslavs, Italians, Bulgarians, Poles, Hungarians, and others settled here. Beginning in 1979, a new wave of immigration brought Southeast Asians to Minnesota and Wisconsin, this time by air, and both states presently record a growing Hispanic population. Even with all this diversity, the Scandinavian/German ethnic personalities of these neighboring states remain predominant. In Minnesota, the more reserved Swedish/Norwegian demeanor tempers the peppery-sausage-making, beer-brewing Germanic heritage; in Wisconsin, it's the other way around.

In recent times, the region's technology and service industries seem far removed from the era of free-roaming Native Americans, explorers, missionaries, voyageurs, and the showy Victorian excesses of wealthy lumber, mining, and railroad barons. But yesterday is not gone. The French and Native American influences of the past have a contemporary presence in the names of cities, lakes, and streets—Menomonie, Fond du Lac, Grand Marais, Minneapolis, Milwaukee, Nicollet and Hennepin Avenues, Mille Lacs Lake, and Lake Winnebago.

THE ARTS

The arts flourish in these two states. (No surprise if you know that Minnesota's historical society predates its statehood.) Architecture from the 1800s is well preserved and displayed in the cities of Milwaukee and Saint Paul. There are also important art deco buildings, many examples of the Prairie School's design influence, and numerous structures created by Wisconsin-born Frank Lloyd Wright.

Artist Georgia O'Keeffe was born in Wisconsin, and Minnesota-born sculptor James Earle Fraser created the buffalo nickel's Indian head. Today you'll find art museums and galleries in nearly every community, a strong regional arts representation, and active arts colonies.

Ethnic dance groups and musicians perform regularly in Minnesota and Wisconsin, and exceptional live theater thrives. Wisconsin's American Players Theatre draws sell-out crowds for Shakespearean

plays in a rural amphitheater; Minnesota's Guthrie Theater and
Children's Theatre Company enjoy nationwide recognition. The larger
cities have fine symphonies and chamber orchestras, along with
respected ballet and modern dance companies. The Twin Cities support
an active jazz scene. Literary notables with regional ties include F. Scott
Fitzgerald, Thornton Wilder, Laura Ingalls Wilder, and contemporary
poet Robert Bly.

CUISINE

Not long ago, dining out yielded no surprises in Minnesota and
Wisconsin. Tastes ran to potatoes and meat, with vegetables more
or less an apologetic afterthought.

But things are changing. Chefs have begun to create inventive
dishes, often using the region's own produce and meats. Wild rice, for
example, a Native American staple harvested here, is enjoying increas-
ing popularity on restaurant menus. You'll find the dark, glossy grain in
soups, crusty breads, and pancakes, and as a delightfully seasoned side
dish for meats.

Ethnic restaurants are prevalent, especially in the cities—from the
fine German restaurants of Milwaukee to the burgeoning Southeast
Asian and East Indian eateries of the Twin Cities. French cuisine also
has a presence. And, of course, the region's German and Scandinavian
heritage means German bratwurst and beer, Norwegian *lefse*, Danish
kringle, and Swedish *pepparkakor.*

With thousands of lakes close at hand, freshly caught walleye and
lake trout appear on many northern resort menus. In dairy-rich
Wisconsin, there's cheese—and more cheese. Stop to nibble samples at
the plentiful cheese houses, and you'll walk out with a tangy wedge of
cheddar or a mellow Brie. The state's fine meat markets are noted for
specialty sausages and cured meats. Breweries and a few wineries offer
tours and tasting sessions.

FLORA AND FAUNA

Trees covered all but the southern third or so of the Minnesota/
Wisconsin region until the lumber industry moved in. Within
decades, almost all the region's virgin timber had been cut. On the
heels of the lumbermen came the farmers, but when much of the
deforested land proved less than ideal for farming, reforestation was

initiated in both Wisconsin and Minnesota, creating vast second-growth forests. Northernmost Minnesota's remote Boundary Waters Canoe Area (BWCA) contains one of the last large tracts of virgin forest in the area. Here, a boreal forest of jack pine, spruce, aspen, and paper birch overlaps a Laurentian forest of white and red pine and hardwoods, including maple.

Pine forest makes up most of the region's legendary North Woods, giving way to hardwood forest further south—the Big Woods of Laura Ingalls Wilder fame. Here, oak, black walnut, butternut, maple, and elm trees offer summer shade and fall color similar to that of New England.

Most of the lush, tall-grass prairie lands in the southern region of both states was once coveted by farmers. Eventually, more than 90 percent of the prairie was plowed, the genesis of the southern half of the region's panorama of farm buildings flanked by rolling fields of grain, beans, and alfalfa. The few patches of remaining virgin prairie are protected; some land is being returned to prairie, and a portion of the forest lands are preserved in state and national parks and forests. Minnesota has close to 70 state parks, one national park, and two national monuments; Wisconsin counts 45 state parks, five official recreation areas, and ten state forests.

In parks and preserves, restored prairies, and along roadsides, you'll encounter wildflowers from white trillium to fall goldenrod. Morel mushroom hunters flock to the woods in spring, and wildflower lovers enjoy bright pink phlox and lavender wild asters, sunny marsh marigolds, and pink-and-white showy lady's slippers, bee balm, columbine, and wood violets.

You may come face to face with a moose lunching on tender willow shoots in a wetland, a white-tailed deer grazing in a meadow at dusk, or a muskrat swimming near a lake shore. Other resident critters include fox, beaver, chipmunk, porcupine, bear, elk, and timber wolves. Both city and country birds keep up constant chatter—cardinals, goldfinches, scarlet tanagers, warblers, nuthatches, bluebirds, woodpeckers, swallows, and more. I've seen large red-crested pileated woodpeckers, noisy as pneumatic drills and spewing sawdust, in remote woods and twice on residential streets in Minneapolis. Wisconsin alone claims more than 330 native bird species.

Abundant water attracts a hefty population of Canadian geese, ducks, herons, and other waterfowl, as it does hunters and fishers. The region has long been the place to come for unequaled walleye, muskie, trout, bass, and crappie fishing. In the Great Lakes, anglers catch herring, lake trout, whitefish, salmon, and perch. It's estimated that half of Minnesota's population goes fishing.

THE LAY OF THE LAND

I ce Age glaciation has much to do with the region's topography: sparkling blue lakes, powerful rivers including the Mississippi, and an extraordinary landscape that includes incredibly fertile farmland based on glacial debris.

Around 75,000 years ago the last southward reach of glacial ice—called the Wisconsin glaciation—extended lobes of ice over all but Minnesota's southeastern corner and Wisconsin's southwestern corner. Devoid of deposits of glacial till and glacial scouring, this region is a world apart—a scenic domain of limestone bluffs and coulees with caves and rushing streams where winding country roads now lead to quaint villages such as Harmony, Choice, Arcadia, and Hillsboro.

As the glacier moved southward over most of the Northern Heartland, it gouged out rocky lake beds, leveled mountains, and occasionally deposited huge boulders called erratics. You'll come across one now and then—a huge mass of rock sitting atop a hill. The glacier also pushed sedimentary, sandstone, dolomite, and limestone layers ahead of it, forming terminal moraines that now mark the glacier's southernmost edge. Moraines snake through Minnesota and Wisconsin as an irregular belt of hillocks and basins with numerous lakes—scenic and also resistant to farming. Upon the glacier's retreat, huge deposits of sand and gravel formed drumlins (long sculpted hills) and eskers (deposits of sand delineating the course of rivers that ran beneath the glacial ice). You can learn about many glaciation phenomena in Wisconsin's Kettle Moraine State Park Northern Unit, one of nine Wisconsin units on the Ice Age Trail, a National Scenic Trail system that follows the glacier's terminal moraine edge.

With the gradual warming of the climate some 13,000 years ago, glacial meltwater filled lake beds and huge chunks of ice were left in depressions or buried in debris to form lakes. Minnesota actually has some 22,000 lakes, though the official count (11,842) is rounded off to 10,000 for Minnesota's oft-repeated moniker, "The Land of 10,000 Lakes." Wisconsin claims 15,000. The region's largest lakes: Lake Michigan on Wisconsin's eastern shore, and Lake Superior, the largest freshwater lake in the world at 288,800 acres and 123 miles of shoreline.

Located near the geographic center of North America, the region's topography in Minnesota ranges from 602 feet above sea level at the Lake Superior shoreline to 2,031 feet above sea level at Eagle Mountain near the North Shore. In Wisconsin, from 580 feet above sea level on the Lake Michigan shore to 1,952 feet at Timms Hill.

OUTDOOR ACTIVITIES

Runners and bikers in Minnesota and Wisconsin enjoy numerous trails in spring, summer, and fall, while snowmobiling, cross-country skiing, and dogsledding take over in the winter. Bikers come from all over to pedal trails such as the 33-mile Elroy-Sparta Trail, routed through tunnels on an abandoned railroad bed in southwestern Wisconsin's unglaciated "driftless" region. Minnesota's railbed trails include the 45-mile Cannon Valley Trail, which winds through south-eastern Minnesota's hardwood-forested bluff country.

For the hardy hiker, sections of the nearly 300-mile Superior Hiking Trail's route are open along Minnesota's North Shore. The 52-mile segment between Castle Danger and Grand Marais and a 91-mile segment from Crosby Manitou State Park to Kodonce River are rugged and challenging. Hundreds of other trails in the region vary in difficulty, and there's abundant hiking for every age and experience level.

Water draws vacationers from all over the world to this region—for fishing, waterskiing, canoeing, sailing, tubing, and kayaking. In fact, the only way you can explore Minnesota's popular roadless Boundary Waters Canoe Area in the Superior National Forest or Voyageurs National Park is by water. A number of companies lead outdoor adventures ranging from white-water rafting and dogsledding to outdoor experiences for women. You can learn to mush a dog team or just cozy into a blanket-laden sled for the ride.

More daring adventurers raft the Flambeau River's rapids in northern Wisconsin and turbulent white water on the St. Louis River in northeastern Minnesota. Backpacking and camping are popular. You can also golf on courses designed by Dye and Robert Trent Jones, or saddle up a horse to explore state parks via riding trails. And if you prefer a leisurely outdoors experience, try one of many city parks or lakeshore trails. Enjoying the outdoors here can be as simple as taking a spontaneous afternoon stroll.

PRACTICAL TIPS

HOW MUCH WILL IT COST?

Northern Heartlanders tend to be practical souls who resist over-spending which, luckily for the traveler, translates into moderate prices for food, lodging, and attractions. In general, prices tend to be higher in the large metropolitan areas, such as the Twin Cities and Milwaukee. Even so, visitors from the East and West coasts and other upscale regions will find even the city prices a bargain. It's possible for a budget-conscious family of four to eat three meals in good, medium-priced restaurants, visit two museums, and take in a play or concert for well under $200. Of course, that requires a discriminating eye when choosing dining spots and amusements.

Many restaurants charge $15 and under for dinner. Most common are restaurants with a $10–$20 price range. Fewer charge $20–$30; a select few charge over $30.

Many museums in this region are free or operate on a donation basis; fees for others are usually under $8. Children and senior-citizen rates are often discounted, and families sometimes receive special rates. Expect higher fees for tours: $10–$25 is not unusual. Admission to each of the Minnesota Historical Society's 22 sites is $2–$4. Admission to four of the State Historical Society of Wisconsin's seven sites (Pendarvis, Stonefield, Villa Louis, and the Wade House and Wesley Jung Carriage Museum) costs from $2–$5. (Exceptions are Old World Wisconsin, $3–$7; Madeline Island Historical Museum, $1.25–$3; and the Old Capitol, no admission.) Purchase of a passport ticket allowing unlimited visits to all sites for the season costs $35 for a family and $25 for an individual. Rates vary from about $5–$25 for popular attractions such as Valleyfair Family Amusement Park near the Twin Cities and Wisconsin's House on the Rock.

State Parks in Minnesota charge a daily permit fee of $4 per vehicle; a yearly pass costs $18. In Wisconsin, state park daily stickers cost $7 for nonresidents and $3–$5 for residents; annual stickers are $25 for nonresidents and $9–$18 for residents. Bikers, equestrians, and cross-country skiers age 16 and older using certain Wisconsin state trails, parks, forests, and recreation areas must have a trail pass. A daily pass costs $3; the annual pass is $10. Passes are sold at park and trail offices, the Bureau of Parks, or Department of Natural Resources (DNR) area and district offices. Some trailheads have self-registration. To order an annual

pass using VISA or MasterCard, call (608) 266-2181 from 7:45 a.m.–
4:30 p.m. Order by mail: Bureau of Parks, P.O. Box 7921, Madison, WI
53707. Minnesota has no trail-use fees.

CLIMATE

M innesota and Wisconsin experience four full-blown seasons with
wide temperature variations. Temperatures from 70 to 85
degrees Fahrenheit are typical in summer months, but the thermome-
ter can shoot up to 90 degrees or even 100 degrees and above.

In general, June and August are a bit cooler than July. Pack light
clothing for summer, but include a lightweight jacket or sweater—just
in case the weather does something unpredictable. An umbrella or rain
gear are advised for spring, summer, and fall.

Winter, on the other hand, is more predictable; it will be long and
cold. Dress for snow and temperatures below 32 degrees Fahrenheit—a
heavy coat, wool hat, scarf, boots, mittens, and long underwear are de
rigueur. On the northern Minnesota border, the January high for

MINNESOTA/WISCONSIN CLIMATE

Average daily high and low temperatures in degrees Fahrenheit.

	Jan.	March	May	July	Sept.	Nov.
Int'l. Falls	12/-10	33/11	65/40	80/54	64/43	33/17
Grand Marais	22/4	35/19	57/39	71/52	65/47	39/26
Duluth	16/-2	33/16	48/29	71/49	64/45	35/22
Twin Cities	21/3	27/9	70/48	84/63	71/50	41/25
Pipestone	21/-1	40/19	70/44	85/59	72/45	42/20
Madison	25/7	42/23	69/45	86/64	71/47	37/20

International Falls averages 14 degrees and the low averages minus 8 degrees; average annual snowfall is 59 inches. The Twin Cities average a 25-degree high and a 6-degree low. In Milwaukee, the January average high is 30 degrees, with an average low of 11 degrees and an average snowfall of 48 inches.

WHEN TO GO

Late spring to early fall is the prime vacation season, and many attractions are seasonal, open from Memorial Day to Labor Day. Summer weekends and holidays can bring crowds to Minnesota's North Shore as well as to bluff and coulee country in southeastern Minnesota and southwestern Wisconsin. Lodging reservations are needed. Make reservations early for Wisconsin's Door Peninsula—a year in advance is not too early.

Radiant fall color brings weekend camera-toting "leaf peekers"to the North Woods, the bluff and coulee country, the Great River Road on both sides of the Mississippi River, and other parts of the region. Accommodations fill quickly. The color peaks around mid- to late September in the north and from late September to early October as you travel south.

Winter has plenty of enthusiasts. Off to the North Woods and lake regions they go, hauling cross-country skis, snowmobiles, or ice-fishing houses. Some lodges and resorts have winter reservation waiting lists, especially along the North Shore and the Gunflint Trail, so plan a winter vacation early—a year in advance is not too soon. Many communities have Christmas-season events with music, concerts, programs, shopping specials, tours of decorated Victorian houses, parades, and lodging packages.

Mid- to late May, when trees and hillsides turn pastel shades of green, is one of my favorite times to travel the region. Visitors are scarce, and so are mosquitoes (summer visits require insect and tick repellant). Since many attractions have yet to open, it's the perfect time to explore town streets and spend time in cafés talking to the local folks.

TRANSPORTATION

Minneapolis/Saint Paul International is the region's major airport. Located off I-494, about 12 miles southeast of downtown Minneapolis and 10 miles southwest of downtown Saint Paul, the airport is served by 12 major airlines and several regional carriers. It is the main hub for Northwest Airlines.

An information center is located on the lower level of the main terminal, across from the baggage claim area. On this level you'll also find free reservation phones for major hotels; limousine, city bus, and taxi service; and car rentals. Major hotels and motels offer complimentary or inexpensive shuttles.

It's wise to reserve a rental vehicle in advance. You'll find all the nationally known car rental agencies in the Twin Cities, including Avis, (800) 831-2847, and National Car Rental, (800) CAR-RENT. Rental recreational vehicles are in high demand during summer months, especially on weekends. A dozen or so Twin Cities metro area companies specialize in recreational vehicle rentals, including Cruise America Motorhome Rental and Sales, (612) 933-6100, and Brambillas', Inc., (612) 445-2611.

Milwaukee's General Mitchell International Airport is served by major airlines including Northwest, TWA, and United, as well as by regional carriers. Limousine, taxi service, and car rentals are also available.

A network of municipally owned airports and seaplane bases facilitate air travel throughout the region. Greyhound Bus Line, (800) 231-2222, has terminals in downtown Minneapolis and Saint Paul, with intercity bus service daily. Twin Cities bus service is provided by Metropolitan Council Transit Operations (MCTO), (612) 373-3333.

Amtrak, (800) 872-7245, serves the region via a major east-west line from Chicago and other eastern cities to Seattle and Portland, with stops in a number of Wisconsin and Minnesota cities. A Twin Cities depot is based in Saint Paul's Midway area, ten minutes from downtown Saint Paul and 15 minutes from downtown Minneapolis.

If you are traveling by auto, you'll find a dependable network of roads in the Northern Heartland. Road conditions are good in spring, summer, and fall, although you'll encounter road repair delays. Winter travelers should carry winter survival kits and blankets and be aware of weather forecasts. Although both states operate excellent snow-removal programs, storms often result in icy, snow-packed roads with low visibility. Travel to remote areas can be difficult or impossible in winter. In Wisconsin, the road condition hotline is (800) 726-3947; in Minnesota, (800) 542-0220. For car travelers, Minnesota and Wisconsin operate visitor information centers near the border, off I-94, and elsewhere.

CAMPING, LODGING, AND DINING

E ach chapter includes camping, lodging, and dining options in a variety of price ranges, from economical to luxurious, for the featured destination city or area. Sources for additional guidance include the Wisconsin Association of Campground Owners' directory of the state's private campgrounds available from Wisconsin Tourism, (800) 432-8747 or (800) 372-2737. The Minnesota Association of Campground Operators publishes a directory of Minnesota's private campgrounds and RV parks, available from the Minnesota Office of Tourism, (800) 657-3700 or (612) 296-5029.

State parks contain excellent campgrounds in both states. Reservations are recommended from late June through Labor Day. In Minnesota, state park camping fees are $8–$12 nightly, based on the individual park's facilities, plus $2.50 for electricity. Reservations can be made up to 90 days in advance, 24 hours a day, seven days a week by calling The Connection at (612) 922-9000 in the Twin Cities or (800) 246-CAMP. There is a $6 reservation fee. For maps and information, call the Department of Natural Resources (DNR) at (800) 766-6000. Campers must also purchase the park's entrance permit, $4 daily or $18 annually.

Wisconsin state parks charge a camping fee of $8–$12 nightly for nonresidents, and $7–$10 for residents, May 1–October 31; rates are based on when you visit and on park facilities. Campsites may be reserved via VISA or Mastercard in most parks by telephoning the park between June 1 and August 31, Monday–Friday, 9 a.m.–4 p.m. Otherwise, call (608) 266-2181 or (608) 267-2752/TDD to receive a DNR reservation form; campsite application forms are accepted between May 1–October 31. There is a $4 reservation fee plus a daily $7 or $25 nonresident annual permit.

High quality, reasonably priced lodging is plentiful in this region. Of course, you can spend $200 for a very pampered one-night stay if that's what you have in mind. The Wisconsin Innkeepers Association and the Wisconsin Bed and Breakfast Homes and Historic House Association publish comprehensive lodging guides available from Wisconsin Tourism. The Minnesota Motel Association and Minnesota Resort Association directories are available from Minnesota Tourism, as is a guide to bed and breakfasts and inns.

You'll find a variety of dining choices, from fast food, ethnic, and traditional Midwestern fare to gourmet. Bed and breakfasts often pamper your taste buds, while resort dining rooms tend to serve above-average food. The Minnesota Restaurant Association's restaurant directory is available from Minnesota Tourism. Wisconsin's restaurant association does not publish a directory. Restaurants are also listed in guidebooks to each locality/destination, available from community chambers of commerce or convention and visitors bureaus.

RECOMMENDED READING

Your best sources of free travel information are the state tourism offices, city/area convention and visitor bureaus or chambers of commerce, and each state's department of natural resources. Phone numbers for these and other travel resources appear in the Resources section of this guide.

Be sure to request *The Minnesota Explorer* from Minnesota tourism—a quarterly newspaper jammed with seasonal events all over the state and travel features. The Minnesota DNR also publishes a small magazine, *The Minnesota Volunteer*, with some of the best nature writing around; subscriptions are free to residents (donations welcomed). For nonresidents, a subscription costs $15, available by writing the Minnesota DNR (address listed in Resources).

Regional magazines and alternative newspapers can be a great way to take the pulse of a city or community. *Wisconsin Trails* is a helpful, fun-to-read magazine with articles on Wisconsin places, people, and restaurants. The magazine also publishes books: *Best Wisconsin Bike Trips: 30 One-Day Tours* by Phil VanValkenberg, *Best Canoe Trails of Southern Wisconsin* by Michael E. Duncanson, and *Great Golf in Wisconsin* by John Hughes and Jeff Mayers are highly recommended and can be ordered by mail or phone. *Minnesota Monthly* magazine runs articles about Minnesota with frequent features on bed and breakfasts, food, and travel. In the Twin Cities, two tabloid-size newspapers—*City Pages* and *The Twin Cities Reader*—offer complete calendars of current activities, theater, art exhibits, music, movies, and more. They're free and can be picked up from racks in many public places such as libraries, restaurants, and small food stores. *Mpls St Paul* magazine is another good resource.

Numerous books have been written about the region. In *Landscape of Ghosts*, a delightful book with photos by Bob Firth, Minnesota writer Bill Holm takes a wry look at rural Minnesota's past and present people, values, and places (Voyageur Press, 1993, 800-888-9653). Maxwell MacKenzie's *Abandonings: Photographs of Otter Tail County, Minnesota* features color photos of abandoned structures built by Scandinavian immigrants and stories told by settlers (Elliott and Clark, 1995).

Conservationist and environmentalist Aldo Leopold recounts his experiences on his farm near Baraboo, Wisconsin in *Sand County Almanac* (New York: Oxford Press, 1949). Not everybody knows that the naturalist responsible for founding the Sierra Club, John Muir, grew up in Wisconsin and attended the state university. You can read about Muir's life in *The Wilderness World of John Muir* by Edwin Way Teale (Boston: Houghton Mifflin Company, 1954).

John Hassler's novels capture the flavor of Minnesota life. Read *Staggerford*, published by Atheneum Books, New York, in 1977. Ole Rolvaag's classic, *Giants in the Earth* (New York: Harper & Brothers, 1928), poignantly details the struggles of pioneer Norwegian farm families on the prairie. For a look at a four-generation Minnesota farm family, read *Mapping the Farm: The Chronicle of a Family* by John Hildebrand (Alfred A. Knopf, 1995).

Probably the most famous books about Minnesota were written by two literary greats, Sinclair Lewis and F. Scott Fitzgerald. *Main Street* by Lewis, first published in 1920, is a thinly disguised portrait of Sauk Centre, the author's hometown. Fitzgerald's classic, *The Great Gatsby*, describes the flamboyant l920s lifestyle of the wealthy in Saint Paul.

Laura Ingalls Wilder's stories of pioneer life in Wisconsin and Minnesota, recounted in her books *Little House in the Big Woods* and *On the Banks of Plum Creek*, first published in the 1930s by Harper & Brothers, are great family travel reading. Then there's Wisconsin's renowned architect Frank Lloyd Wright. One of many books about Wright is *The Prairie School: Frank Lloyd Wright and his Midwest Contemporaries* by Allen H. Brooks (New York: W.W. Norton, 1972).

RESOURCES

Minnesota Office of Tourism
100 Metro Square, 121 7th Place East
Saint Paul, MN 55101
(800) 657-3700 or (612) 296-5029
Outdoor activity guides, the Boundary Waters Canoe Area, travel directories, calendar of events.

Wisconsin Department of Tourism
Box 7976, 123 W. Washington Avenue

Madison, WI 53707
(608) 266-2161 or (800) 372-2737 (Wisconsin and neighbor states),
(800) 432-TRIP (national)
Travel, historic sites, and recreation guides; calendar of events.

Minnesota Department of Natural Resources Information Center
500 Lafayette Road
St. Paul, MN 55155-4040
(612) 296-6157 or (800) 766-6000
Information on state parks, hunting, fishing, and boating. Licensing,
regulations.

Wisconsin Department of Natural Resources
Box 7921
Madison, WI 53707-7921
(608) 266-2181
State parks, forests, and trail information; campground reservation forms.
Call (608) 266-2621 for fishing, boating, and hunting regulations and
licensing.

Chambers of Commerce and Convention and Visitors Bureaus:
Minnesota
Alexandria Lakes Area (800) 235-9441
Bemidji Area (800) 458-2223
Brainerd Lakes Area (800) 450-2838
Chatfield (507) 867-3966
Detroit Lakes Region (800) 542-3992
Duluth (800)-4-DULUTH
Ely (800) 777-7281
Fergus Falls (800) 726-8959
Grand Marais (800) 622-4014
Grand Portage (218) 475-2592 or (800) 232-1384 (U.S.),
   (800) 543-1384 (Canada)
Greater Minneapolis (612) 348-7000 or (800) 445-7412
Gunflint Trail Association (800) 338-6932
Harmony (800) 247-MINN
Historic Bluff Country (800) 428-2030
International Falls (800) 325-5766
Iron Trail Convention and Visitors Bureau (800) 777-8497
La Crescent (800) 926-9480
Lake City (800) 369-4123
Lake of the Woods Area (800) 382-FISH
Lanesboro (800) 944-2670
Lutsen-Tofte (218) 663-7804 or (800) 322-8327
Mille Lacs (800) 346-9375
Perham Area (800) 634-6112
Pipestone (507) 825-3316 or (800) 336-6125
Prairie Lands/Minnesota: Luverne Area (507) 283-4061

Red Wing (800) 498-3444
Redwood Falls Regional Tourism and Convention Bureau (800) 657-7070
Saint Paul (612) 297-6985 or (800) 627-6101
Taylors Falls (800) 447-4958
Tip of the Arrowhead Tourism Association (800) 622-4014
Voyageurs National Park (218) 283- 9821
Voyageurs National Park Visitor Center at Ash River (218) 374-3221
Voyageurs National Park Visitor Center at Crane Lake (218) 993-2481
Voyageurs National Park Visitor Center at Kabetogama Lake
   (218) 875-2111
Voyageurs National Park Visitor Center at Rainy Lake (218) 286-5258
Wabasha (800) 565-4158
Winona (800) 657-4972

Chambers of Commerce and Convention and Visitors Bureaus:
Wisconsin
Bayfield (800) 447-4094
Bayfield County (800) GRAND FUN
Birchwood Area (800) 236-2252
Cumberland (715) 822-3378
Dodgeville (608) 935-5993
Door Peninsula/Wisconsin: Door County (800) 52-RELAX or
   (414) 743-4456
Governor Dodge State Park (608) 935-2315
Greater Madison Convention and Visitors Bureau (800) 373-6376
Greater Milwaukee Convention and Visitors Bureau (800) 231-0903
Kettle Moraine State Forest Headquarters, North Unit (414) 626-2116
Lac du Flambeau Tribal Natural Resources Dept. (715) 588-3303
La Crosse (800) 658-9424
Lake Winnebago, Horicon Marsh, and the Kettle Moraine/Wisconsin:
   Fond du Lac (800) 937-9123
Madeline Island (715) 747-2801 or 747-2051.
Minocqua-Arbor Vitae-Woodruff Area (800) 446-6784
Mount Horeb Area (608) 437-5914
Northern Highland-American Legion State Forest (715) 356-5211
Oshkosh (800) 876-5250
Rice Lake (800) 523-6318
Shell Lake (715) 468-4477
Spooner (715) 635-2168 or 466-2845
Spring Green (800) 588-2042
Stockholm (715) 442-2015
Stone Lake Area (800) 639-6822
Trempealeau (608) 534-6780
Washburn County (800) 367-3306

1
THE TWIN CITIES: MINNEAPOLIS AND SAINT PAUL

The Twin Cities, Saint Paul and Minneapolis, actually have quite distinct personalities. The pulse of Minneapolis races in the city's compact, 12-block-radius downtown, despite the romantic meander of Nicollet Avenue, an outdoor pedestrian mall with fountains and statues, flowers, trees, and summertime musicians. Minneapolis is home to Fortune 500 companies including General Mills and Honeywell and is a noted center for the arts, with two major art museums and a wealth of performing arts companies. In genteel Saint Paul, to the east, baroque domes and venerable sandstone buildings sit on hills and steep river bluffs; modern skyscrapers flank historic steeples and towers. Streets angle and curve through downtown's three distinct sections: Historic Lowertown, Saint Paul's birthplace, with a village green and resident arts community; the central business district; and a cultural district on the western side. ∎

TWIN CITIES REGION

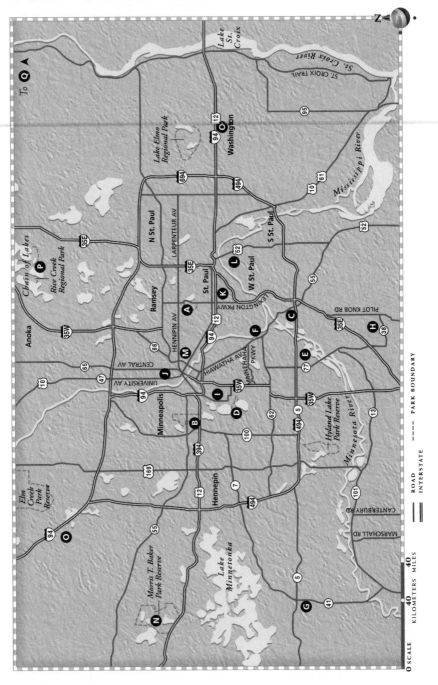

SCALE
40 KILOMETERS
40 MILES

— ROAD
═ INTERSTATE
---- PARK BOUNDARY

Sightseeing Highlights

Ⓐ Como Park, Zoo, and Conservatory

Ⓑ Eloise Butler Wildflower Garden

Ⓒ Historic Fort Snelling

Ⓓ Lyndale Park Gardens

Ⓔ Mall of America

Ⓕ Minnehaha Falls and Minnehaha Parkway

Ⓖ Minnesota Landscape Arboretum

Ⓗ Minnesota Zoo

Food

Ⓘ Egg & I

Ⓙ Emily's Lebanese Delicatessen

Lodging

Ⓚ Chatsworth Bed and Breakfast

Ⓛ The Covington Inn

Ⓜ Econo Lodge–Minneapolis

Camping

Ⓝ Baker Park Reserve

Ⓞ KOA campgrounds

Ⓟ Rice Creek Campground

Ⓠ William O'Brien State Park

A PERFECT DAY IN THE TWIN CITIES

Start with a walk around Lake Harriet, one of Minneapolis' 22 lakes. Breakfast at Nicollet Island Inn above St. Anthony Falls, explore the quaint island village, and take a self-guided tour of Mississippi Mile's old milling district. Next visit the Minneapolis Institute of Arts, then head for Saint Paul's historic Summit Avenue. Lunch at W.A. Frost, tour the James J. Hill House, and explore the Minnesota History Center. Stroll the Mississippi River walkways, dine at the classy Saint Paul Grill, and end the day with a concert or musical at the Ordway Music Theatre.

SIGHTSEEING HIGHLIGHTS

☆☆☆ **American Swedish Institute**—"There are more Swedish artifacts here than in museums in Sweden," a Swedish visitor once commented. The cherished possessions of Swedish immigrants and their descendants are carefully preserved and displayed in a 33-room castle-like mansion with turrets, towers, and exquisitely carved woodwork. Admission: $2–$3, under 6 free. Hours: Tuesday, Thursday–Saturday, noon–4 p.m; Wednesday, until 8 p.m.; Sunday, 1–5 p.m. Address: 2600 Park Ave., Minneapolis. Phone: (612) 871-4907. (1–2 hours)

☆☆☆ **Frederick R. Weisman Art Museum**—The museum's Frank Gehry–designed aluminum building has been called "a tin can" and generated controversy when it opened in 1993 on the banks of the Mississippi River. Inside, you'll find a beautiful interior display space with skylights. The museum features a large collection of Marsden Hartley works, pop-art murals created by Roy Lichtenstein for the 1965 World's Fair, and works by Robert Motherwell and James Rosenquist. Admission: Free. Charge for special events. Hours: Tuesday–Friday, 10 a.m.–5 p.m.; until 8 p.m., Thursday; Saturday and Sunday, 11 a.m.–5 p.m. Address: 333 East River Rd. on the University of Minnesota Campus. Phone: (612) 625-9494. (1 hour)

☆☆☆ **Historic Fort Snelling**—At Fort Snelling, costumed interpreters reenact fort life in stone buildings and a stockade restored to the fort's 1827 appearance. Visitors can converse with cooks and soldiers and watch military drills and other events on bluffs high above the juncture of the Mississippi and Minnesota Rivers. Admission: $2–$4. Hours:

MINNEAPOLIS

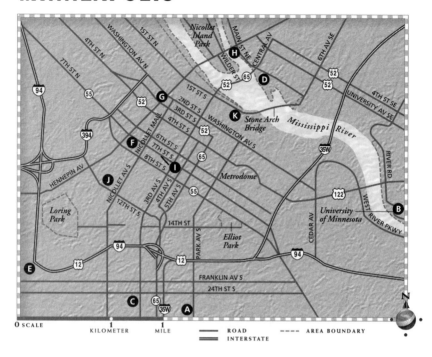

Sightseeing Highlights

Ⓐ American Swedish Institute

Ⓑ Frederick R. Weisman Art Museum

Ⓒ Minneapolis Institute of Arts

Ⓓ St. Anthony Falls Historic District

Ⓔ Walker Art Center and Minneapolis Sculpture Garden

Food

Ⓕ Goodfellows

Ⓖ New French Café & Bar

Ⓗ Nicollet Island Inn

Ⓘ Peter's Grill

Lodging

Ⓙ Hotel Luxeford Suites

Ⓗ Nicollet Island Inn

Ⓚ The Whitney Hotel

Note: Items with the same letter are located in the same place or area.

May–October, 10 a.m.–5 p.m., Monday–Saturday; Sunday, noon–5 p.m. History center open all year; weekdays October–May, 9 a.m.–4 p.m. Address: Off Highways 5 and 55, Saint Paul. Phone: (612) 725-2413. (2–3 hours)

★★★ **Lyndale Park Gardens**—On rolling lawns with venerable shade trees, park visitors stroll paths through a rose garden, a rock garden, and a bird sanctuary near Lake Harriet and glimpse a slice of the South Minneapolis lifestyle. Admission: Free. Hours: Sunrise–10 p.m. Address: Roseway Road between E. Lake Harriet Pkwy. and Kings Highway. Phone: (612) 370-4900 or (612)661-4800; (612) 661-4875 for events. (½ hour)

★★★ **Minneapolis Institute of Arts**—The internationally known institute displays 80,000 objects of fine and decorative arts spanning 4,000 years. Admission: Free; fee for special exhibits, except free Thursday, 5–9 p.m. Free tours Tuesday–Sunday, 2 p.m.; 7 p.m. Thursday; 1 p.m. Saturday and Sunday. Hours: 10 a.m.–5 p.m., Tuesday–Saturday; until 9 p.m. Thursday; noon–5 p.m. on Sunday. Closed Monday. Address: 2400 3rd Ave. S. Phone: (612) 870-3131. (1–2 hours)

★★★ **Minnesota History Center in St. Paul**—This new architectural gem features clever interactive displays that tell the story of Minnesota. The center's Café Minnesota offers exceptional food (lunch and brunch only). Admission: Free. Hours: 10 a.m.–5 p.m., Tuesday–Saturday; until 9 p.m., Thursday; noon–5 p.m., Sunday. Closed Monday, but open Monday holidays. Address: 345 Kellogg Blvd., at the junction of I-35E and I-94 in Saint Paul, at the corners of Kellogg and John Ireland Blvds. Phone: (612) 296-6126 or (800) 657-3773. (1–2 hours)

★★★ **St. Anthony Falls Historic District**—Take a guided tour from the Minnesota Historical Society's visitor center or follow the St. Anthony Falls Heritage Trail markers to see the only falls on the Mississippi and the old milling district's remaining buildings and ruins. The Upper Lock and Dam Visitor Center (open April through November, at Portland and W. River Parkway) has views of the falls and river activity. Admission: Historical Society tours, $2–$4, under 6 free. Hours: Historical Society Visitor Center, 9 a.m.–5 p.m., Wednesday–Sunday, May–October. Address: 125 S.E. Main St. Phone: (612) 627-5433. (1–2 hours)

★★★ **Walker Art Center and Minneapolis Sculpture Garden**—
This cutting-edge contemporary art center is the third most-visited
museum in the United States. "Galleries" are defined by trees in the
adjacent 11-acre garden, which houses more than 40 sculptures. The
museum is noted for the *Spoonbridge and Cherry* sculpture by Claes
Oldenburg and Coosje Van Bruggen. Admission: Art Center, $3–$4, 11
and under free; free Thursday and first Saturday each month. Walking
tours at 2 p.m., Thursday and weekends, also 6 p.m. on Thursday, free
with admission. Sculpture garden, free. Hours: Art Center, 10 a.m.–5 p.m.,
Tuesday–Saturday; until 8 p.m. Thursday; 11 a.m.–5 p.m., Sunday.
Closed Monday. Garden, 6 a.m.–midnight, daily. Address: 725 Vineland
Place. Phone: (612) 375-7600. (2 hours)

★★ **Como Park, Zoo, and Conservatory**—Expansive 150,000-acre
grounds contain a Victorian floral conservatory, a free zoo, Japanese
gardens, an 18-hole golf course, ski trails, bike and canoe rentals at
Lakeside Pavilion, a 1½-mile walking trail that winds around the lake,
and an amusement park. Admission: Park and zoo, free; conservatory,
25–50 cents, 10 and under free. Fee for rides in amusement park.
Hours: Zoo grounds, 8 a.m.–5 p.m., daily. Buildings, 10 a.m.–4 p.m.
Conservatory, 10 a.m.–6 p.m. daily, April–September; until 4 p.m., winter. Address: Take I-94 to Lexington Pkwy. in Saint Paul, go north 2
miles, turn left at zoo/conservatory sign. Phone: (612) 266-6400;
Conservatory, (612) 489-1740; Zoo, (612) 488-5571. (1–3 hours)

★★ **Eloise Butler Wildflower Garden in Theodore Wirth Park**—
This delightful wildflower garden with free educational programs nes-
tles in the park's acres of wooded, rolling hills. Admission: Free. Hours:
7:30 a.m.–dusk, April–October. Address: half block north of I-394
on Theodore Wirth Parkway, Minneapolis. Phone: (612) 370-4903.
(¾ hour)

★★ **James J. Hill House**—Great Northern Railroad magnate James J.
Hill's massive Richardsonian Romanesque home stands like a fortress
on Saint Paul's Summit Avenue, a 4½-mile boulevard lined with showy
late nineteenth- and early twentieth-century mansions. Nearby stands
the ornate 1915 St. Paul Cathedral, modeled after St. Peter's in Rome,
with tours Monday, Wednesday, and Friday at 1 p.m. Hill House
admission: $2–$4, 5 and under free. Hours: Wednesday–Saturday, 10
a.m.–3:30 p.m. year-round, guided tours. Reservations preferred.

Address: 240 Summit Ave. Phone: (612) 297-2555. (1½ hours)
Cathedral admission: Free. Hours: 7 a.m.–6 p.m. Address: 239 Selby
Ave. Phone: (612) 228-1766. (½–¾ hours)

★★ **Minnehaha Falls and Minnehaha Parkway**—The spectacular
falls of Minnehaha Creek tumble into a canyon in wooded Minnehaha
Park. Walking trails lead from the park to the Mississippi River; hiking
and bike paths run along along Minnehaha Creek. Other attractions
include a picnic area, a historic depot, and historic houses. Be sure to
drive a portion of Minnehaha Parkway, which runs west following the
creek and is bordered by grassy spaces and picnic spots. Admission:
Free. Hours: 6 a.m.–11 p.m. Address: 4825 Minnehaha Ave. Phone:
(612) 661-4817 or (612) 661-4800. (1 hour or more)

★★ **Minnesota Landscape Arboretum**—Walk trails and/or drive to
see more than 675 acres of plants, landscaped gardens, and restored
prairie. The flowering crabapple and cherry trees are magnificent in the
spring. The central building houses a library and a tearoom. Admission:
$1–$4, 5 and under free. Hours: Grounds, 8 a.m. to sunset daily; building, until 4:30 p.m. Address: 3675 Arboretum Dr., 9 miles west of I-494
on Highway 5, Chanhassen. Phone: (612) 443-2460. (1–3 hours)

★★ **Minnesota Zoo**—This natural habitat zoo offers special programs
and holiday events. Admission: $4–$8, 2 and under free. Hours: 9 a.m.–
6 p.m., daily; until 8 p.m., Sunday; closes at 4 p.m. Labor Day–April.
Address: 13000 Zoo Blvd.; ten minutes south of the Mall of America,
off Highway 77; signs direct you. Phone: (612) 432-9000. (2 hours–
all day)

★★ **Science Museum of Minnesota** and **William L. McKnight 3-M
Omnitheater**—Popular with all ages, the museum holds interactive science exhibits and the Dinosaur and Fossils Hall. The Omnitheater
shows science- and nature-based films on its 76-foot domed screen.
Admission: $4–$7. Hours: Monday–Saturday, 9:30 a.m.–9 p.m.; Sunday,
10 a.m.–9 p.m. Closed Monday from Labor Day–mid-December.
Address: 30 E. Tenth St., off I-94 and I-35E, at the corner of Exchange
and Wabasha. Phone: (612) 221-9444. (2½ hours)

★ **Mall of America**—Minnesota is home to the largest mall in the
United States. Along with about 150 specialty shops are anchor stores

Bloomingdale's, Macy's, Nordstrom, and Sears. Kids will head for the enclosed amusement park, Knott's Camp Snoopy, and the LEGO showcase/hands-on building area. Admission: Free. Prices for amusement park rides vary. Hours: Mall doors open 7 a.m.–2 a.m.; store hours are 10 a.m.–9:30 p.m., Monday–Saturday; 11 a.m.–7 p.m., Sunday. Address: Bloomington, off I-494 and Cedar Ave./Highway 77. Phone: (612) 883-8800. Camp Snoopy: (612) 883-5600. (1–4 hours)

✸ **Minnesota Children's Museum**—This museum features hands-on exhibits and a simulated storm complete with thunder and lightning. Admission: $3.95–$5.95, infants free. Hours: 9 a.m.–5 p.m., Tuesday–Sunday; until 8 p.m., Thursday; open Mondays from Memorial Day–Labor Day only; closed holidays. Address: 7th Street between St. Peter and Wabasha Streets. Phone: (612) 225-6050 weekends; (612) 225-6001 weekdays. (1 hour)

✸ **State Capitol in Saint Paul**—This imposing edifice, built by Cass Gilbert in 1905, claims the world's largest unsupported marble dome. Free tours leave daily on the hour and are packed with Minnesota history. Admission: Free. Hours: Monday–Friday 9 a.m.–4 p.m.; Saturday, 10 a.m.–3 p.m.; Sunday 1–3 p.m. Address: Cedar and Aurora Streets in Saint Paul. Phone: (612) 296-3962; tours (612) 296-2881. (1 hour)

FITNESS AND RECREATION

The Twin Cities boast miles of interconnecting paths and parks that are used by hikers, bikers, and skiers alike. **Minneapolis Parks and Recreation Board** maintains nearly 40 miles of walking paths and almost 40 miles of biking paths, which are described in the board's summer activities guide (for information, call 612-661-4875 or 612-661-4800). Additionally, **Hennepin Parks**, (612) 559-9000, publishes a free parks guide. Parks with hiking and biking include **Hyland Lake Park Reserve** (5½ miles of hiking/biking trails and 4½ miles of bike-only trails) in Bloomington, (612) 941-4362. **Saint Paul Parks and Recreation**, (612) 266-6400, maintains more than 40 miles of parks, parkways, and trails; call for the *Bike, Hike and Jog User Guide*. In Saint Paul, go to **Crosby Farm-Hidden Falls Regional Park**, (612) 488-7291, at Shepard Road and Mississippi River Boulevard, to hike through woods and along the river banks on more than 7½ miles of trails. The region has more than 100 public and private golf courses.

SAINT PAUL

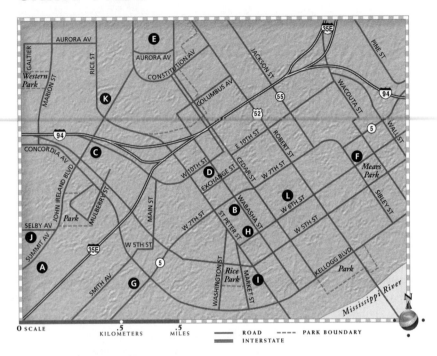

Sightseeing Highlights
- **A** James J. Hill House
- **B** Minnesota Children's Museum
- **C** Minnesota History Center
- **D** Science Museum of Minnesota and William L. McKnight 3-M Omnitheater
- **E** State Capitol in Saint Paul

Food
- **F** Café da Vinci
- **G** Cossetta's Italian Market & Pizzeria
- **H** Sakura
- **I** Saint Paul Grill
- **J** W.A. Frost & Co.

Lodging
- **K** Best Western Kelly Inn
- **L** Radisson Inn Saint Paul
- **I** Saint Paul Hotel

Note: Items with the same letter are located in the same place or area.

Lakes with popular public swimming beaches include **Lake Harriet** and **Lake Calhoun** in south Minneapolis; Lake Calhoun, (612) 370-4964, has canoe rentals, as well. Downhill ski areas include **Hyland Hills,** (612) 835-4250, in Bloomington and **Afton Alps** in Hastings, (612) 436-5245.

Fans can experience **Minnesota Twins baseball,** (612) 375-1116, and **NFL Vikings football,** (612) 333-8828, in the **Hubert H. Humphrey Metrodome,** (612) 332-0386, 900 S. Fifth St., Minneapolis.

FOOD

Executive chef Kevin Cullen creates award-winning regional cuisine, including Minnesota venison, at **Goodfellows,** in the heart of the downtown Minneapolis hotel district, (612) 332-4800, with meals from $19–$29. At the **New French Café & Bar**, 128 N. 4th St., Minneapolis, (612) 338-3790, excellent nouvelle French cuisine costs $16 to $24. The "in" breakfast spot, from $1.50–$5.75, in south Minneapolis is the **Egg & I**, 2828 Lyndale Ave., (612) 872-7282; and when President Clinton came to town, he ate old-fashioned home cooking at **Peter's Grill**, Baker Center, 114 S. 8th St., (612) 333-1981, where meals cost from $6.65–$14.95.

You can count on professional service and innovative cuisine, such as salmon with apple dill couscous, at **Nicollet Island Inn,** (612) 331-1800, with river views and dinner from $12.50–$29. **Emily's Lebanese Delicatessen**, 641 University Ave. N.E., Minneapolis, (612) 379-4069, is a casual place to dine on fantastic tabbouleh salad, spinach pie, and lamb kebabs for under $10.

In Saint Paul, **W.A. Frost & Co.**, 374 Selby Ave., (612) 224-5715, has a great summer garden patio; prices range from $6.95 to $20. The spacious **Café da Vinci**, 400 Sibley St., (612) 222-4050, is loaded with artsy atmosphere and specializes in Italian pasta dishes ($7.95–$15.95); while **Cossetta's Italian Market & Pizzeria**, 211 W. 7th St., (612) 222-3476, has award-winning pizza and great deli fare for under $10. The handsome **Saint Paul Grill**, Saint Paul Hotel, 350 Market St., (612) 224-7455, offers excellent food only a short Rice Park stroll away from the Ordway Music Theatre; prices run $10.50 to $25 a la carte. Also convenient to the Ordway is **Sakura**, 34 W. 6th St., (612) 224-0185, with Japanese cuisine and a sushi bar from $8–$15.

LODGING

For sophisticated luxury lodging, stay at the **Saint Paul Hotel**, 350 Market St., (800) 292-9292, with rooms from $145–$160 and suites, $175–$675; or the **Whitney Hotel**, 150 Portland Ave., Minneapolis, (612) 339-9300, with rooms for $155–$165 and suites, $190–$200. For a funkier experience, try Saint Paul's **Covington Inn** bed and breakfast on a historical line boat docked at Pier One on Harriet Island, with rooms from $115–$150, (612) 292-1411. A black cat sleeps on a window seat at the **Nicollet Island Inn**, 95 Merriam St., (612) 331-1800, a charming country inn on an island in the heart of Minneapolis, with rooms from $110–$145. The **Chatsworth Bed and Breakfast**, 984 Ashland Ave., Saint Paul, (612) 227-4288, occupies a 1902 Victorian house, with rates from $65–$125.

Saint Paul's **Best Western Kelly Inn-State Capitol**, 161 St. Anthony Blvd., (800) 528-1234, has rooms from $76–$79. In the **Econo Lodge-Minneapolis**, 2500 University Ave., (800) 424-4777, rooms range from $45–$77; and at Minneapolis' **Hotel Luxeford Suites**, 1101 LaSalle Ave., (612) 332-6800, rooms are $85–$170. The **Radisson Inn Saint Paul** in downtown Saint Paul, 411 Minnesota, (612) 291-8800, offers rooms for $79–$160 with a full breakfast and cocktails.

CAMPING

The greater metro area has close to two dozen campgrounds, private and public. **Baker Park Reserve** on Lake Independence in Maple Plain, (612) 559-6700, has 210 sites, 27 with electricity, for $11–$15. **William O'Brien State Park**, 16 miles north of Stillwater via State 95, (612) 433-0500, has 125 campsites—62 with electricity, wheelchair accessible showers, and flush toilets. **Rice Creek Chain-of-Lakes Regional Park Reserve's Rice Creek Campground** in north metro Lino Lakes, 3 miles west on County 14 off I-35E, (612) 757-3920 or (612) 767-2868, has 79 sites—39 with hookups, restrooms, and showers for $10 to $14. You'll find private **KOA campgrounds** in Rogers, 15 miles northwest on I-94W, exit 213; 2 miles west on County 30 and 1 mile north on Highway 101, (612) 420-2255; and east of Saint Paul in Woodbury, on County 19 off I-94E, (612) 436-6436.

NIGHTLIFE AND SPECIAL EVENTS

Order the *Dining and Entertainment Guide* from Minnesota Tourism, (800) 657-3700 or (612) 296-5029, as well as the latest *Twin Cities* visitor's guide. Then pick up *The Twin Cities Reader* and *City Pages*, along with the Friday Variety section of the *Twin Cities Star Tribune* for current happenings. Musical offerings include **Minnesota Orchestra**, 1111 Nicollet Mall, Minneapolis, (612) 371-5656; **Saint Paul Chamber Orchestra**, usually at the Ordway in Saint Paul, (612) 291-1144; **Minnesota Opera**, (612) 333-2700; and touring Broadway shows at the restored **Historic Orpheum Theatre**, 910 Hennepin Ave. S., Minneapolis, (612) 339-7007, and **Ordway Music Theatre**, 345 Washington St., Saint Paul, (612) 224-4222. In Saint Paul, jazz music accompanies original and wonderful "Minnesota cuisine" at the **Dakota Bar and Grill**, 1021 Bandana Blvd. E., east of Snelling Ave., (612) 642-1442, and at the hot Greenwich Village–mood **Artists' Quarter**, 366 Jackson St., (612) 292-1359, which has hosted Mose Allison and Benny Golson. **Fine Line Music Café**, 318 First Ave. N., Minneapolis, (612) 335-8181 or 338-8100, swings with jazz and rock bands of local and national repute. Dance companies perform at Minneapolis' historic **Hennepin Center for the Arts**, 528 Hennepin, (612) 332-4478, and elsewhere. In Minneapolis, go to the **Guthrie Theater**, 725 Vineland Place, (612) 377-2224, a noted repertory theatre for the classics, or to **Mixed Blood**, 1501 S. 4th St., (612) 338-6131, for fun, startling, and bold plays that are always good. Also try the renowned **Children's Theatre Company** at 2400 3rd Ave. S. in Minneapolis, (612) 874-0400, for plays applauded by children and adults. There are also theaters and nightclubs at the **Mall of America**, off I-494 and Highway 77 in Bloomington, (612) 883-8800. Casinos considered close to the Twin Cities include **Mystic Lake**, 2400 Mystic Lake Blvd., Prior Lake, (800) 262-7799; and **Treasure Island**, off Highway 61 between Hastings and Red Wing, (800) 222-7077.

Scenic Route: St. Croix River Valley Drive

Take I-35W or I-35E (they meld into I-35) north of the Twin Cities to State Highway 97, just south of Forest Lake. Follow 97 east to the Swedish town of Scandia and visit the Swedish-heritage **Gammel-garden Museum** (612-433-5053, weekends, May– October).

Continue east to the St. Croix River, a national scenic riverway, and head north on State Highway 95, which winds along the bluffs of the St. Croix. In Taylor Falls, follow signs to the **Historic Angel Hill District**, a New England–style village with white-frame houses and a prim, tall-steepled 1861 church. Tour the restored 1855 Greek Revival/Federal-style **Folsom House** daily, 1– 4:30 p.m., from Memorial Day weekend to mid-October. At **Interstate Park** (across from downtown), hike trails past glacial potholes, up rocky bluffs for river views, and through the woods. Take a river cruise to view the scenic rock cliffs of the Dalles of the St. Croix.

To return to the Twin Cities, follow U.S. Highway 8 west from Taylor Falls through lake country. Stop in **Lindstrom** to browse at Gustaf's Fine Gifts, World of Christmas, and Department 56 Village Place. Dine on the Dinnerbel's deck, continue west to I-35 and take the interstate south to return to the Twin Cities. ◩

ST. CROIX RIVER VALLEY DRIVE

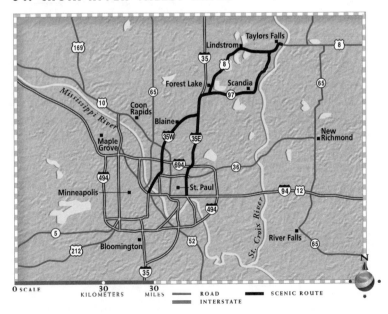

2

DULUTH AND
MINNESOTA'S NORTH SHORE

D uluth and the Lake Superior North Shore lie in the northeastern Minnesota Arrowhead region, home of the magnificent, nearly 3 million-acre Superior National Forest. This land of rocky outcroppings contains exposed Precambrian rocks more than 2.5 billion years old. Fur trade once flourished in this area; a major fur trading post was established at Grand Portage by 1776 and is now honored as a national monument.

About 150 miles south of Grand Portage, perched on rocky cliffs overlooking Lake Superior, world port Duluth has a large natural harbor and is a railway and shipping hub. Ships arrive via the St. Lawrence Seaway from more than 30 countries to take on cargoes of coal, grain, crude oil, and iron ore. The harbor was critical to Minnesota's once-booming iron ore mining industry, masterminded by powerful men such as John D. Rockefeller and Andrew Carnegie. Most of the high-grade iron ore is gone now, but taconite mining continues on the Iron Range. Iron-ore wealth helped build the architectural treasures that line the streets of Duluth today. The rugged terrain in this region provides some of the best and most challenging hiking and skiing in the state, as well as unparalleled scenic beauty. ◄

NORTH SHORE REGION

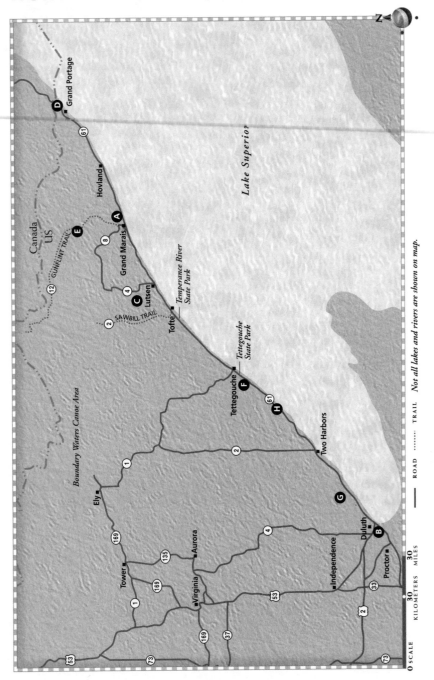

Not all lakes and rivers are shown on map.

— ROAD ...... TRAIL

SCALE
KILOMETERS
0   30
MILES
0   30

Lake Superior

Canada
US

Boundary Waters Canoe Area

Grand Portage

Hovland

Grand Marais

Lutsen

Tofte

GUNFLINT TRAIL

SAWBILL TRAIL

Temperance River State Park

Tettegouche State Park

Tettegouche

Two Harbors

Ely

Tower

Aurora

Virginia

Independence

Duluth

Proctor

61

8

12

4

2

1

169

135

169

1

169

37

53

2

33

2

73

53

73

4

A B C D E F G H

Sightseeing Highlights

Ⓐ Cook County Museum

Ⓑ Duluth

Ⓑ Enger Park

Ⓑ Glensheen Mansion

Ⓒ Gondola Sky Ride/Alpine Slide/Mountain Bike Park

Ⓐ Grand Marais

Ⓓ Grand Portage National Monument

Ⓓ Grand Portage State Park

Ⓔ Gunflint Trail

Ⓐ Johnson Heritage Post Art Gallery

Ⓑ Lake Superior & Mississippi Railroad

Ⓕ Lake Superior North Shore

Ⓖ North Shore Scenic Drive

Ⓑ Skyline Parkway

Ⓗ Split Rock Lighthouse State Park

Note: Items with the same letter are located in the same place or area.

A PERFECT DAY IN DULUTH

Start your visit to Duluth amid the flocks of seagulls at the Marine Museum and learn about the genesis of the famed Aerial Lift Bridge. Then walk to the lighthouse, where resident swallows swoop and dive; explore the shops near Canal Park; and stroll the lakewalk. Go to the Transportation Museum, try a Greek lunch at Natchio's, and head for Jay Cooke State Park. Cross the St. Louis River on a swinging bridge and hike a trail or two. Catch Skyline Drive's harbor views, then get a closer look on a dinner harbor cruise, followed by a lakeside amble.

SIGHTSEEING HIGHLIGHTS

★★★ **Duluth**—In recent years, Duluth has spiffed up its downtown harbor area with a lakewalk and the renovation of old buildings, while maintaining its hardworking, seafaring atmosphere. Go to the **Marine**

Museum and Canal Park for a recap of maritime history via pictures, a film show, and artifacts. Watch gigantic vessels pass through the canal and under the Aerial Lift Bridge, which rises 138 feet to allow ships to enter and leave the harbor. Free. Hours: Daily, 10 a.m.– 9 p.m., late May–early September; other seasons, open until 4:30 p.m. daily, except only Friday–Sunday mid-December–April. Address: Canal Park. Phone: (218) 727-2497. Boat-watcher's hot line: (218) 722-6489. (1 hour)

Visitors and residents alike enjoy strolling along the lake through four city parks. For panoramic views of the shoreline and harbor 600 feet below, drive the 30-mile **Skyline Parkway** and stop in **Enger Park** to stroll in Japanese gardens and climb 5-story Enger Tower. For more Lake Superior drama—thundering waves crashing at the foot of rocky cliffs backdropped by towering pine and spruce—take the 26-mile Scenic Highway 61 **North Shore Drive** from Brighton Beach up to Two Harbors. You can tour **Glensheen Mansion** in Duluth, a 39-room Jacobean Revival mansion built by millionaire Chester Congdon. Reservations are recommended. Admission: $4–$8.75, under 5 free. Hours: 9:30 a.m.–5 p.m. daily, Memorial Day–mid-October. Address: 3300 London Rd. Phone: (218) 724-8864 or (218) 724-8863. (2 hours)

The **Lake Superior Museum of Transportation** features railroad equipment and a huge steam locomotive in The Depot. Admission: $3–$5, under 3 free or a $15 family rate. One fee admits you to the Depot's children's museum, the Duluth Art Institute, and the transportation museum (1 hour; 2–3 hours for all three museums). Hours: Mid-May–mid-October, 10 a.m.–5 p.m. daily; other seasons, the same schedule except 1–5 p.m. Sunday. Address: 506 W. Michigan St. Phone: (218) 727-8025. The transportation museum also operates the **North Shore Scenic Railroad**, with North Shore two- and six-hour excursions. Call the museum for the schedule.

Lake Superior & Mississippi Railroad offers trips along the St. Louis River on a vintage train with 1911–1912 coaches. Admission: $4–$6. Hours: Mid-June–early September, Saturday, and Sunday, 11 a.m. and 2 p.m. Phone: (218) 624-7549 or 727-0687. (1½ hours)

You can also tour the *William A. Irvin*, flagship of the USS Great Lakes Fleet (1 hour). Admission: $3.50–$6, under 3 free. Address: Duluth Entertainment Convention Center dock, Harbor Drive. Phone: Call for tour times, (218) 722-5573. Or take a **Vista Fleet** cruise and tour the harbor. Admission: $4–$8.50, under 3 free. Hours: 9:30 a.m.– 7:30 p.m. daily, mid-May–mid-October; tours leave hourly from 11:30 a.m.–3:30 p.m., otherwise every two hours. Address: Harbor

Drive at the Entertainment Convention Center dock. Phone: (218)
722-6218. (2 hours)

★★★ **Grand Marais**—This picturesque North Shore fishing village
on Highway 61 shelters an arts colony and has a natural harbor with a
lighthouse you can reach by walking on the breakwater (800-622-
4014). Visit the **Johnson Heritage Post Art Gallery** to see the work
of North Shore artists. Admission: Free. Hours: 10 a.m.–5 p.m.,
Monday–Saturday, 11 a.m.–4 p.m., Sunday, in summer; noon–4 p.m.
daily in winter. Address: On Wisconsin St., downtown. Phone: (218)
387-2314. (½ hour)
    Nearby is the **Cook County Museum**, which houses artifacts and
history on area logging and commercial fishing. Admission: Free.
Hours: Mid-May–mid-October, 10 a.m.–5 p.m., Monday–Saturday, and
noon–4 p.m., Sunday; closed in winter. Address: Wisconsin St., downtown. Phone: (218) 387-2838 or (800) 622-4014. (½ hour)

★★★ **Lake Superior North Shore**—The rugged, heavily wooded
shoreline that begins in Duluth is protected from development by a
string of eight state parks with hiking and ski trail systems, rocky
gorges, waterfalls, and cascades off Highway 61 between Two Harbors
and Grand Portage. The narrow, challenging Superior National
Recreation Hiking Trail runs atop ridgelines above the North Shore;
some 200 of the trail's 300 miles from Duluth to the Canadian border
are open for hiking. To hike sections of the trail, watch for brown
highway signs depicting the trail logo and an arrow pointing to parking
or access roads. The Lutsen-Tofte Association offers lodge-to-lodge
hiking/transportation packages, (800) 322-8327. The Superior National
Forest U.S. Forest Service has trail information, (218) 663-7280 or
(218) 327-1750, as do Tip of the Arrowhead, (800) 622-4014, and
Superior Hiking Trail Association, (218) 834-4436.

★★★ **Split Rock Lighthouse State Park**—You can tour the lighthouse and keeper's quarters in summer months at this lighthouse, which
sits on the edge of a craggy cliff. Admission: $2–$4, under 6 free, in lieu
of park permit. Hours: Mid-May–mid-October, 9 a.m.–5 p.m. daily.
Visitor Center only is open from noon–4 p.m. Friday–Sunday other
months with no admission but a park permit is required. Closed
December. Address: On Highway 61, 20 miles northeast of Two
Harbors. Phone: (218) 226-4372. (1 hour)

DULUTH

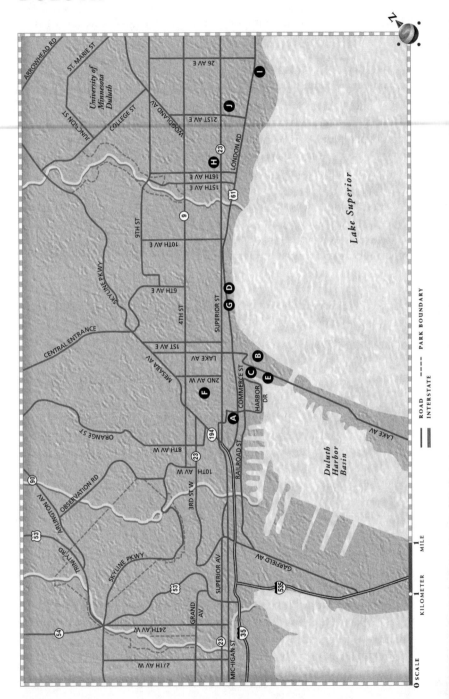

Sightseeing Highlights

Ⓐ Lake Superior Museum of Transportation

Ⓑ Marine Museum and Canal Park

Ⓐ North Shore Scenic Railroad

Ⓒ *William A. Irvin*

Food

Ⓓ Augustino's

Ⓔ Grandma's

Ⓕ Natchio's Greektown Restaurant

Ⓖ Pickwick Restaurant

Lodging

Ⓗ A. Charles Weiss Inn

Ⓘ Best Western Edgewater East

Ⓙ The Ellery House

Ⓓ Fitger's Inn

Note: Items with the same letter are located in the same place or area.

⭐⭐ **Grand Portage National Monument**—The site contains the reconstructed North West Fur Company Trading Post, complete with stockade, great hall, and furnishings. There are daily demonstrations of fort activities. You can also hike the portage used by Native Americans and voyageurs, but it's a demanding, often muddy, not especially scenic trek—nearly 9 miles, five hours one way. Admission: $2, under 16 free; $5 family rate. Hours: 8 a.m.–5 p.m. daily, mid-May–mid-October. Address: Off Highway 61, 36 miles north of Grand Marais; watch for the sign after you pass the casino. Phone: (218) 387-2788. (at least 1 hour)

⭐⭐ **Grand Portage State Park**—Hike boardwalk trails to view the 120-foot High Falls of the Pigeon River, the state's highest waterfall. This young state park opened in 1994 as a day-use facility with interpretive programs jointly operated by the DNR and the Grand Portage Band of Ojibwa. Admission: Park Permit. Hours: Daytime. Address: On the upper side of Highway 61, just past the town of Grand Portage. Phone: (218) 475-2360.

⭐⭐ **Gunflint Trail**—This 63-mile road leads north and west from Grand Marais into the BWCA wilderness and Superior National Forest's close to 3 million acres of public land. You'll find highly rated wilderness lodges, fishing, wildlife (including moose and eagles), lots of hiking, and winter skiing. Bring your hiking boots and lots of mosquito repellent if you're visiting this area during the summer months. The Gunflint Trail Association puts out helpful guides. Phone: (800) 338-6932.

⭐ **Gondola Sky Ride/Alpine Slide/Mountain Bike Park**—Gondola rides climb to the Moose Mountain summit at Lutsen Mountains ski area and offer excellent ridgeline views, especially scenic during fall color season. There are hiking trails here, as well as an alpine slide and a mountain-bike park. Admission: Gondola ride: $4.75–$6.75, under 7 free. Alpine slide: $3.75–$16.50. Mountain biking trail pass: $9 with one gondola ride to $16.50 for one day. Bike rental: $8 an hour, $24 all day. Combination daily pass: $20. Hours: Memorial Day–Labor Day, opens at 10 a.m., closing varies, open until 7 p.m. July weekends. Late May and early to mid-October, weekends, 10–5 p.m. Address: 90 minutes northeast of Duluth, off Highway 61. Phone: (218) 663-7281. (1 hour–all day)

FITNESS AND RECREATION

Hiking and skiing (cross-country and downhill) dominate the recreation scene. Duluth's visitor's guide, (800) 438-5884, lists eight hiking and five ski trails with their locations, along with bike, canoe, and snowmobile rental sources. **Lutsen Mountains** ski area, (800) 360-7666, has the best downhill skiing in the Midwest and offers various ski packages. There's also downhill skiing at **Spirit Mountain** in Duluth, (800) 642-6377. You can hike segments of the **Superior Hiking Trail** which, when completed, will stretch from Duluth to the Canadian border. Seasoned hikers can try the 75-mile BWCA **Border Route Trail** from Kekekabic Trail on the Gunflint Trail to the Pigeon River below South Fowl Lake, state park and other area trails, or loop combinations. The U.S. Forest Service, (218) 387-1750, and Tip of the Arrowhead, (800) 622-4014, publish a hiking guide listing 33 hikes, including the 6-mile **Temperance River** trail with pools and rocky ledges; the 2-mile **Devils Kettle** trail at Judge C.R. Magney State Park with waterfalls, rapids, and a disappearing 50-foot waterfall; and the short but steep **Honeymoon Bluff Trail** off County 66 at the Flour Lake Campground entrance with an overlook on Hungry Jack Lake. For more detailed information, get the *Guide to Lake Superior Hiking* sold in local shops or available from the Lake Superior Hiking Association, (218) 834-4436. Head to **Village Inn-Resort's Homestead Stables** at Lutsen Mountains for guided horseback rides, (218) 663-7241. Golf courses include **Superior National Golf Course** in Lutsen, (218) 663-7195, with 18 holes of championship golf. You'll find numerous charter fishing companies in Duluth, including **England's Charters**, (218) 721-3976, and **Lake Superior Sport Fishing Charters**, (218) 724-4214 or (218) 724-9104. The area also offers kayaking, rock-climbing, and canoeing. Winter sports include cross country and downhill skiing, dogsledding, and yurt-to-yurt or lodge-to-lodge skiing: Contact the Gunflint Trail Association, (800) 338-6932, and Lutsen-Tofte Association, (218) 663-7804.

FOOD

You'll find excellent food here. In Duluth, go to **Natchio's Greektown Restaurant**, 109 North Second Ave. W., (218) 722-6585, for souvlaki and meals for $5.50–$21.95. Duluth's **Pickwick Restaurant**, 508 E. Superior St., (218) 727-8901, is a classic establishment that has been family-operated since 1914, offering good steaks and traditional fare

NORTH SHORE REGION

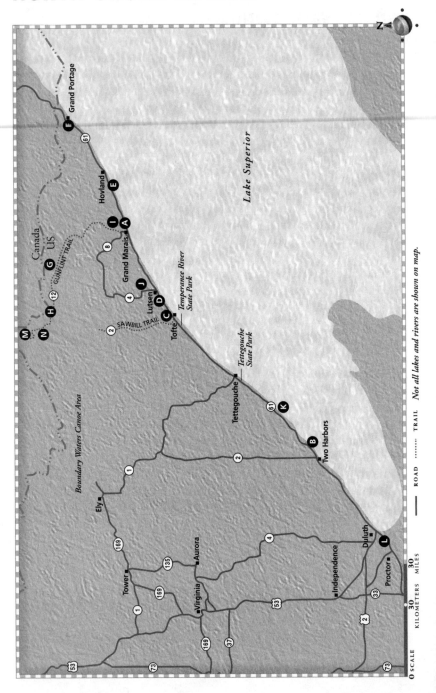

Lake Superior

Grand Portage

Hovland

Grand Marais

Canada
US

GUNFLINT TRAIL

Lutsen

Temperance River
State Park

Tofte

SAWBILL TRAIL

Tettegouche
State Park

Tettegouche

Two Harbors

Boundary Waters Canoe Area

Ely

Tower

Aurora

Virginia

Independence

Duluth

Proctor

N

ROAD ········ TRAIL   *Not all lakes and rivers are shown on map.*

SCALE   0   30   KILOMETERS
        0   30   MILES

Food

Ⓐ Angry Trout

Ⓑ Betty's Pies

Ⓒ Bluefin Restaurant

Ⓐ Blue Water Café

Ⓓ Lutsen Resort

Ⓔ Naniboujou Lodge

Ⓕ Starlight Room

Ⓐ Sven and Ole's

Ⓘ Indian Point Campground

Ⓛ Jay Cooke State Park

Ⓔ Judge C.R. Magney State Park

Ⓜ Trail's End Campground

Ⓝ Voyageur Outfitters

Lodging

Ⓖ Bearskin Lodge

Ⓐ Econolodge

Ⓕ Grand Portage Lodge

Ⓗ Gunflint Lodge

Ⓓ Lutsen Resort and Sea Villas

Ⓘ Pincushion Mountain
    Bed and Breakfast

Ⓐ Seawall Motel

Ⓑ Superior Shores

Ⓙ The Woods Bed and Breakfast

Camping

Ⓖ East Bearskin Campground

Ⓚ Gooseberry Falls State Park

Ⓐ Grand Marais Recreation
    Area RV Park-Campground

Ⓕ Grand Portage Campground
    and Marina

Ⓗ Gunflint Pines Resort

Note: Items with the same letter are located in the same town or area.

from $7–$21.95. **Grandma's**, 522 Lake Ave. S., Duluth, (218) 727-4192, serves sandwiches, soups, steaks, and pasta in a casual, fun atmosphere for $8–$25. **Augustino's**, (218-722-2787, in Fitger's Inn at 600 E. Superior St.), serves Italian pasta and seafood for $6.95–$17.95. **Bluefin Restaurant**, on the North Shore near Tofte, (218) 663-7297, features locally caught fish and exceptional cuisine for $7–$18.95. Travelers make a beeline for **Betty's Pies**, 215 Highway 61 E. in Two Harbors, (218) 834-3367, for wonderful pie and Lake Superior trout. Northshore area lodges serve fantastic meals. Try the wild-rice soup and raisin rye bread in **Lutsen Resort's** Scandinavian dining room, off Highway 61 at Lutsen, (218) 663-7212; dinner costs from $9.95–$19.95. Afternoon tea, from 3–5 p.m. daily, with scones and shortbread cookies for $6.25, is a delight at **Naniboujou Lodge**, 15 miles east of Grand Marais via Highway 61, (218) 387-2688, a former private club with a great hall decorated in Cree Indian motif. The **Angry Trout** in Grand Marais, (218) 387-1265, serves pasta, fish, and salads with attention to healthy preparation. The town's **Blue Water Café**, (218) 387-1597, is where local folks gather, and **Sven and Ole's**, (218) 387-1713, may be the only place you'll find Scandinavian pizza; meals cost from $4–$12. There's also Grand Portage Casino's **Starlight Room**, with dinners from $5.50–$23.

LODGING

At **Fitger's Inn**, 600 E. Superior St., Duluth, (800) 726-2982, you'll lodge in a renovated 1857 brewery for $72–$245. Duluth's **Best Western Edgewater East**, 2400 London Road, (800) 777-7925, is on the lakewalk with rooms from $69–$121. The **Ellery House**, 28 S. 21st Ave. E., Duluth, (800) 355-3794, is an 1890 Victorian bed and breakfast with a full breakfast and rooms from $69-$125; the **A. Charles Weiss Inn**, 1615 E. Superior St., (218) 724-7016, furnished with antiques, has rooms from $85 to $125. **Superior Shores**, 1 mile north of Two Harbors, (800) 242-1988, is beautifully redone with lake homes and condominiums from $69–$229. The **Woods Bed & Breakfast**, on Caribou Trail near Lutsen, 1½ miles from Highway 61, (218) 663-7144, has rooms for $59–$79. **Lutsen Resort and Sea Villas**, (800) 258-8736, on the Lake Superior North Shore, has lodge guestrooms, new log cabins, and townhomes for $55–$239. **Gunflint Lodge**, 45 miles up the Gunflint Trail, (800) 328-3325, has been run by the Kerfoot family since 1927 and has cabins with modern conveniences for $149–$309 for

two people. **Bearskin Lodge**, 275 Gunflint Trail, (800) 338-4170, is a
highly regarded upscale resort with lakefront log cabins, townhouses
and a lodge with dining for $670–$1,050 weekly. It's a cross-country ski
resort in winter, often booked a year ahead. **Pincushion Mountain
Bed and Breakfast**, 220 Gunflint Trail, (800) 542-1226, has rooms for
$80–$90, with May and June discounts. **Grand Portage Lodge** in
Grand Portage, (800) 543-1384, has double rooms for $56.95, under 18
free. The **EconoLodge**, East U.S. Highway 61, Grand Marais, (800)
247-6020, has a fireside lakeview lobby and rooms from $59–$110.
Seawall Motel, U.S. Highway 61 and 3rd Ave. W., Grand Marais,
(800) 245-5806, is a modest, clean motel with a harbor view and rooms
for $42–$64.

CAMPING

Private campgrounds include **Grand Portage Campground and
Marina** with full hookups on Lake Superior at Grand Portage, (800)
543-1384; rates from $10–$17 or $250 per month. Among the lodges
on Gunflint Trail offering campsites with hookups and showers are
Gunflint Pines Resort, 45 miles up the Gunflint Trail, (800) 533-5814,
with 18 sites, boat/motor rental, a lodge, playground, and swimming for
$17–$21; and **Voyageur Outfitters**, on Seagull River, (800) 777-7215,
with 12 sites, boat/motor rental and groceries for $5–$20 for two people, two-day minimum stay. Private campgrounds near Duluth with
showers, electricity, and full hookups include **Indian Point Campground**, 75th Avenue W. and Grand Ave. (Highway 23), on the St.
Louis River Bay near the zoo, (218) 624-5637, with 50 sites and wheelchair accessible facilities. Public camping options are nearly overwhelm-
ing. **Jay Cooke State Park**, (218) 384-4610, south of Duluth off I-35
near Carlton, exit 235, then take County 1, has beautiful stands of birch
and St. Louis River views, 80 sites, 20 with electricity, and handicapped
accessible showers.

Many of the eight state parks lining the North Shore have campsites: **Judge C.R. Magney**, (218) 387-2929, has 33 drive-in sites, showers but no electricity; **Gooseberry Falls**, (218) 834-3855, has 70 sites
with showers but no electricity. It is imperative to have weekend campsite reservations on the North Shore in summer and fall. (See Practical
Tips for camping reservation information and phone numbers.) Fifteen
Forest Service-run campgrounds have water but no electricity or showers, with the exception of **East Bearskin**, (218) 388-2292, which is on

County 12 (Gunflint Trail), and **Trail's End**, (218) 388-2212, also on County 12 (Gunflint Trail), which have showers. Trails End will also take reservations. The **Grand Marais Recreation Area RV Park-Campground**, W. Highway 61, on the west end of the harbor in Grand Marais, (218) 387-1712, has 300 campsites from tenting to full RV hookups, bathhouses, and an indoor pool for $13.50–$18; (800) 998-0959 for reservations.

NIGHTLIFE AND SPECIAL EVENTS

Sleep is the top-rated evening activity after hiking on the North Shore or Gunflint Trail. Some lodges and state parks do have evening nature walks, campfire talks, and naturalist-led programs. Casinos have become very popular in this region. You'll find **Fond-du-Luth Casino** in Duluth at 129 E. Superior St., (800) 873-0280, and **Grand Portage Casino** at Grand Portage, (800) 543-1384. Duluth's **Bayfront Festival Park** hosts musical events all summer long, including the **Bayfront Blues Festival** in August, (800) 438-5884. **Grand Slam-Adventure World** with indoor baseball, softball, and amusement rides in Canal Park, 395 Lake Ave., (218) 722-5667, is popular with kids; there are also dinner cruises of the harbor, (218) 722-6218. Check out performing arts events at **The Depot**, 506 W. Michigan St., (218) 727-8025, in Duluth, and the **Grand Marais Playhouse** in Grand Marais, (218) 387-1648. There's also the **Waltzing Bear Booksellers and Coffee Brewers**, (218) 387-9199, in Grand Marais, a fun place to spend time reading literary and small-press books over an espresso coffee drink and dessert.

Scenic Route: Lake Superior North Shore Drive

Follow Highway 61 up the north shore for spectacular views of waves crashing on the rocky Lake Superior shore. The spectacle of storms on the North Shore can be almost magnetic. Storms quickly transform clouds, sky, and lake from benign to threatening and make for a grand show, backdropped by tall pines and spruce. Stop to hike in the numerous state parks; at Gooseberry Falls State Park, the Gooseberry River tumbles over a series of waterfalls. In Temperance River State Park, the river courses through a black-walled gorge and you can see potholes created long ago. Tettegouche State Park contains the Baptism River's falls and cascades, as well as lush inland forests of maple, basswood, and spruce. Spend some time in Grand Marais with its picturesque lighthouse, good restaurants, and arts community. Continue on Highway 61 to Grand Portage, visit the monument and state park, then backtrack to Grand Marais and drive the wilderness terrain of the Gunflint

LAKE SUPERIOR NORTH SHORE DRIVE

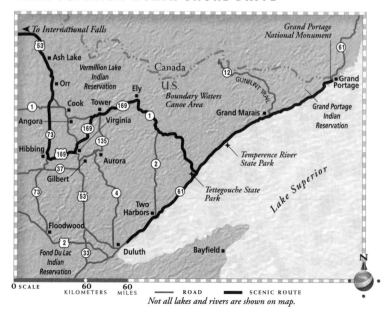

Trail. Overnight in one of the fine lodges and decide where to go next. Options include taking 61 back to Duluth to catch the state parks you missed on the way up, or take 61 to Scenic Highway 1, at Tettegouche State Park, and follow it to Ely. From Ely, take Highway 1 southwest to Soudan and Tower, take the underground mine tour at Soudan Underground Mine State Park, then follow State 135 south about 18 or so miles to County 21. Stop at the visitor center at the intersection and sign up for a tour of Finnish pioneer homesteads and saunas given at 10 a.m. and 2 p.m. daily, from Memorial Day–Labor Day, $2–$5: The guide rides with you in your car on the 15-mile, two- to three-hour trip. Then backtrack (north on 135) to State 1/169. Take 169 west to Iron World near Chisholm for a colorful introduction to mining history and Iron Range culture via exhibits, demonstrations, ethnic costumes, and food. From Chisholm, take State 73 and U.S. Highway 53 north to International Falls and Voyageurs National Park. ◼

3
MINNESOTA'S NORTHERN WILDERNESS REGION

The roadless Boundary Waters Canoe Area (BWCA) lies at the top of the Arrowhead region in the Superior National Forest and contains some 2,000 lakes. The 1.3 million-acre BWCA stretches along the U.S.–Canadian border for 150 miles, adjoining Voyageurs National Park. The national park's 218,000 acres embrace a similar water-and-woods roadless wilderness; however, motorized craft are allowed in Voyageurs—which is not the case in the BWCA. BWCA explorers travel by canoe, just as the French Canadian voyageurs did when the water served as their highway between Lake Superior and Lake of the Woods.

A fluke of cartography awarded Minnesota a separate chunk of land bordering Lake of the Woods, known as the Northwest Angle. To drive there, you pass through a portion of Manitoba. Or you can go by boat, across huge and temperamental Lake of the Woods, north from Warroad. Voyageurs and Native Americans—first Cree, Monsonis, and Assiniboine, then Dakota (Sioux) who were displaced by the Ojibwa—were the only regular occupants of these wilderness lands for many years. Eventually, logging, agriculture, and tourism arrived. Resorts and outfitters thrive in this sparsely populated remote region. The permanent dwellers are independent, hardy, self-reliant individuals with a genuine affinity for the outdoors and solitude. ◧

NORTHERN WILDERNESS REGION

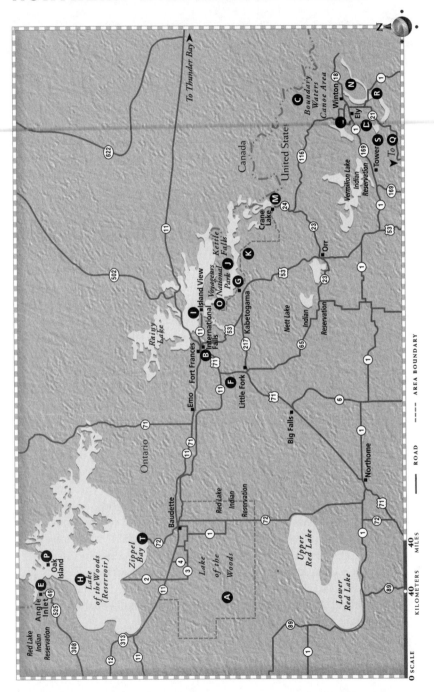

Sightseeing Highlights

Ⓐ Beltrami Island State Forest

Ⓑ Border Country Traders

Ⓒ BWCA

Ⓓ Ely

Ⓔ Fort St. Charles

Ⓕ Grand Mound History Center

Ⓑ International Falls

Ⓖ Kabetogama Lake Visitor Center

Ⓑ Koochiching County Historical Museum/Bronko Nagurski Museum

Ⓗ Lake of the Woods

Ⓘ Rainy Lake Visitor Center

Ⓙ Voyageurs National Park

Ⓑ Voyageurs National Park Headquarters

Food

Ⓚ Ash Trail Lodge

Ⓖ Bait 'n Bite

Ⓛ Burntside Lodge

Ⓑ Grandma's Pantry

Ⓑ Hummingbird Café

Ⓘ Island View Lodge

Ⓜ Nelson's Resort

Ⓝ Silver Rapids Lodge

Lodging

Ⓔ Angle Outpost

Ⓞ Arrowhead Lodge and Resort

Ⓟ Bonnie Brae Resort

Ⓠ Finnish Heritage Homestead

Ⓜ Nelson's Resort

Ⓔ Prothero's Trading Post

Ⓘ Rainy Lake Houseboats

Ⓡ River Point Resort

Ⓝ Silver Rapids Lodge

Ⓑ Super 8 Motel

Ⓜ Voyageur Houseboats

Camping

Ⓢ Bear Head Lake State Park

Ⓣ Morris Point Resort

Ⓝ Silver Rapids Lodge and Campground

Ⓚ Sunset Resort Campground

Ⓞ Woodenfrog Campground

Ⓣ Zippel Bay State Park

A PERFECT DAY IN THE NORTHERN WILDERNESS

Breakfast in Ely, visit the Wolf Center, and drive to Voyageurs National Park. Take the narrated boat tour on the *Pride of Rainy Lake*, see the exhibits at the visitor center, check into a lodge, go for a hike, go fishing, or hire a small plane for an aerial view of the park. Then fill up on good home cooking in the lodge dining room and hear anglers exchange fishing tales. At dusk, go for another walk, keeping an eye out for bears. At night, sit on the dock listening to loons and waves lapping the shore. Go to bed and sleep, sated with the fresh clean air.

SIGHTSEEING HIGHLIGHTS

✮✮✮ **Boundary Waters Canoe Area (BWCA)**—More than 1 million acres of wilderness and 1,500 miles of water trails await canoeists. Permits are required for entrance, so contact the permit station/headquarters. Headquarters hours: 6:30 a.m.–5 p.m. daily; mid-May–October, until 6 p.m. Address: east of Ely on Highway 169, in the International Wolf Center building. Phone: (218) 365-7681.

✮✮✮ **Ely**—Ely is the launching point for BWCA adventures, so the town is filled with outfitters and guides who can supply everything you need for a canoe trip into the wilderness. The advent of Northwest Airlines service to Ely from May through September makes getting to the remote BWCA as easy as a 45-minute flight from the Twin Cities. For details on area happenings and attractions, call (800) 777-7281.

On guided walking tours of Ely, you'll learn why 41 languages were once spoken in this former mining town. Admission: $7. Hours: 9:30–11 a.m., Monday, Wednesday, and Friday from June–mid-September. Address: Meet at the community center/library, First Avenue E. and Harvey Street; reservations required. Phone: (218) 365-4809. (1½ hours)

✮✮✮ **Lake of the Woods**—This vast lake claims 65,000 miles of shoreline and 14,000 islands. People come here for walleye, muskie, and northern pike fishing. They also come to get away—really away. Lake of the Woods is as far north as you can go in the contiguous United States. To immerse yourself in the countryside, take the Wilderness Drives in 669,030-acre **Beltrami Island State Forest**, including Homesteader's Drive on Bankton Forest Road, with old cemeteries and lilacs abloom near ruined buildings on old homesteads. Try Blueberry Picker's Drive for the best picking—along roadsides or small forest clearings where jack pines grow. Main entrances to the drive are at Williams and Baudette. Get a detailed Wilderness Drives map from Lake of the Woods Tourism on Highway 11 in Baudette, (800) 382-FISH. (2 hours or more)

There's also **Fort St. Charles**, a restored fort on the site of the original log fort and trading post erected in 1732 by French voyageurs and commanded by Pierre La Verendrye. Reachable by boat. Open 24 hours. (½ hour)

✯✯✯ **Voyageurs National Park**—More than a third of the park's 218,000 acres are under the waters of four major lakes—Rainy, Kabetogama, Sand Point, and Namakan—and some 26 smaller ones with countless rocky islands. Leave your car at one of the park's four entry points and explore the park by water in your own boat, via resort boats or the visitor centers' excursion boats, canoe trips, and programs.

At **Kabetogama Lake Visitor Center**, *Sight-Sea-Er* tour boat offers naturalist-guided tours of the lakes, from a six-hour trip to historic Kettle Falls Hotel ($20 –$30) to a two-hour sunset cruise ($8–$12). Address: From U.S. 53, take County 122 north to Kabetogama Lake Center. Phone: (218) 875-2111. **Rainy Lake Visitor Center** has displays about the park and *Pride of Rainy Lake* cruises with a naturalist aboard, (218) 286-5470 for reservations. Included are a 1½-hour gold mine tour ($5.75–$10) and a two-hour bald-eagle-watch tour ($6.50–$12). Address: From International Falls, follow Highway 11 east 12 miles. Phone: (218) 286-5258. Both centers have free naturalist-guided canoe trips and evening programs. **Voyageurs National Park Headquarters** is at 3131 Highway 53, the south end of International Falls; (218) 283-9821.

✯✯ **Dorothy Molter Cabin**—The original cabins of Dorothy Molter, "The Root Beer Lady," have been reconstructed in Ely. Molter lived alone on Knife Lake in the BWCA for more than 50 years and served homemade root beer to canoeists who stopped by. Admission: $1–$2; $5 for a family. Hours: 10 a.m.–6 p.m. daily, May through September. Address: On Highway 169, a quarter mile east of Ely. Phone: (218) 365-4451. (½–1 hour)

✯✯ **International Falls**—Located in the heart of the wilderness, this city of 8,300 was—and still is—shaped by forestry and logging. The **Koochiching County Historical Museum/Bronko Nagurski**

ELY

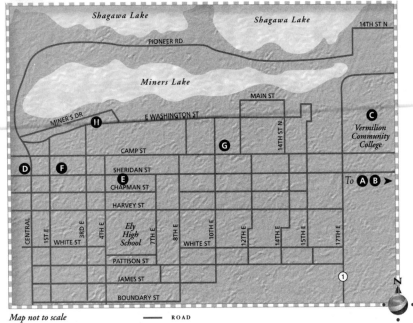

Map not to scale   —— ROAD

Sightseeing Highlights

- **Ⓐ** Dorothy Molter Cabin
- **Ⓑ** International Wolf Center
- **Ⓒ** Vermilion Interpretive Center

Food

- **Ⓓ** The Chocolate Moose
- **Ⓔ** Minglewood Café
- **Ⓕ** Vertins Café, Pub, and Supper Club

Lodging

- **Ⓖ** Budget Host Motel
- **Ⓗ** Trezona House

Note: Items with the same letter are located in the same or town area.

Museum tells the colorful story of gold-rush days, logging, and homesteading—and NFL football legend and native son Nagurski. Admission: $1–$3, under 5 free. Hours: 11 a.m.–5 p.m., Monday–Saturday; Sunday and holidays, 1–5 p.m. Address: 3rd St. and 6th Ave., in Smokey Bear Park. Phone: (218) 283-4316. (1 hour)

Grand Mound History Center interprets the Laurel Indian culture, from 200 B.C. to A.D. 800, and tracks succeeding Indian cultures. It is the site of the largest prehistoric burial mound in Minnesota. Walk through lovely woods to see other mounds. Admission: $2, under 6 free. Hours: May–Labor Day, 10 a.m.–5 p.m., Monday–Saturday; noon–5 p.m., Sunday. Labor Day–mid-October, 10 a.m.–5 p.m. Saturday; noon–5 p.m. Sunday. Address: 17 miles west of International Falls on Highway 11. Phone: (218) 279-3332. (1 hour)

Be sure to stop at **Border Country Traders**, which sells everything from fresh fish to art to taxidermy services. Address: 200 Second Ave. Phone: (218) 283-4414.

★★ **International Wolf Center**—You can actually howl with the resident pack of wolves at the center that features a "Wolves and Humans" exhibit, other displays, ongoing wolf research, and educational programs. Admission: $2.50–$5, under 6 free. Hours: May–mid-October, 9 a.m.–5 p.m. daily, open until 6 p.m. in July and August. Open Friday and Saturday, 10 a.m.–5 p.m., and Sunday until 3 p.m. other seasons. Address: Highway 169, on the east edge of Ely. Phone: (218) 365-4695 or (800) ELY-WOLF. (1 hour)

★ **Vermilion Interpretive Center**—The center covers 12,000 years of local history and tells the story of the Vermilion Iron Range. Admission: $1–$2, under 5 free. Hours: Memorial Day–Labor Day, 10 a.m.–4 p.m., daily; winter by appointment. Address: 1900 E. Camp St., Vermilion Community College Campus in Ely. Phone: (218) 365-3226. (½ hour)

FITNESS AND RECREATION

Fishing is the big recreation here. We're talking big fish—8-, 10-, 20-, 30-, and even 40-pounders. Visitors are sure to see eagles, osprey, pelicans, and cormorants, and possibly moose and bear. Blueberry-picking is a popular pursuit—for bears and for humans. More than 22 outfitters base in Ely to provide supplies and guidance for canoe trips in the BWCA. Among them are 75-year-old **Wilderness Outfitters**,

1 E. Camp St., (800) 777-8572; **Canoe Country Outfitters**, operating since 1946, 629 E. Sheridan, (800) 752-2306; and **Piragis Northwoods Outfitting**, 105 N. Central Ave., (800) 223-6565. You can walk or ski around Miners Lake in Ely on the 4-mile **Trezona Trail**, which connects to the International Wolf Center. **Zippel Bay State Park** on Lake of the Woods has 3,000 acres with a 3-mile sand beach and 6-mile trail system for hiking and horseback riding, 3½ miles of ski trails and 5 miles of snowmobile trails, and abundant wildlife. (See Camping for location.) **Bear Head Lake State Park,** near Ely, offers 4,375 acres with hiking, skiing, and snowmobile trails, plus boat and canoe rentals at the park contact station. (See Camping.) If you come in winter, try mushing your own dogsled team. Companies offering dogsled outings include **White Wilderness Sled Dog Adventures** with naturalist/guides and heated tents or lodge-to-lodge trips from Ely, (800) 701-6238; and **Outdoor Adventure Dog Sled Trips** based in Ely offering day trips, winter camping, and cabin/lodge accommodations, (800) 777-8574. For helpful information, read *Boundary Waters Journal* magazine, 9396 Rocky Ledge Rd., Ely; (800) 548-7319.

FOOD

In Ely, the **Chocolate Moose**, Central and Main, (218) 365-6343, serves homemade muffins, wild-rice pancakes, cappuccino, walleye, and buffalo. **Minglewood Café**, 528 E. Sheridan St., Ely, (218) 365-3398, offers a health food focus; and **Vertins Café, Pub, and Supper Club** at 145 E. Sheridan, (218) 365-4041, has three dining rooms and is noted for homemade soups, steaks, and sticky buns. Visit **Burntside Lodge**, 2755 Burntside Lodge Rd., Ely area, (218) 365-3894, for walleye and steak in an historic lodge with lakeside dining. **Silver Rapids Lodge**, 5 miles from Ely via Highways 58/16, offers sunset views with its prime rib and a Sunday brunch, (218) 365-4877. **Grandma's Pantry** in tiny Ranier (Voyageurs National Park area), 3 miles east of International Falls on Highway 11, (218) 286-5584, serves wonderful homemade soups and meals. Ranier's **Hummingbird Café**, (218) 286-1192, is also good, and there are some fun shops and galleries here. In the Lake Kabetogama area, the **Bait 'n Bite** restaurant's owner has a sense of humor: "Eat Here and Get Worms" reads the sign! It's actually a family dining place with good homemade soups and dinners from $6.95–$10.95, on County 122/9634 Gappa Rd., (218) 875-2281. You can pick up tackle and bait here, too. Resorts in this area with public dining rooms include **Ash Trail Lodge**, 25 miles south of International Falls on U.S. 53, then follow County 129/Ash River Trail, (218) 374-3131; **Nelson's Resort**, 7632 Nelson Rd. on Crane Lake, (218) 993-2295, with home-style cooking and a five-course meal for $14–$18, by reservation only; and overlooking Rainy Lake, **Island View Lodge** with fine dining, 12 miles east of International Falls via Highway 11, (218) 286-3511 or (800) 777-7856.

LODGING

In Ely, the 1869 **Trezona House**, 315 E. Washington St., (800) 430-5434, has rooms furnished in hunting, mining, fishing, and North Woods cabin themes. The full breakfast cooked by co-owner Jim Macdonald, transplanted from Scotland, includes Scottish potato "stovies" and his "internationally acclaimed omelet." Rates range from $55–$75. Another unusual and fun lodging choice west of Ely is the **Finnish Heritage Homestead** bed and breakfast, (218) 984-3318, 4776 Waisanen Rd., Embarrass (take Highway 21 west from Ely to Embarrass, go south on County 362/Waisanen Rd. half a mile), on an 1891 farm complete with animals and a wood-fired sauna. Guest rooms have handmade quilts, bathrobes, and thoughtful touches for around $58.50; inquire about packages. Area motels include the **Budget Host Motel**, 1047 E. Sheridan St., (218) 365-3237, with double rooms from $43.95–$59.95. Ely area resorts include **Silver Rapids Lodge** on White Iron Lake Chain, (800) 950-9425, and **River Point Resort** at Kawishiwi River/Birch Lake, (800) 456-5580. In the Voyageurs National Park area, lodging includes **Nelson's Resort** on Crane Lake, (218) 993-2295, an exceptional resort that wins raves with log cabins and lodge dining rooms with fireplaces. Rates range from $103 per person daily with three meals to $90 with dinner only, June–September. May and September rates are $87–$77. There are full-week-stay discounts. Fishing guides cost $245 per day for three people, and boat rentals are $55–$95 per day. To get there, take U.S. 53 to Orr, go east on County 23 about 28 miles to the resort sign and Nelson Rd.

   Arrowhead Lodge and Resort on Kabetogama Lake, (218) 875-2141, is a traditional Minnesota lake fishing-resort lodge with lodge rooms and two meals from $184 per person for two days to $620 for seven days. Cottages and two meals range from $205 for two days to $695 for seven days per person. Rates include a boat and motor, dock service, and maid and linen service. To get there, take U.S 53 to County 122, go east to Waltz Road, turn right, and go 2 miles to Arrowhead.

Houseboat rentals are also a popular way to experience the lakes: **Voyageur Houseboats** on Crane Lake, (800) 882-6287, rent from $210–$745 daily and $975–$3,850 a week. To get there, follow County 23 and County 24 east from U.S. 53 at Orr. **Rainy Lake Houseboats** on Rainy Lake, (218) 286-5391, rent for $210–$505 daily and $1,055–$2,545 weekly. To get there, take Highway 11 east for 10 miles from International Falls.

In International Falls, motels include the **Super 8 Motel**, on U.S. 53, (800) 800-8000, with rooms from $48.88–$50.88. In the Lake of the Woods area, **Prothero's Trading Post** at Angle Inlet, (800) 376-3151, has handcrafted housekeeping log cabins with window boxes and log furniture. You'll find reading material as well as the history of long-time owners Grace and Dale Prothero in the trading post sitting area. Rates are $380 a week for two people, $50/$40 for each additional adult/child under 12. A boat is included, and motors rent for $18 a day. There are few stores here so bring food with you. Reserve early; this resort fills quickly. **Angle Outpost** on Lake of the Woods is owned and run by Diane and Paul Edman, who make you feel at home and serve excellent food, (800) 441-5014. Cabins rent from $24–$45 per person a night for housekeeping; $35–$55 with dinner; $48–$69 with three meals. They are open for ice fishing in the winter at lower rates. To reach Prothero's and Angle Outpost, take Highway 313 north from Warroad; it turns into Highway 12 in Canada. At Sprague, Manitoba, go right on Highway 308 which becomes a gravel road. Turn right on 525 and drive 20 minutes to the resort area. Dan McClanathan's **Bonnie Brae Resort**, (800) 772-8411, on pretty Oak Island has attractive housekeeping condominium units, log fourplex units, three semi-modern cabin units, a log lodge, hiking trails, and lots of pelicans winging overhead. Rates of $205–$310 per person for three days and nights include a 25-minute fly-in from Baudette or boat-in from Young's Bay on Northwest Angle, plus a boat, motor, and gas. Bring your groceries with you.

CAMPING

Some resorts in this area also have camping. Private campgrounds near Ely include **Silver Rapids Lodge and Campground**, (218) 365-4877, on the White Iron Chain, via Highway 169 east of Ely, then right on Highways 58/16, with 15 lakeside full hookup sites, 19 electricity/water,

and two tent sites, a restaurant, and activities, from $15–$22 a night or
$90–$135 a week. **Bear Head Lake State Park**, between Tower and Ely
off State 169/1, south on County 128, (218) 365-7229, has 73 drive-in,
53 backpack, and one canoe-in sites; no electricity; handicap accessible
showers and flush toilets. In the BWCA, camping is allowed on designated campsites identified on your BWCA maps.

In the Voyageurs National Park area, private campgrounds include
Sunset Resort Campground on Ash River, (800)232-3161, via County
129/Ash River Trail, with six full-hookup and 35 wooded tent sites with
electricity, water, and showers for $14–$18. Public **Woodenfrog
Campground** on Kabetogama Lake off of County 122 has 60 secluded,
wooded sites with water and a good beach but no showers or electricity
for $7; (218) 875-2602 or (218) 757-3274. Lake of the Woods area pri-
vate campgrounds include **Morris Point Resort**, north of Baudette via
Highway 172, then left on County 8, on a 300-acre peninsula, with 20
sites with electricity, 20 for tenting, and a new shower building for
$12–$20; (218) 634-2570. Public camping is available at 2,906-acre
Zippel Bay State Park, 10 miles northeast of Williams on Lake of the
Woods, off County 8, with 57 rustic sites, showers but no electricity,
(218) 783-6252.

NIGHTLIFE AND SPECIAL EVENTS

Frankly, folks don't come here for the nightlife. However, hanging out
in a bar—which is likely to sport mounted fish, pine paneling, and
lighted beer signs—can be a fun way to meet the local people and learn
what it's like to live in this remote place. Resorts often have games and
pool tables. **Nelson's Resort** on Crane Lake, (218) 993-2295, has
entertainment in the lounge Thursday–Saturday. In the Ely area, you
can go to **Fortune Bay Casino** in Tower, (800) 992-7529, for evening
activity. A fun summer event is Ely's **Blueberry Arts Festival** in July,
(800) 777-7281. January brings the International Falls-to-Orr **Sled Dog
Race and Weight Pull**, (800) 325-5766.

THE NORTH WOODS LAKES
OF MINNESOTA

This is the pine forest known as the home of Paul Bunyan and his blue ox, Babe—the lakes and wetlands created by glacial moraine and glacial meltwater. It is also what most Minnesotans identify as "the lakes region." Less rugged and wild than the landscape at the top of the state, the North Woods Lakes region has become a vacation playground. Here, in more or less the midsection of Minnesota, resorts range from small and secluded to upscale and posh. Nearby cities and towns contain shopping, amusement parks, casinos, and plenty of other entertainment to occupy vacationers.

Although fishing is not the only thing to do here, it does have a significant presence. In fact, Mille Lacs Lake, the second largest Minnesota lake at 20 miles across and with 100 miles of shoreline, is renowned for good walleye fishing. Near Bemidji, the headwaters of the mighty Mississippi River lie in Itasca State Park, which was discovered in 1832 by Henry Schoolcraft and his guide, Chief Ozawindib. Here, as it begins its 2,348-mile trip to the Gulf of Mexico, the Mississippi River is a shallow stream that is easy to cross. East of Bemidji stretches the vast Chippewa National Forest, a habitat for bald eagles and numerous other wild creatures. ◼

A PERFECT DAY IN THE MINNESOTA NORTH WOODS LAKES REGION

Start with an early morning bog walk in Lake Bemidji State Park to catch the songbirds' serenade. Grab breakfast in Bemidji, stock up on picnic food, and head for Itasca State Park. Visit the Mississippi Headwaters and hike the Schoolcraft Trail. Take the Wilderness Drive; hike to remote Bohall Lake and eat a picnic lunch. From Douglas Lodge, hike the 2-mile Dr. Robert's Trail, or hike to the observation tower. Take the Lake Itasca boat tour, eat dinner at Douglas Lodge, then cozy into your own log cabin for a night in the Itasca State Park woods.

SIGHTSEEING HIGHLIGHTS

★★★ **Bemidji**—Northeast of the Mississippi River Headwaters and Itasca State Park, this city of 11,245 lays claim to being the first city on the Mississippi. Logging in the area orginally attracted the railroad and led to the growth of Bemidji, which was named for the first settler here, an Indian who lived on the south shore of the lake. Legend attributes the creation of the river and surrounding 1,000 lakes to the Minnesota North Woods' fabled resident, Paul Bunyan. That's why 18-foot statues of Bunyan and Babe The Blue Ox stand on the shore of Lake Bemidji.

You can acquaint yourself with local flora and fauna on **Lake Bemidji State Park's bog walk**, a 1,200-foot boardwalk through a bog rich in plant life, including lady's slipper orchid and pitcher plant. The park has six other trails that wind through old-growth maple-basswood forest, lowland forest, and pine forest, and offers naturalist-guided tours. Admission: Park permit. Hours: 8 a.m.–10 p.m. Address: 3401 State Park Rd. NE, Bemidji, at the north end of the lake on County 20. Phone: (218) 755-3843. (½–1 hour)

Bemidji Woolen Mills sells wool goods including woodsman pants, knitting yarns, and Hudson Bay Point blankets. Hours: Year-round, 8 a.m.–5:30 p.m., Monday–Saturday; 10 a.m.–5 p.m., Sunday. Address: 301 Irvine Avenue. Phone: (218) 751-5166. (½ hour)

You can visit 11 antique shops in the area and numerous gift and novelty shops. Stop at Chocolates Plus for truffles and other goodies freshly made. Hours: Year-round, 10 a.m.–9 p.m., Monday–Saturday; noon–5 p.m., Sunday. Address: 102 First St. Phone: (218) 759-1175. The Old Schoolhouse holds the work of 500 area artists. Hours: 10 a.m. to

NORTH WOODS LAKES REGION

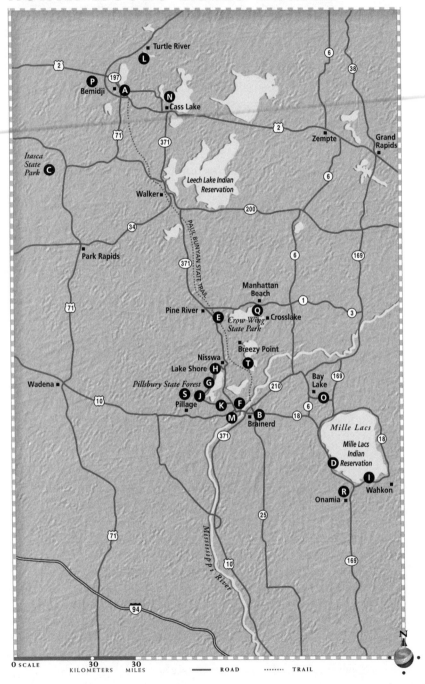

Turtle River

L

P Bemidji

A 197

N Cass Lake

2

38

6

Grand Rapids

Zempte

Itasca State Park **C**

Leech Lake Indian Reservation

Walker

200

6

34

Park Rapids

371

71

PAUL BUNYAN STATE TRAIL

Manhattan Beach

6

169

1

3

Pine River **E** Crow Wing State Park **Q** Crosslake

Breezy Point

Nisswa **T**

Lake Shore **H**

Pillsbury State Forest **G**

Wadena

10

S **J** Pillage

K **F** 210

M **B** Brainerd

Bay Lake

O 169

18

6

Mille Lacs

Mille Lacs Indian Reservation **D**

18

I Wahkon

R Onamia

25

71

Mississippi River

10

94

169

O SCALE
30 KILOMETERS   **30 MILES**   —— ROAD   .... TRAIL

N

Sightseeing Highlights

- Ⓐ Bemidji
- Ⓑ Brainerd
- Ⓑ Brainerd International Raceway
- Ⓑ Crow Wing County Historical Society Museum
- Ⓒ Itasca State Park
- Ⓓ Mille Lacs Indian Museum and Trading Post
- Ⓔ Minnesota Resort Museum
- Ⓕ Northland Arboretum
- Ⓖ Swedish Timber House

Food

- Ⓒ Douglas Lodge
- Ⓓ Grand Casino Mille Lacs
- Ⓗ Grand View Lodge
- Ⓘ Izaty's Golf and Yacht Club
- Ⓙ Kavanaugh's Resort and Restaurant
- Ⓚ Madden's on Gull Lake
- Ⓖ Quarterdeck Resort and Restaurant

Lodging

- Ⓛ A Place in the Woods
- Ⓜ Brainerd Days Inn
- Ⓑ Econo Lodge Motel
- Ⓝ Finn 'n Feather Resort
- Ⓗ Grand View Lodge
- Ⓒ Itasca State Park
- Ⓘ Izaty's Golf and Yacht Club
- Ⓙ Kavanaugh's Resort and Restaurant
- Ⓚ Madden's on Gull Lake
- Ⓖ Quarterdeck Resort and Restaurant
- Ⓠ Ruttger's Bay Lake Lodge

Camping

- Ⓟ Bemidji KOA
- Ⓠ Greer Lake Campground
- Ⓒ Itasca State Park
- Ⓡ Mille Lacs Kathio State Park
- Ⓢ Rock Lake Campground
- Ⓣ Wilderness Point Resort

Note: Items with the same letter are located in the same town or area.

5:30 p.m., Monday–Saturday. Address: 1 mile south of Bemidji via State 197, then 1 mile west on Old Schoolhouse and Carr Lake Road. Phone: (218) 751-4723. (½ hour)

Contact the Bemidji Convention and Visitor Bureau for information about Bemidji. Address: 300 Bemidji Ave. Phone: (800) 458-2223 or (218) 759-0164.

★★★ **Itasca State Park**—Established in 1891 to protect remnant stands of virgin pine and the Mississippi River source, this 32,690-acre park has an interpretive program with naturalist-led activities, including hikes and tours. The main attraction is the Mississippi River Head-waters. The park's historic Douglas Lodge has a dining room open daily, rooms, and cabin rentals May–September. There are also daily narrated naturalist tours of Lake Itasca on the boat *Chester Charles* at 11 a.m., and 1 and 3 p.m. daily, July–mid-August (Sundays, 1 and 3 p.m.); 1 and 3 p.m. mid- to late June and mid-August to September; at 1 p.m. late May–early June and in September. Tours cost $7, 3 and under free; (218) 732-5318 or (218) 266-2101. In Preacher's Grove, you can see a stand of red pines more than 250 years old. Take the 10-mile Wilderness Drive past a 2,000-acre wilderness of virgin forest including Minnesota's largest white pine. Admission: Park permit. Hours: 8 a.m.–10 p.m. Address: 20 miles north of Park Rapids on U.S. 71. Phone: (218) 266-2114.

★★ **Brainerd**—Brainerd, with a population of some 12,300, has been a popular vacation destination for many years. Resorts are the primary attraction here (see Lodging), and tourism flourishes. For information, contact the Brainerd Lakes Area Chamber of Commerce. Phone: (800) 450-2838, or (218) 829-2838. The **Crow Wing County Historical Society Museum**, housed in a 1917 sheriff's residence and jail, offers a glimpse of a sheriff's lifestyle and details about the history of the region, including Native American and logging artifacts. Admission: $3, children free. Hours: Memorial Day–Labor Day, 9 a.m.–5 p.m. Monday–Friday, until 1 p.m. on Saturday; Labor Day–Memorial Day, 1–5 p.m., Monday–Friday and 9 a.m.–1 p.m. Saturday. Address: 320 Laurel St., Brainerd. Phone: (218) 829-3268. (½–1 hour)

The **Minnesota Resort Museum** at Driftwood Family Resort has displays on early resort life in a 6,500-square-foot building. Admission: $1–$2. Hours: 10 a.m.–5 p.m. daily, May–September. Address: Pine River, on the Whitefish Chain of Lakes; 5½ miles north of Jenkins, off County 15. Phone: (218) 568-4221. (½–1 hour)

The **Brainerd International Raceway** hosts national competitions in NHRA drag and AMA motorcycle racing. There's also on-track camping. Admission: Varies with event. Hours: All-day events. AMA racing in July and August, NHRA drag racing in August. Address: Highway 371N, Brainerd. Phone: (612) 475-1500 or (218) 829-9863.

The **Swedish Timber House** sells Scandinavian gifts in a log house that was constructed in Sweden, dismantled, and shipped to the U.S. Hours: 10 a.m.–5 p.m. daily, May–late October; same hours, Friday–Sunday, December until Christmas. Address: 7678 Interlachen Rd., Lakeshore, Nisswa. Phone: (218) 963-7897.

At **Northland Arboretum**, 3,000 species of plants and a Nature Conservancy jack-pine savanna are contained on 600 acres with 12 miles of hiking/ski trails: The Paul Bunyan Recreational Trail starts here. Admission: $1–$3. Hours: Gates open 24 hours. Gatehouse hours are 8 a.m.–4 p.m., Monday–Friday. Honor system box on porch for fee if gatehouse is closed. Address: Off State 210 between Brainerd and Baxter, on West 7th St., or enter on Conservation Road in summer. Phone: (218) 829-8770. (½ hour)

✯ **Mille Lacs Indian Museum and Trading Post**—The exhibit hall focuses on the history of the Mille Lacs band of Ojibwa in this excellent new facility. The Four Seasons Room has dioramas depicting Ojibwa life, and the trading post sells American Indian–made wares. Admission: $2–$4, under 5 free; $10 family rate. Hours: May–October, 10 a.m.–5 p.m., Monday–Saturday; Sunday, noon–5 p.m. Address: North of Onamia 12 miles, on U.S. 169. Phone: (612) 532-3632. (1 hour)

FITNESS AND RECREATION

The **Paul Bunyan Trail**, a recreational corridor for biking, hiking, and snowmobiling, begins in Brainerd and connects to the Blue Ox Trail from Bemidji, which leads north to International Falls, (800) 450-2838. There is, of course, fishing for prized muskie, northern pike, largemouth bass, brown and rainbow trout, and panfish. Hunting for wild strawberries, raspberries, and blueberries is also popular. Golf courses at Madden's on Gull Lake and Grand View Lodge resorts (see Lodging) are among the finest in the Midwest. Winter sports range from cross-country and downhill skiing to curling and snowshoeing. You'll find 33 miles of hiking trails and a 17-mile bicycle route at **Itasca State Park**, plus boat, canoe, bike, and snowshoe rentals, (218) 266-2114; Itasca Sports Rental is across from the park headquarters on the main park drive. You can rent a multispeed mountain bike for $3.50 an hour or $20 a day—there's a family rate for five people or more of $12 per person per day—or rent a canoe or rowboat for $3 an hour or $18 a day. **Lake Bemidji State Park** offers 14 miles of hiking trails, 9 miles of ski trails, and 3 miles of snowmobile trails, and has boat and snowshoe rentals, (218) 755-3843. There are also amusement park attractions and waterslides near Brainerd. Near but not on the southwestern end of Mille Lacs Lake, 10,585-acre **Mille Lacs Kathio State Park** has miles of hiking, horse, ski, and snowmobile trails—plus boat, canoe, ski, and snowshoe rentals; (612) 532-3523. The park is 5 miles northwest of Onamia on County 26.

FOOD

The best places to eat here are resort dining rooms open to the general public as well as to guests. **Kavanaugh's Resort and Restaurant**, 2300 Kavanaugh Dr., (800) 562-7061 or (218) 829-5226, is one of my favorites, with well-prepared food from $14.95–$22.95 in a pleasant dining room with views of Sylvan Lake. Once from our dining room table, we were entertained by baby loons diving from their mother's back. There's a romantic, more formal North Woods resort atmosphere and gourmet dining in the **Grand View Lodge** dining room, $22 for a set-price five-course dinner, off Highway 77 north of Brainerd, (800) 432-3788 or (218) 963-2234. Near Brainerd, food is excellent at the **Quarterdeck Resort and Restaurant** ($7.95–$22.95) on Gull Lake, (218) 963-7537 or (218) 963-2482; **Madden's on Gull Lake**, 8001 Pine Beach Peninsula, ($12–$18), (218) 829-2811; and **Izatys Golf and Yacht Club** ($5–$22) on Mille Lacs Lake's south shore, (800) 533-1728 or (612) 532-3101. And you can hardly beat the $8.40 price for the good dinner buffet at **Grand Casino Mille Lacs**, Highway 169 on Mille Lacs Lake's west shore, (800) 626-LUCK. There are numerous dining spots in Bemidji: For great burgers and chili from $2.75–$5 in a North Woods setting, go to **Slim's Bar & Grill**, 142 Anne St., (218) 751-8196. Order walleye at **Douglas Lodge** in Itasca State Park, (218) 266-2114; dinner costs $7–$15.95.

LODGING

Resorts are as plentiful as lakes here, and the larger ones have numerous planned activities and recreation programs. In the Brainerd area, **Madden's on Gull Lake**, 8001 Pine Beach Peninsula (take U.S. 371

north and County 77 west out of Brainerd), (800) 642-5363, is a large golf resort on expansive landscaped grounds with 45 holes of golf, six tennis courts, pools, and saunas. Guests stay in cottages, lodges, and villas. Rates for a lodge room are $79–$200 for two people; a two-bedroom cottage costs from $220–$255 for two people, each additional person pays $15.

A stroll down a flower-lined walk brings you to a fine sand beach at **Grand View Lodge**, South 134 Nokomis, Nisswa, (14 miles north on Highway 371 out of Brainerd, take a left on County 77 and another left at the Grand View sign), (800) 432-3788. The emphasis here is on golf (27 holes of championship golf) and tennis (11 courts and free children's clinics). This highly rated resort nestled in the woods has a main lodge on the National Historic Registry; rates for two people per night, two-night minimum, are $125–$240.

Kavanaugh's Resort and Restaurant, 2300 Kavanaugh Dr. SW, Brainerd, on Sylvan Lake in the Pine Beach area, (800) 562-7061, is a smaller-scale resort than Madden's or Grand View, offering cottages and townhomes with fireplaces and kitchens, tennis, and indoor pool and spa. For two people, a one-week stay ranges from $615–$1,375. There's a three-night to one-week minimum during summer. Ask about packages. At **Quarterdeck Resort and Restaurant** on Gull Lake in the Brainerd lakes area, (800) 950-5596, guests stay in lakeside units or luxury villas, from $86–$126 per night for two people in a lakeside home; $166–$224 for two people in a luxury villa. The resort has fishing boats, a guide service, and a lakeside dining room.

In the Bemidji area, **A Place in the Woods**, on Turtle River Lake, 14 miles north of Bemidji on Highway 71, (800) 676-4547, occupies a 45-acre wooded peninsula. Handsome log cabins have round-log walls, porch/decks, cathedral ceilings, and log stairs up to a loft; a cabin for two people costs $500 for three nights, then $165 each night, or $920 for a week. The lodge has a fieldstone fireplace and a library. At **Finn 'n' Feather Resort**, a highly rated family housekeeping resort on Lake Andrusia in the Bemidji area, (800) 776-3466, attractive new log homes have screen porches and fireplaces; rates start at $145 for two people and $205 for four people. Resort amenities include a lodge, beaches, and water sports equipment. From Bemidji, take U.S. 2 south to Roosevelt Road/Highway 8, go east 9 miles to the resort, on your left. Guests stay in a renovated 1917 country house on 130 acres of woods, meadow, and wetland at **Meadowgrove Inn Bed and Breakfast**, 13661 Power Dam Road in Bemidji, (218) 751-9654, with a hearty

BEMIDJI

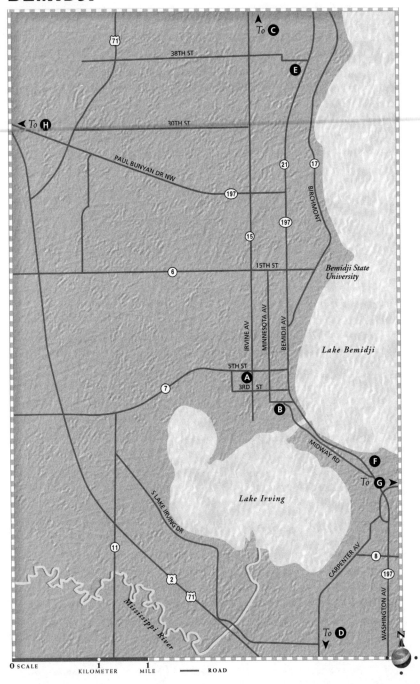

To **C**

38TH ST

E

71

30TH ST

To **H**

PAUL BUNYAN DR NW

21 **17**

197

197

BIRCHMONT

15

15TH ST

6

Bemidji State University

IRVINE AV

MINNESOTA AV

BEMIDJI AV

Lake Bemidji

5TH ST

A

3RD ST

B

7

MIDWAY RD

F

To **G**

S LAKE IRVING DR

Lake Irving

CARPENTER AV

8

197

11

2

71

Mississippi River

WASHINGTON AV

To **D**

N

0 SCALE   1 KILOMETER   1 MILE   ———— ROAD

Sightseeing Highlights

A Bemidji Woolen Mills

B Chocolates Plus

C Lake Bemidji State Park

D The Old Schoolhouse

Food

E Slim's Bar & Grill

Lodging

F Edgewater Motel on Lake Bemidji

G Meadowgrove Inn Bed and Breakfast

H Super 8 Motel

Camping

C Lake Bemidji State Park

Note: Items with the same letter are located in the same town or area.

breakfast for $50–$55, and a 10 percent discount for over three days. **Itasca State Park**, (218) 266-2126 or (218) 266-2114, offers lodge, motel, and cabin lodging, from $44–$68 for two people. Motels in the Bemidji area include **Super 8 Motel**, with a sauna and whirlpool, 1815 Paul Bunyan Drive NW, (800) 800-8000, with double rooms from $44.98–$54.98, and **Edgewater Motel on Lake Bemidji**, 1015 Paul Bunyan Drive NE, (800) 776-3343, with a sand beach and rates from $35–$71.

On the south shore of Mille Lacs Lake, **Izatys Golf and Yacht Club**, 40005 85th Ave., (800) 533-1728, has a picturesque lodge, beach villas, cottages, lakeside townhomes, a Dye-designed 18-hole golf course, and rentals for water sports and fishing. Rates for two people range from $125–$255.97 per night. In the Brainerd Lakes region, **Ruttger's Bay Lake Lodge**, on Highway 6 near Deerwood, (800) 450-4545, enjoys a picturesque, wooded setting with quality accommodations, an 18-hole championship golf course and a nice beach; doubles range from $94–$176 per night. Brainerd area motels include **Brainerd Days Inn**, 1630 Fairview, Baxter, (800) 329-7466, with summer rates from $38–$69, and **Econo Lodge Motel**, Hwy. 371S, Andrew Street, (800) 553-2666, with rooms from $48.95–$53.95.

CAMPING

You'll find pleasant, wooded campsites in state parks here. See the Practical Tips chapter for reservation and fee information. **Itasca State**

Park, 20 miles north of Park Rapids on U.S. Highway 71, (218) 266-2114, has showers, flush toilets (wheelchair-accessible), two campgrounds with a total of 198 sites: 100 with electricity, 11 backpack and 11 cart-in sites. Reserve early!! **Mille Lacs Kathio State Park**, just south of the southwestern edge of Mille Lacs Lake on County 26, (612) 532-3523, has 70 sites, six with electricity, 20 horse camp sites, wheelchair accessible showers, and flush toilets. **Lake Bemidji State Park**, on County 20 about 6 miles northeast of Bemidji, (218) 755-3843, has 98 sites, 43 with electricity, wheelchair-accessible showers, and flush toilets. This is a deservedly popular campground, so plan ahead for a visit. For private campgrounds, try **Wilderness Point Resort**, 2 miles north of Nisswa on Highway 371, then right on County 107/Wilderness Road, go 3 miles. The resort is on a point at the end of the road; (800) 231-4050. There are six lakefront tent sites, 30 shaded, secluded sites with water and electricity, showers, a swimming beach, and boat rentals; rates range from $15–$18 per night, $85–$100 per week. There's also the **Bemidji KOA**, at 5707 U.S. Highway 2W, 2 miles east of Wilton, (218) 751-1792, with pine-shaded tent sites, a range of hookups, hot showers, flush toilets, and a playground.

State forests in the area have primitive campgrounds. Campers pay $7 a night on the honor system, and most sites have pit toilets and drinking water from hand pumps. Pillsbury State Forest's **Rock Lake Campground**, with 18 sites, is west of Pillager. Take State 210 west from Pillager one-half mile, turn right on County 1, go 6 miles, turn left, and follow the road around the lake, (218) 828-2565. To get to Crow Wing State Forest's **Greer Lake Campground** from Crosby, take State 6 north 12 miles to County 36, go west 3 miles to County 14, go south 1½ miles, then turn right and follow the signs for 2 miles. There are 34 campsites, (218) 828-2565.

NIGHTLIFE AND SPECIAL EVENTS

The Paul Bunyan Playhouse, (218) 751-7270, has popular summer-theater productions in the historic Chief Theatre in downtown Bemidji. If you're in the mood for gaming, go to **Grand Casino Mille Lacs** on Highway 169, west shore of Lake Mille Lacs, (800) 626-LUCK, for blackjack, slots, video games, and a huge all-you-can-eat buffet.

5
MINNESOTA'S
OTTER TAIL COUNTRY

Only in recent years has tourism begun to make its way into Otter Tail Country, a lush green land of hardwood forest and country roads angling and curving past blue lakes—a breathtakingly pretty place. This is the western central Minnesota lakes region, a broad swath of moraine lakes far enough south for the forests to be predominantly deciduous. So far, efforts to attract tourists have had a gentle impact, tending more toward a smattering of regional arts and crafts shops in small towns and modest cities, and one-of-a-kind attractions encountered now and then along a country road. For example, a retired farmer indulges his passion for flowers by creating glorious open-to-the-public gardens on a former farm feedlot, and a rural town with an ambitious cultural center hosts a nationally recognized annual Great American Think-Off philosophy competition. There's a picturesque old mill surrounded by trees and verdant sweeps of grass, and a town that draws all manner of media coverage for its annual summer turtle races. Here, amusement parks and waterslides are scarce.

People have been coming to Otter Tail Country resorts for years—usually to fish. These quiet resorts are mostly small operations, comfortable and well-kept, beloved by owners and guests but not fancy. In the communities highlighted by this guide, visitors will discover unusual sights and extraordinary finds in the most unexpected places. ◼

OTTER TAIL COUNTRY

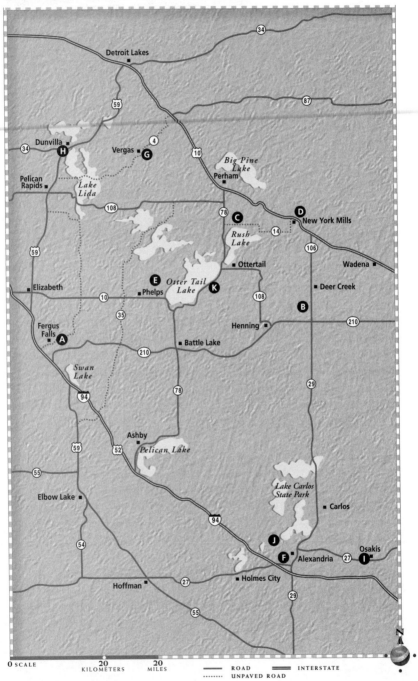

Detroit Lakes

34

59

87

Dunvilla **H**
34
Vergas ■ **G**
4
10
Big Pine Lake
Perham ■

Pelican Rapids ■
Lake Lida
108
78 **C**
14
D ■ New York Mills

Rush Lake
106

59
■ Ottertail
Wadena ■

Elizabeth ■
E
Otter Tail Lake
■ Phelps
K
108
■ Deer Creek

10
35
B
Henning ■
210

Fergus Falls ■ **A**
210
■ Battle Lake
29

Swan Lake
78

94

59
Ashby ■
52
Pelican Lake

55

Elbow Lake ■
Lake Carlos State Park
■ Carlos

54
94
J
F ■ Alexandria
27
Osakis ■ **I**

Hoffman ■
27
■ Holmes City
29

55

N

O SCALE   20 KILOMETERS   20 MILES   ━━ ROAD   ══ INTERSTATE
·········· UNPAVED ROAD

Sightseeing Highlights

Ⓐ Fergus Falls

Ⓑ Finn Creek Open Air Museum

Ⓒ Floralane Gardens

Ⓓ New York Mills

Ⓓ New York Mills Regional Cultural Center

Ⓐ Otter Tail County Historical Society Museum

Ⓔ Phelps Mill County Park

Ⓐ Prairie Wetlands Learning Center

Ⓕ Runestone Museum

Food

Ⓕ Becky's Coffee House

Ⓖ Billy's Bar

Ⓗ Dunvilla in the Country

Ⓘ Just Like Grandma's Tea Room

Ⓙ Lake Café

Ⓐ Mabel Murphy's Eating & Drinking Establishment

Ⓚ The Pier Supper Club

Note: Items with the same letter are located in the same place or area.

A PERFECT DAY IN OTTER TAIL COUNTRY

Start off with a walking tour of Fergus Falls, then visit the outstanding Otter Tail County Historical Society Museum. Buy picnic lunch supplies in town, bring along a good book, and spend a couple of peaceful hours at beautiful Phelps Mill County Park. Then go to Floralane via County 14 and see Clarence Bjorklund's flowers. Backtrack to Otter Tail Lake for an early dinner at The Pier, then drive to Vergas via State 78, U.S. 10, and State 228. Take County 4 west to the Log House and Homestead, where a rose and a tray laden with fruit, cheese, and cakes awaits your arrival.

SIGHTSEEING HIGHLIGHTS

✪✪✪ **Floralane Gardens**—Clarence Bjorklund's gardens are a creation born of love for blooming plants and shrubs. "I should have been a gardener all along," says Bjorklund, a retired farmer of Swedish descent. Garden paths lead past beds of perennials and annuals in which Bjorklund has built fountains and placed sculptures, including a pair of geese "flying" overhead and a bizarre arch made of wagon wheels welded together. Talking to the spirited, feisty farmer/gardener is part of the fun. There's also a sales room with dried flower arrangements. Admission: A $1 donation is appreciated. Hours: Late May or early June–October, daylight hours. The flowers are prime between July 10 and August 10. Address: Floralane Gardens is located on Otter Tail County Road 14, 1 mile east off Highway 78. Phone: (218) 346-6724. (½ hour)

✪✪✪ **Phelps Mill County Park**—This is one of the most beautiful and most photographed spots in Minnesota. The old Phelps Mill, one of the first to use roller mill technology, stands on the lush banks of the broad meandering Otter Tail River in an expansive park. Shade trees and picnic grounds flank the mill. It's not been in use since 1939, but you can walk through the mill and read interpretive displays explaining how the mill once worked. The interior is being restored by the Friends of Phelps Mill/Otter Tail County Historical Society, and you are on your own to explore. Admission: Free. Hours: Daylight hours. Address: Phelps is 4 miles west of Otter Tail Lake. At the northeast edge of Fergus Falls, catch County Highway 1N. Follow County 1 north to the County 10 intersection; go east to the mill. Phone: (218) 736-6038.

✪✪✪ **Otter Tail County Historical Society Museum**—This highly regarded historical society museum places interpretive displays in natural settings. There's a comprehensive agricultural wing complete with a lifelike sow nursing her piglets and a farmer driving a yesteryear tractor, as well as an interesting Native American exhibit. A scarecrow guards the pioneer garden planted in front of the museum. Admission: 50 cents–$2. Open year round, 9 a.m.–5 p.m., Monday–Friday, 1–4 p.m. Saturday; also open Sunday, 1 a.m.–4 p.m. from June–September. Address: 1110 Lincoln Ave. West, Fergus Falls. Phone: (218) 736-6038. (¾–1½ hours)

★★ **Fergus Falls**—Downtown streets have floral planters and statues in this city of 12,300. The Otter Tail River runs through downtown with a secluded river walk, and I'm a bit partial to Lake Alice in the heart of town. You can take a walking tour of the historic downtown and homes on Lake Alice via guidebooks (1–1½ hours). The Fergus Falls Convention and Visitors Bureau in City Hall—the red brick building with a white cupola by the river on Washington Avenue between Mill and Court Streets—is a good information source. Location: Fergus Falls is in west central Minnesota, off I-94 at exits 54 through 61, near the junction of I-94 with State 210 and U.S. 59. It is 96 miles directly west of Brainerd via State 210. Phone: Visitor and Convention Bureau, (800) 726-8959 or (218) 739-0125.

★★ **Runestone Museum**—A larger-than-life Viking statue towers above the museum that holds the famed and controversial Kensington Runestone—a large stone inscribed with runic inscriptions found by a Swedish farmer near the town of Kensington, Minnesota, in 1898. Was the inscription made by Vikings? If so, that means they visited here in 1362. Or is the inscription a fake—a bit of trickery on the part of the Swedish farmer and his minister, who were up on Viking lore and known to enjoy a good laugh? The controversy has lasted for years. Alexandria has preserved the stone and its story in a museum which also includes community settlement history and pioneer buildings. Wheelchair-accessible. Admission: $2–$4, under 6 free. Hours: Memorial Day–Labor Day, 9 a.m.–5 p.m. Monday–Saturday, noon–5 p.m. on Sunday. Other seasons, 9 a.m.–5 p.m., Monday–Friday, noon–5 p.m., Saturday. Address: 206 Broadway in Alexandria. Phone: (612) 763-3160. Alexandria is a city of 8,000, off I-94 at the intersection of State 29 and State 27; 52 miles southeast of Fergus Falls via I-94; (800) 235-9441. (½–1 hour)

★★ **New York Mills**—Near New York Mills, you can visit **Finn Creek Open Air Museum**, an early 1900s farmstead complete with original Finnish home and sauna. Admission: Donation welcome. Hours: Daily in summer during daylight hours. Address: 3 miles east of New York Mills on U.S. Highway 10, then 3 miles south on Highway 106 toward Deer Creek, then one-half mile west on a gravel road. A sign directs you. Phone: (218) 385-2233. (½–1 hour)

In downtown New York Mills, the **New York Mills Regional Cultural Center** has a fine art gallery, performance space, gourmet coffee nook, and gift shop. There's a regional art show yearly, and the center hosts numerous cultural programs and activities, including the annual Great American Think-Off (to bring philosophy down to the common person's level), culminating in a debate in June by the final four contestants. Center admission: Free. Special events and shows have a moderate charge. Hours: Year round, 10 a.m.–5 p.m, Tuesday–Saturday; 1–5 p.m. Sunday. Address: 24 North Main Ave., New York Mills. Phone: (218) 385-3339. New York Mills is on U.S. 10, about 56 miles northwest of Brainerd. (¼–½ hour)

✿ **Prairie Wetlands Learning Center**—This 300-acre tract of land includes 23 wetlands, 19 acres of virgin prairie with big bluestem grass, and approximately 175 acres of restored prairie grasslands. You can drive or walk the rather rough road through the prairie. The center conducts educational programs. Admission: Free. Hours: Daylight hours. If the gate is open, you are welcome to come in and walk the trails. Otherwise, call to arrange a visit. Address: Adjacent to the Otter Tail County Fairgrounds, west of Pebble Lake Road, south of State 210, at the south edge of Fergus Falls. Phone: (218) 739-2291 or call the Fergus Falls Convention and Visitors Bureau, (800) 726-8959. (½–¾ hour)

FITNESS AND RECREATION

Fishing is the top recreation in this region. Which lake is best? That depends on who you talk to and what you want to catch. Big Pine Lake, according to contest statistics, has yielded good-sized walleye, northerns, and crappie in recent years. Other diversions include summer boating, waterskiing, hiking, and horseback riding; as well as winter snowshoeing, snowmobiling, and cross-country skiing. Several state parks in the area have trails. **Maplewood State Park** has 25 hiking trail miles, plus horse, ski, and snowmobile trails; and **Lake Carlos State Park** has 12.6 hiking trail miles along with horse, ski and snowmobile trails (see Camping for directions to these parks). **Glendalough State Park**, 4 miles north of Battle Lake off State 78, (218) 864-5403, has 4 miles of hiking trails. Golf options include **Perham Lakeside Country Club**, 1 mile north of Perham on County 51 or 8, (218) 346-6070, an 18-hole championship course; **Radisson-Arrowwood**, (612) 762-1124, (see Lodging for location) with 18 holes in Alexandria; and **Pebble Lake Golf Course**, with 18 holes, 2 miles south of Fergus

Falls via Pebble Lake Road, (218) 736-7404. Fergus Falls has 7 miles of marked bikeways in the city. Northeast of Fergus Falls, one bike path follows County 1N. The Pebble Lake bike route runs south from Vernon Ave./ Adams Park. The visitors bureau puts out a free area guide with marked bikeways, (800) 726-8959.

FOOD

The **Pier Supper Club** on Highway 78 near Ottertail, (218) 367-2260, has a dining room with wide lake views—great for watching the sunset. The club's salmon with pineapple-tomato salsa is excellent; don't miss the cheesecake! Dinner, the only meal served here, costs from $10.95–$15.95. Fish is a specialty. There's a dock if you come by boat, and casual, limited-menu deck dining supplements the main dining room. At **Just Like Grandma's Tea Room**, 115 W. Main, Osakis, (612) 859-4505, you can get wild-rice salad and other dishes based on home-style recipes that could have come from a church congregation's cookbook. Soups, salads, sandwiches, good breads, and several hot entrees are available, plus ice cream, great pie, and other desserts, served in a combination tearoom/bed and breakfast in a restored 1902 Victorian home. Gifts and the works of regional artisans are sold in an adjacent vintage schoolhouse, barn, annex, and summer kitchen. The fragrance of potpourri, cinnamon, and spices lingers in the buildings. At **Mabel Murphy's Eating & Drinking Establishment**, Highway 210W and I-94, Fergus Falls, (218) 739-4406, prime rib and steak are the specialties in a rambling many-roomed restaurant. It's busy and popular, and serves large portions of good food for $8.95–$21.95 in an upbeat atmosphere. The attractive **Lake Café** in the Radisson-Arrowwood, Alexandria, (612) 762-1124, serves breakfast, lunch, and dinner. Try the coco shrimp or the filet mignon; dinner costs $6.95–$27.95. **Becky's Coffee House**, 518 Broadway, Alexandria, (612) 762-8535, features gourmet coffees, teas, Italian sodas, cappuccino, and other coffee drinks, as well as soups and sandwiches. The food gets praise at **Dunvilla in the Country**, (218) 863-1625, a summer-only restaurant in a Spanish-style hacienda overlooking Lake Lizzie, off U.S. 59 and State 34, 6 miles north of Pelican Rapids. Vergas residents recommend the hamburgers at **Billy's Bar**, downtown across from the hardware store, (218) 342-2451. Decorated with neon beer signs and mounted deer heads, it's a busy place where local people convene.

OTTER TAIL COUNTRY

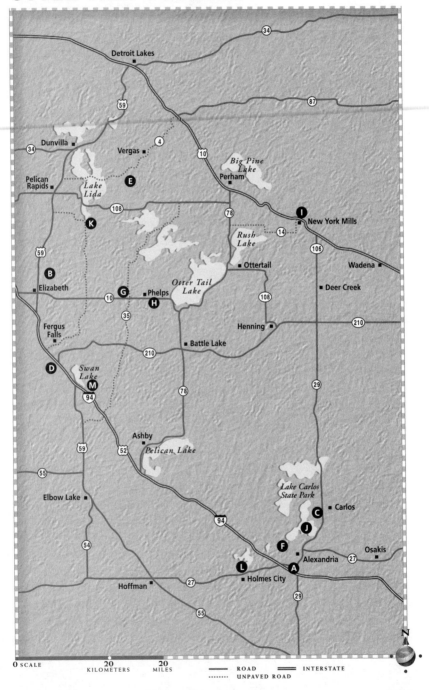

Detroit Lakes

34

59

87

Dunvilla

34

Vergas
4

10

Big Pine
Lake
Perham

Pelican
Rapids

E

Lake
Lida

108

K

78

I New York Mills

Rush
Lake

14

106

Wadena

59

B

Elizabeth

G

Phelps

H

10

Otter Tail
Lake

Ottertail

108

Deer Creek

35

Fergus
Falls

210

Battle Lake

Henning

210

D

Swan
Lake

M

94

210

78

29

59

52

Ashby

Pelican Lake

55

Elbow Lake

Lake Carlos
State Park

C Carlos

54

J

F

Osakis

L

Alexandria

27

A

Hoffman

27

Holmes City

29

55

N

O SCALE   20
KILOMETERS   20
MILES

ROAD   INTERSTATE
UNPAVED ROAD

Lodging

Ⓐ AmericInn

Ⓑ Bakketopp Hus

Ⓒ Carrington House

Ⓓ Day's Inn

Ⓔ The Log House & Homestead on Spirit Lake

Ⓕ Radisson-Arrowwood

Ⓓ Super 8 Motel

Ⓖ Weslake Resort

Ⓗ Whispering Waters

Ⓘ Whistle Stop Inn Bed and Breakfast

Camping

Ⓙ Lake Carlos State Park

Ⓚ Maplewood State Park

Ⓛ Sun Valley Resort and Campground

Ⓜ Swan Lake Resort

Note: Items with the same letter are located in the same place or area.

LODGING

The **Log House & Homestead on Spirit Lake** near Vergas is a charming place to go for pampering with all sorts of extra touches, right down to the water-filled crystal vase waiting to receive the rose that's laid on each guest's pillow. You'll receive first-rate service, a morning newspaper at your door, and gourmet food. Owners Yvonne and Lyle Tweten have traveled the world and bring the best of what they've experienced. Rates for four rooms and a suite run from $85–$135. They have a wonderful Christmas tea in December. To get there, take County 4 west out of Vergas for about 4 miles, enter the driveway, and follow the gravel road to the right of the Homestead. Pass the Log House and go to the house at the dead end over the hill for registration, (800) 342-2318. **Radisson-Arrowwood**, on Lake Darling, 2100 Arrowwood Lane, Alexandria, (800) 333-3333 or (612) 762-1124, is a superb resort with something for everyone—formal and casual dining, golf, tennis courts (indoor and outdoor), volleyball courts, 30-horse riding stable, whirlpool, fitness center, walking/jogging paths, bike and snowmobile rentals, and a playground. There are organized activities for all ages. Rates range from $89–$239. From I-94, take the Alexandria exit, go north on State 29, west on County 82, and north on 22 to Arrowwood Drive. **Carrington House**, 4974 Interlachen Drive, Alexandria, (612) 846-7400, built in 1911, is on Lake Carlos, a southern lakeside home with private baths and a honeymoon cottage for $85–$130. You can sleep in a caboose or a room in a 1903 house for $39–$69 at the **Whistle Stop Inn Bed and Breakfast**, (800) 484-9532, ext. 7528, one block south and one block east of the four-way stop sign in New York Mills. In Fergus Falls, **Bakketopp Hus** on Long Lake, (218) 739-2915, is a chalet-style home with a fireplace, spa, and suites. You'll eat breakfast on antique china. Rates are from $65–$95. **Whispering Waters** is the quintessential Minnesota mom-and-pop fishing resort. It's clean and quiet, run by Jan and Don Gladson, who are friendly, helpful folks. You'll find basic lodging but nothing fancy here. Rates are $350–$505 for one week; a minimum stay of two days, $140 to $202, is required; open mid-May–September on the northeast shore of East Lost Lake. From Fergus Falls, go 16 miles east on County 1/10. Cross Otter Tail River, turn right at the resort sign. It's near Phelps Mill. (218) 495-2552. **Weslake Resort**, on West Lost Lake, (800) 258-9056, is run by Gary and Sharon Nelson and their two children, Karine and Chris. You'll find cabins and a large family lodge for big groups, pleasant grounds, and fireplaces in some cabins. There's a small store, lots of activities, and more attention to decor than in some area fishing resorts—but don't expect upscale and posh. Rates for late June through mid-August start at $645 per week for one to four people in a two-bedroom cabin on the lake. Rates are less in spring and fall. Motels in the area include **Day's Inn** at the intersection of Highway 210 and I-94, Fergus Falls, (800) 528-5495, with rates from about $37–$75, and the **Super 8 Motel**, I-94 and Highway 210 junction, exit 54, Fergus Falls, (800) 800-8000 or (218) 739-3261, with rates from $38.88–$47.88. In Alexandria, rates at the **AmericInn**, 4520 Highway 29, (800) 634-3444, are $57–$63 for rooms and $92–$105 for suites.

CAMPING

Public campgrounds are located in several state parks. **Maplewood State Park**, 21 miles north of Fergus Falls via Highway 59 to Pelican Rapids, then 7 miles east on Highway 108, (218) 863-8383, has 9,250 heavily forested acres with 60 drive-in sites, no electricity, handicapped-accessible showers, and flush toilets. **Lake Carlos State Park**, north of

© Minnesota Office of Tourism

Alexandria off Highway 29, (612) 852-7200, has 126 drive-in sites, 68 with electricity, handicapped accessible showers, and flush toilets. These are popular parks, so reserve early. Private campgrounds include **Swan Lake Resort**, near Fergus Falls: From I-94 exit 61, take Highway 59 south for three-quarters of a mile, then County 82 east for 2 miles, then County 29N for 1½ miles, (218) 736-4626. The resort offers 30 shaded sites with hookups, ten tent sites, free showers, a swimming beach, and 20 acres with trails for $13–$18 per night. On Mill Lake, **Sun Valley Resort and Campground**, 10045 State 27W (7 miles west from Alexandria), (612) 886-5417, has 30 shaded sites, hookups, and showers, and charges $16–$18 a night for two people and $1 for each additional person.

NIGHTLIFE

Check the local tourism guides and newspapers for current happenings. Your best bets are the motel/hotel lounges, which may have live music. Some supper clubs also have live music, and local festivals sometimes have evening activities. Phelps Mill County Park is the site of the popular **July at the Mill** arts festival, (218) 739-2884. Finn Creek Open Air Museum holds a **Summer Folk Festival** the last weekend in August, with dancers, musicians, threshing, and blacksmithing, (218) 385-2233. You can also participate in **turtle races** in Perham. Sponsors of the races supply the turtles for the town's headline event, held every Wednesday morning starting at 10:30 a.m. from May 31–August 30, (218) 346-7710. A major music festival happens in Detroit Lakes: **WE FEST**, held in early August, is billed as "the country music and camping event of the summer." The fest draws thousands to festival grounds on Soo Pass Ranch, (218) 847-1681 or (218) 847-1340.

THE PRAIRIE LANDS OF MINNESOTA

A green and gold checkerboard of fields stretches across the gently rolling land of southwestern Minnesota below the Minnesota River—until you reach the extreme southwest, where Minnesota becomes more Western than Midwestern. This is the Coteau des Prairies, a glacial drift upland rising from 500 feet to 800 feet above the plains. Under the Coteau lie tilted ridges of Precambrian sandstone and Sioux Quartzite in hues of pink and red—remnants of a previous mountain range. The quartzite, estimated to be 1.5 billion years old, is dramatically exposed in Pipestone National Monument, the Jeffers Petroglyphs, and Blue Mounds State Park. Native Americans have long quarried the quartzite for its softer red stone layer, which they fashion into pipes. Hence the red stone's name: pipestone. Today, Native Americans alone are allowed to quarry the pipestone at Pipestone National Monument. Reddish-pink quartzite buildings are everywhere, including downtown Pipestone's National Historic Registry District. South of Pipestone, in Blue Mounds State Park, virgin prairie grass and prickly-pear cactus grow on land that slopes upward and ends abruptly in a cliff; The cliffline extends 1½ miles and is 90 feet high at some points. In the same region, the Jeffers Petroglyphs preserve ancient rock carvings dating to 3,000 B.C. and older. ◨

PRAIRIE LAND REGION

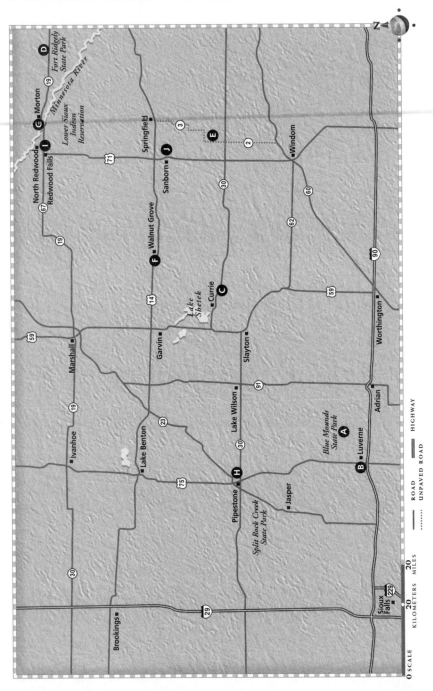

N

Fort Ridgely State Park

D

Morton

19

Minnesota River

G

Lower Sioux Indian Reservation

Springfield

3

E

2

Windom

North Redwood

I

71

Redwood Falls

Sanborn

J

67

19

Walnut Grove

F

30

60

14

Currie

C

62

Lake Shetek

90

Marshall

Garvin

Slayton

59

Worthington

59

19

91

Adrian

Ivanhoe

23

Lake Wilson

30

Blue Mounds State Park

A

Lake Benton

75

H

Luverne

Jasper

B

Pipestone

Split Rock Creek State Park

30

Brookings

Sioux Falls

229

29

SCALE

0   20
KILOMETERS

0   20
MILES

— ROAD   ═══ HIGHWAY

······· UNPAVED ROAD

Sightseeing Highlights

Ⓐ Blue Mounds State Park

Ⓑ Carnegie Cultural Center

Ⓒ End-O-Line Railroad Park & Museum

Ⓓ Fort Ridgely State Park

Ⓔ Hinkly House Museum

Ⓔ Jeffers Petroglyphs

Ⓕ Laura Ingalls Wilder Dugout Site and Museum

Ⓖ Lower Sioux Agency

Ⓑ Luverne

Ⓗ Pipestone

Ⓗ Pipestone County Museum

Ⓗ Pipestone National Monument

Ⓘ Redwood County Historical Society Museum/Minnesota Inventors Hall of Fame

Ⓘ Redwood Falls

Ⓑ Rock County Courthouse

Ⓙ Sod House on the Prairie

Note: Items with the same letter are located in the same place or area.

A PERFECT DAY IN THE PRAIRIE LANDS OF MINNESOTA

Eat a hearty breakfast at The Pantry in Luverne, pack a picnic, and head for Blue Mounds State Park. Stop to browse at the visitor's center, then hike through the prairie to the cliffline. Hike the upper cliffline trail to Lower Mound Lake, eat a picnic lunch, and go for a swim. Hike the lower trail back. Then drive to Jeffers via State 30 east and visit the Jeffers Petroglyphs. Go to Sanborn via State 30E and U.S. 71N, eat dinner at Springfield, then spend the night in the Sod House on the Prairie bed and breakfast. Listen to the chorus of insects as you fall asleep, as pioneers once did.

SIGHTSEEING HIGHLIGHTS

★★★ **Blue Mounds State Park**—This park's 2,028 acres encompass prairie and grassland, a dramatic cliffline, lush wildflowers and wildlife, and a bison herd. Some say Native Americans drove buffalo over the cliff to effect a kill (piles of buffalo bones were once found at the base of the cliff). Patches of prickly-pear cactus atop quartzite outcrops bloom yellow in late June and early July. Coyotes, meadowlarks, white-tailed deer, and nighthawks live here; on late summer days, swallows dive, crickets create a shrill chorus, and grasshoppers leap everywhere. A scramble up rocky crevices leads to an overhang overlooking the broad valley below. Park lands are thick with goldenrod, lacy pink this-tle, prairie cordgrass, milkweed pods bursting with white silk-bearing seeds, flowering white Queen Anne's lace, and monarch butterflies by the hundreds. The 13 miles of hiking trails lead through prairie with tall big bluestem grass and side oats grama, pass two lakes, and enter oak woods. Stop at the interpretive center for program and guided hikes information. There is a swimming beach, fishing, and camping. Admission: Park permit. Hours: 8 a.m.–10 p.m. Address: Located 6 miles north of I-90 and Luverne, and 16 miles south of Pipestone in Rock County: Enter the park off U.S. Highway 75. Phone: (507) 283-4892

★★★ **Jeffers Petroglyphs**—In the midst of virgin prairie, these rock carvings span 5,000 years. More than 2,000 figures and designs are carved on a red quartzite outcrop some 700 feet long—probably carved by different peoples who lived here over several centuries. Operated by the state historical society, a new interpretive center and trails will open in 1997. Admission: Free. Hours: Open Friday and Saturday, 10 a.m.–5 p.m., Sunday noon–5 p.m., May 1–Labor Day, Friday and Saturday; also open Saturday and Sunday in September. Address: 3 miles east of U.S. Highway 71 on County 10, then 1 mile south on County 2. Phone: (507) 877-3647 or (507) 678-2311. (1 hour)

★★★ **Pipestone National Monument**—Digging at this quarry began in the 1700s and pipe-carvers prized the red stone. Dakota (Sioux) con-trolled the quarries and distributed the stone only through trade. The T-shaped calumet pipes became known as peace pipes because they were used by Native Americans at treaty ceremonies. Pipes came into white society via trade, and as contact with whites increased, pipes also became a source of income. Pipestone Monument was created in 1937, open to the public but with quarrying restricted to Native Americans. A circle tour passes active and old quarry sites, Winnewassa Falls, Leaping Rock, craggy outcroppings, a clear stream, and pioneer inscriptions in the stone. Bright yellow and pink wildflowers and meadow sedge flank the paths, and river bulrush grows near the stream. Native Americans carve pipes in the cultural resource center from Memorial Day to Labor Day. Admission: $2–$4; free to Native Americans and children under 16. Hours: 8 a.m.–6 p.m., Monday–Thursday Memorial Day–Labor Day; Friday–Sunday, 8 a.m.–8 p.m. Other seasons, open daily 8 a.m.– 5 p.m. Wheelchair access to visitor center and self-guided trail. Address: Just north of Pipestone; follow signs from U.S. 75, State 23, or State 30. Phone: (507) 825-5464. (1–2 hours or more)

☆☆ **End-O-Line Railroad Park & Museum**—After the town of Currie bought some railroad property, including the turntable at the north end of town, they added a caboose, motorcar, locomotive, plus an engine house, a twentieth-century section foreman's house, an 1873 furnished general store, a school, lots of railroad memorabilia, and more. Thus was born a museum that continues to be supported by an involved community. Admission: Suggested donation of $1–$5, under 6 free. Hours: Memorial Day–Labor Day or by special arrangement, Monday–Friday, 10 a.m.–noon and 1–5 p.m., Saturday and Sunday, 1–5 p.m. Last tour at 4 p.m. Address: South of Shetek State Park in Currie. Currie is on State 30, at the intersection with County 38. Follow County 38 north of town to the museum. Phone: Louis Gervais at (507) 763-3113 or Dorothy Ruppert at (507) 763-3409. (1 hour)

☆☆ **Laura Ingalls Wilder Dugout Site and Museum**—In the town of Walnut Grove, the Wilder museum interprets Laura's life on the prairie. You can drive a few miles to the actual site of the dugout in which Laura and her family lived on the banks of Plum Creek. The popular and crowded Wilder pageant, "Fragments of a Dream," is held in a natural outdoor amphitheater on three weekends in July. Pageant admission: $6–$7. Hours: Gates open at 7 p.m. Phone: (507) 859-2174. Museum admission: $1. Dugout site suggested donation is $2 per car. Hours: Memorial Day–Labor Day, 10 a.m.–7 p.m.; May and September, until 5 p.m.; April and October, until 3 p.m. Address: Walnut Grove is on State 14. The museum is at 330 Eighth St. Phone: (507) 859-2358 or 859-2155. (1–2 hours)

★★ **Sod House on the Prairie**—Visitors can tour two authentic sod houses (built in 1987 and 1988 by Stan McCone) to compare a "rich" man's soddy and a dugout. The site has restored prairie grasses and information about sod-house pioneers and life on the once-treeless prairie. (The rich man's soddy also operates as a bed and breakfast, open all year.) Admission: $3, under 7 free. Hours: April through October. Address: 1 mile east, one-quarter mile south of junction of Highways 71 and 14, 20 miles east of Walnut Grove. Phone: (507) 723-5138. (½–1 hour)

★ **Luverne**—Home to 4,300 plus, Luverne makes a logical base for forays into Blue Mounds State Park. Notable quartzite structures include the imposing **Rock County Courthouse**, on Luverne between Cedar and McKenzie Streets, and the **Hinkly House Museum**. The house, at 217 N. Freeman Ave., was built by the family, who mined local quartzite for many buildings; it has underground caverns for storing dynamite. Admission: $1, free for children with adults. Hours: Sunday, Tuesday, and Thursday, 2–5 p.m., June–August. Phone: (507) 283-2115. (½ hour)

Near the Hinkly House stands the **Carnegie Cultural Center**, 205 N. Freeman, with displays of arts, crafts, and historical items. Admission: Donation. Hours: Daily from 2–5 p.m., Thursdays until 9 p.m. Address: 205 N. Freeman. Phone: (507) 283-8294. (¼ hour)

★ **Pipestone**—This town is renowned for its historic downtown district with 20 quartzite buildings, including one adorned with gargoyles. A walking-tour map is included in the community's free guide. **Pipestone County Museum** is located in the former city hall (built in 1896 out of Sioux quartzite) and has exhibits on the county's history, pioneer artifacts, a Native American gallery, and a library/reading room. Admission: $2, under 12 free. Hours: 10 a.m.–5 p.m. daily; until 8 p.m. during the Hiawatha Pageant. Address: 113 S. Hiawatha. Phone: (507) 825-2563. Pipestone is at the intersection of U.S. 75 and State 30 and 23. The Chamber of Commerce/Convention and Visitors Bureau near the intersection offers information, (507) 825-3316. (½ hour)

OTHER SIGHTS

Redwood Falls offers hiking and camping in 217-acre Alexander Ramsey Park. The **Redwood County Historical Society**

Museum/Minnesota Inventors Hall of Fame occupies the former County Poor Farm facility. Admission: $1. Hours: May–September, Wednesday through Sunday, from 1–5 p.m. Address: Highway 19W. Phone: (507) 637-3329/2828. (½–1 hour) Redwood Falls is on U.S. 71 and State 67/19; (800) 657-7070. Fort Ridgely State Park has a restored commissary and marked fort building foundations. The interpretive center has displays emphasizing military strategy of the U.S.-Dakota Conflict of 1862. Admission: State park permit. Hours: May through Labor Day, 10 a.m.–5 p.m., Tuesday–Saturday, (also Monday holidays); noon–5 p.m., Sunday. Address: 7 miles south of Fairfax, off State Highway 4. Phone: (507) 426-7888 or 697-6321. (1 hour) Lower Sioux Agency is the site of first battle of the U.S.-Dakota Conflict of 1862. Starvation and poor treatment led to retaliation by Dakota confined on this reservation. An excellent interpretive center thoughtfully explores the genesis of the conflict. A stone agency warehouse remains, and a path leads to the Redwood Ferry site. Admission: $1–$2, under 12 free. Hours: Open 10 a.m.–5 p.m. daily, May–Labor Day. After Labor Day–October, 1–5 p.m. daily. Address: on Redwood County Highway 2, 9 miles east of Redwood Falls. Phone: (507) 697-6321. (1–1½ hours)

FITNESS AND RECREATION

Blue Mounds State Park has 13 miles of hiking trails. Split Rock Creek State Park, 6 miles south of Pipestone off State 23 and County 2, and Lake Shetek State Park, north of Currie off County 38, also have hiking trails. Luverne has a city park with tennis courts on the banks of the Rock River and an indoor community swimming pool. In Pipestone, Ewert Recreation Center at 115 N. Hiawatha, (507) 825-5834, open to the public, has a swimming pool, weight/exercise room, whirlpool, racquetball/handball courts, steam room, golf practice net, gym, and tanning bed. Redwood Falls' exceptional Alexander Ramsey Park and Zoo has both easy and challenging trails, plus a waterfall.

FOOD

You'll find good quality food locally, but limited fine dining. Expect roasted chicken, burgers, and steak fare; dinner here costs about $6–$14. Prices are lower in town cafés. In Pipestone, try Day's Inn Historic

PRAIRIE LAND REGION

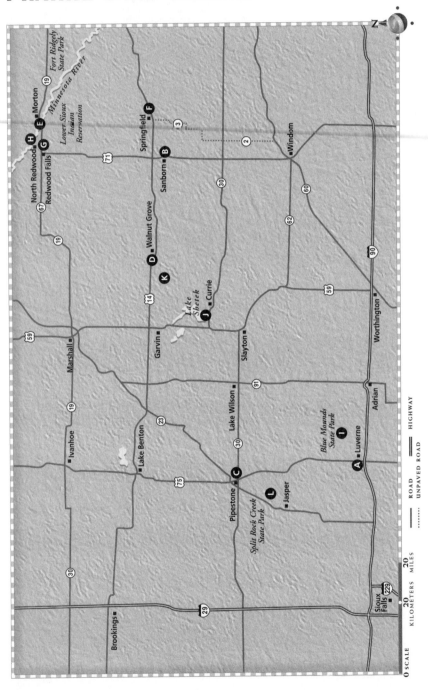

Fort Ridgely
State Park

Minnesota River

Morton

North Redwoods

Redwood Falls

Lower Sioux
Indian
Reservation

Springfield

Sanborn

Windom

Walnut Grove

Currie

Lake
Shetek

Garvin

Slayton

Worthington

Marshall

Lake Wilson

Adrian

Ivanhoe

Blue Mounds
State Park

Lake Benton

Luverne

Pipestone

Jasper

Split Rock Creek
State Park

Sioux
Falls

Brookings

SCALE

20 KILOMETERS   20 MILES

ROAD ——— HIGHWAY
UNPAVED ROAD

Food

Ⓐ Blue Mound Inn
Ⓑ Corner Corral
Ⓒ Day's Inn Historic Calumet Restaurant
Ⓓ Diane's Bakery and Café
Ⓓ Dorothy's Café
Ⓒ Gannon's
Ⓔ Impressions
Ⓐ Magnolia Steak House
Ⓐ The Pantry
Ⓕ Ruby's Heritage House
Ⓕ Victorian Gardens

Lodging

Ⓒ Arrow Motel
Ⓖ The Dakota Inn
Ⓒ Day's Inn Historic Calumet Hotel
Ⓐ Hillcrest Motel
Ⓐ Luverne Super 8 Motel
Ⓗ Redwood Inn
Ⓑ Sodhouse on the Prairie
Ⓖ The Stanhope
Ⓐ Sunrise Motel
Ⓒ Super 8 Motel Pipestone
Ⓗ Super 8 Motel Redwood Falls

Camping

Ⓖ Alexander Ramsey Park and Zoo
Ⓘ Blue Mounds State Park
Ⓙ Lake Shetek State Park
Ⓒ Pipestone RV Campground
Ⓚ Plum Creek Park
Ⓛ Split Rock Creek State Park

Note: Items with the same letter are located in the same town or area.

Calumet Restaurant at 104 W. Main, (507) 825-5871, with meals from $5.95–$12.95, or **Gannon's** at U.S. 75 and State 23 intersection, (507) 825-3114. In addition to the usual assortment of fast-food options, Luverne's **The Pantry**, downtown at 214 E. Main, (507) 283-9321, serves breakfast, daily specials, homemade pies, and soups. There's also the **Blue Mound Inn**, 2 miles north of Luverne on U.S. 75, with a noon ($5.85) and evening ($8.50) buffet Tuesday–Saturday and a Sunday smorgasbord; closed Monday; (507) 283-2718. Locals recommend **Magnolia Steak House** at I-90 and U.S. 75, Luverne, (507) 283-9161. **Impressions**, located in the Jackpot Junction Casino (800-WIN CASH), in Morton, is one dining option. Sanborn has the **Corner Corral** at the junction of Highways 71 and 14, (507) 648-3740, a burger-and-fries café. Near Sanborn in Springfield, **Victorian Gardens**, 8 W. Central, (507) 723-6594, has gourmet coffee drinks and sandwiches, and **Ruby's Heritage House**, 11 S. Marshall, (507) 723-4716, serves full meals. In Walnut Grove, go to **Dorothy's Café**, 550 Highway 14, (507) 859-2384, for good food and pie or **Diane's Bakery and Café**, (507) 859-2140, on Main Street downtown.

LODGING

In the Pipestone area, **Day's Inn Historic Calumet Hotel**, 104 W. Main St., (800) 535-7610, is a renovated 1888 Sioux quartzite hotel, with rooms furnished in antiques; rates from $46–$90. The hotel is adjacent to the Center for Performing Arts, so inquire about theater and romantic getaway packages. **Super 8 Motel**, 605 8th Avenue SE, Pipestone, at the juncture of Highways 75, 23, and 30, has rooms for $45.88–$59.88, (800) 800-8000 or (507) 825-4217. The **Arrow Motel**, U.S. 75N, Pipestone, (800) 825-3331, has rooms for $21–$37 and a free continental breakfast. Luverne area lodging includes the **Luverne Super 8 Motel**, located at I-90 (Exit 12) and U.S. 75S, (800) 800-8000; $53.88 for a double; **Hillcrest Motel**, near Blue Mounds State Park (I-90 Exit 12, go north 20 blocks on Highway 75), (800) 588-3763, with rooms for $24.50–$34; and the small, remodeled **Sunrise Motel**, near a park at 114 S. Sunshine (from U.S. 75, west on Main St. six blocks), (800) 868-4748, with rooms from $24 to $36. In Sanborn, the one-room **Sodhouse on the Prairie** replicates an 1880 structure with two double beds, rocking chair, oil lamps, wood stove, and nearby outhouse. Open year-round, $75–$125, (507) 723-5138. In the Redwood Falls area, the **Dakota Inn** is a lodge-style hotel owned by Jackpot Junction

Casino, with gaming packages and free casino shuttle, (800) WIN-CASH.
Rooms run $75–$150. There's also the **Super 8 Motel**, (800) 800-8000,
1305 E. Bridge St., with rooms at $46, and the **Redwood Inn**, (507)
637-3521, 1303 E. Bridge, with rates of $39–$46. **The Stanhope**, off
State 19 on the east edge of Redwood Falls, a country home bed and
breakfast with shared baths, has free horse pasturage and a continental
breakfast; rooms are $45; (507) 644-2882.

CAMPING

Three area state parks have campgrounds; however, they are in
demand in summer so reserve early. **Blue Mounds State Park** has 73
semimodern sites, 40 with hookups, 14 cart-in sites, a swimming
beach, 13 miles of hiking trails, lake fishing, canoeing, 7 miles of
snowmobile trails, wheelchair-accessible showers, and flush toilets.
(See Practical Tips chapter for fee/reservation details.) The park
headquarters phone is (507) 283-4892; interpretive center, (507)
283-4548. **Split Rock Creek State Park** has 28 sites, 19 with electricity, wheelchair-accessible showers and flush toilets, 4 miles of hiking
trails, boat and canoe rentals, 6 miles south of Pipestone via Highway
23, (507) 348-7908. **Lake Shetek State Park**, off U.S. Highway 59,
south of U.S. 14, on 1,109 acres, has 98 drive-in sites, 67 with electricity, ten walk-in sites, wheelchair-accessible showers, and flush toilets, plus a camping cabin that can be reserved and 8 miles of hiking
trails; (507) 763-3256. **Pipestone RV Campground**, 919 N.
Hiawatha Ave., (507) 825-2455, has 50 sites, 49 with electricity, also
tent and tepee camping and a heated outdoor pool. **Plum Creek
Park**, southwest of Walnut Grove on the site of the original walnut
grove that gave the city its name, has a campground with 40 wooded
and electrified sites with showers; (507) 859-2358. **Alexander Ramsey
Park and Zoo** in Redwood Falls has 28 sites, some with electricity, no
reservations, and a fee of $10; exit State 19 and go north on Grove
Street or Lincoln Street, (507) 637-5755.

NIGHTLIFE AND SPECIAL EVENTS

Festivals take place all summer long in this part of Minnesota. Luverne
hosts the **Tri-State Band Festival** for marching bands the first
Saturday in September. The town's **Buffalo Days** celebration includes
a parade, an arts and crafts fair, free buffalo burgers, and an open house

at Blue Mounds State Park (first weekend in June; 507-283-4061). Luverne's **Palace Theater**, a 1915 vaudeville house revived as a movie theater on Main Street, hosts performances by the **Green Earth Players**, a local theatrical performing group, (507) 283-4061. Pipestone's biggest event is the popular **Hiawatha Pageant**, held in an outdoor amphitheater north of Pipestone. The 200-member cast puts on its colorful show on Friday, Saturday, and Sunday, the last two weekends in July, and the first weekend in August. Admission is $7, under 7 free; (507) 825-4126 or (507) 825-3316. (If you aren't a Henry Wadsworth Longfellow *Song of Hiawatha* fan or you dislike crowds, avoid these weekends.)

There's also the **Pipestone County Fair** in August and a full calendar of entertainment in the **Pipestone Center for Performing Arts,** a state-of-the-art theater in an historic building on Main Street. Programs include community theater and classics. For tickets and information, call the Days Inn Historic Calumet Hotel, (800) 535-7610.

For music and late night activity, try Jackpot Junction Casino's **Dakota Room**, featuring entertainers such as the Oak Ridge Boys, Crystal Gayle, and Wayne Newton. There are five- and six-piece bands weekly, Wednesday through Sunday, (800) WIN-CASH. For a slice of pioneer prairie life, catch the **Laura Ingalls Wilder Pageant, "Fragments of a Dream,"** in Walnut Grove's outdoor amphitheater, the last weekend in June and first two weekends in July, Friday, Saturday, and Sunday. Gates open at 7 p.m.; admission is $6-$7. Phone: (507) 859-2174.

7

MINNESOTA'S BLUFF COUNTRY

Southeast of Rochester, in the Richard J. Dorer Memorial Hardwood Forest, lies a magical land of deep valleys and river gorges, limestone cliffs and swift-running trout streams, caves, and sinkholes—the unglaciated bluff country. Although this land was spared glacial abrasion, meltwater rushed in, downcutting and carving the bluffs and valleys in which small farms and villages thrive today. It's a little pocket of New England-in-Minnesota, with white-painted Victorian houses; old stone buildings; narrow churches with tall steeples; hills forested in oak, maple, and black walnut; and undulating, winding country roads. This far southeastern corner of Minnesota enjoyed obscurity for years. Only morel mushroom hunters, berry-pickers, farmers (including a community of Amish), wood-carvers, and artists called it home. That changed with the advent of the Root River Trail, a 35-mile blacktopped state bicycle trail from Fountain to Rushford. Swarms of weekend bicyclists pedal the trail, back roads, and once-quiet streets now bustle with activity. Nearly every village has bed and breakfasts or inns and shops selling Amish goods and regional artisans' work. Even so, it is still possible to go there midweek in spring and late fall, or anytime in the winter, and find solitude hiking the state trail; hear a wild turkey gobbler; spot hawks, white-tailed deer, and bald eagles; and see few other "outsiders" on village streets. ◪

BLUFF COUNTRY

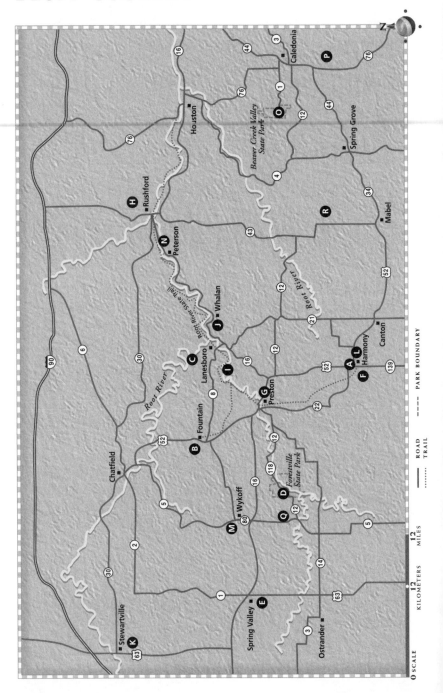

Z

Caledonia

P

76

44

16

3

72

1

O

12

44

Spring Grove

Beaver Creek Valley State Park

Houston

4

34

Rushford

H

Mabel

R

43

52

Peterson

N

Root River

12

Root River State Trail

Whalan

J

21

Lanesboro

C

12

I

16

52

A

L

Harmony

Canton

6

30

Fountain

8

G

Preston

52

F

139

90

B

Root River

22

52

Chatfield

12

118

Forestville State Park

5

D

16

Wykoff

Q

12

M

80

14

2

5

5

1

E

63

30

Spring Valley

3

Stewartville

K

Ostrander

63

63

SCALE

ROAD   PARK BOUNDARY

TRAIL

0   12
KILOMETERS

0   12
MILES

Sightseeing Highlights

Ⓐ Amish Country Tours
Ⓑ Fillmore County Historical Center
Ⓒ Forest Resource Center
Ⓓ Forestville/Mystery Cave State Park Museum
Ⓔ Methodist Church Museum
Ⓕ Michel's Amish Tours
Ⓖ Spring Valley
Ⓐ Village Depot & School
Ⓔ Washburn-Zittleman House

Food

Ⓖ The Branding Iron
Ⓕ Country Bread Basket
Ⓗ The Mill Street Inn Restaurant
Ⓘ The Old Barn Resort
Ⓙ The Overland Inn

Lodging

Ⓚ AmericInn Motel
Ⓙ Besta's Hus
Ⓘ Carrolton Country Inn
Ⓛ Country Lodge Motel
Ⓜ The Historic Wykoff Jail Haus
Ⓗ Meadows Inn B & B
Ⓝ Wenneson Hotel

Camping

Ⓞ Beaver Creek Valley State Park
Ⓟ DunRomin' Park
Ⓓ Forestville State Park
Ⓠ Maple Springs Campground
Ⓘ The Old Barn Resort, Hostel, and Campground
Ⓡ Supersaw Valley Campground

Note: Items with the same letter are located in the same place or area.

A PERFECT DAY IN MINNESOTA S BLUFF COUNTRY

Hike or bike part of the Root River Trail early in the morning, or go to the Forest Resource Center to watch for raptors and hike down the steep bluff to the river. Take a leisurely walking tour of Lanesboro, then drive to Harmony. Eat lunch amid local folks at the Country Bread Basket and take an Amish country tour. Return to Lanesboro via a scenic route. Dine at the remarkable Victorian House restaurant in Lanesboro. Perhaps go to a Commonweal Theatre play. Then settle into a cozy room in Mrs. B's Historic Lanesboro Inn or any of the town's excellent bed and breakfasts.

SIGHTSEEING HIGHLIGHTS

★★★ **Forest Resource Center**—Picturesquely situated on a bluff high above the Root River, the center is a great spot to see raptors cruising the valley below. The John Schroeder Renewable Resource Center offers information on programs and research conducted at the center, as well as a map of the demonstration areas and 7-mile trail system. One trail leads down to the Root River. There's also a bat condominium, a raptor perch, and an osprey nesting platform. Ongoing programs include a shiitake mushroom growing project. Admission: Hiking trails and center are free. Tours and programs, by reservation only, have varying fees. Hours: 8 a.m.– 4:30 p.m., Monday–Friday year round; Saturday and Sunday, 10 a.m.– 5 p.m., April–October, until 3 p.m. in winter. Address: Northwest of Lanesboro, about 5 miles. From Lanesboro, take County 8 west for 2 miles to County 21. Follow 21 northwest 1.2 miles to the FRC sign. Follow the signed gravel road north 2 miles to FRC. Phone: (507) 467-2437. (1–3 hours)

★★★ **Lanesboro**—Backdropped by sheer bluffs in a deep valley, Lanesboro, a town of about 1,000 on State 16, sits on the banks of the meandering Root River. Its downtown streets hold many of the original brick and stone buildings erected by German, Irish, and Scandinavian settlers in the middle to late 1800s. Phone: (800) 944-2670. Attractions in the compact downtown historic district on Parkway Avenue N. and Coffee Street include **Scenic Valley Winery**, (507) 467-2958, specializing in wines made from locally grown fruit; **Cornucopia Art Center and Gallery**, (507) 467-2446, showcasing regional artists' work; specialty shops; the restored art deco–style **St. Mane Theater**, hosting performances of the

Commonweal Theatre Company, (800) 657-7025, a professional acting company; **River Valley Cheese Factory**, (507) 467-7000, with cheese made from Amish farm milk; **Lanesboro Historical Preservation Society Museum**, (507) 467-2177, free, 10 a.m.– 5 p.m., May–October, flexible hours otherwise; and the **DNR Root River Trail Office**, (507) 467-2552. There's also a livestock auction barn at the edge of town (off Coffee Street/Highway 8) and **Avian Acres**, (800) 967-BIRD, a native bird supply store and petting zoo southwest of town on Norway Drive.

✻✻✻ **Other Root River Trail Towns**—Fountain is at one end of the Root River Trail, a biking and hiking trail in an abandoned railroad bed that leads from Fountain through Lanesboro, Whalen, Peterson, and Rushford. Each town is unique; most offer food and lodging. In Fountain, the **Fillmore County Historical Center** displays farm implements and regional history. Admission: Donations welcome. Hours: Monday–Friday, 9 a.m.–4 p.m. year-round; also weekends, 1–4:30 p.m. from mid-June–mid-October. Address: On U.S. 52 and County 8. Phone: (507) 268-4449. (½–1 hour) Rushford has a historic city mill and depot, (507) 864-7560 or (507) 864-2444.

✻✻ **Forestville/Mystery Cave State Park**—This state park is an attraction in its own right, with excellent brown-trout streams, tours of Mystery Cave, and the restored 1899 townsite of Forestville. In summer months, costumed interpreters inhabit the stocked brick store, the Meighen residence, and farm buildings. Admission: Park permit. Site hours: Open May 27–Labor Day, 10 a.m.–5 p.m., Tuesday–Friday; 11 a.m.–6 p.m., Saturday; noon–5 p.m., Sunday. Open Monday holidays. Also open Saturday, 10 a.m.–5 p.m., and Sunday, noon–5 p.m., from September–early October. Tours of Mystery Cave's linear corridors and passages are offered by the state park through Labor Day for $3–$5, under 5 free (1 hour). Park wildlife includes wild turkey, red and gray fox, raccoon, opossum, snapping turtle, and deer. Remnant stands of white pine remain, and black walnut trees send down volleys of green-clad nuts in the fall. Park admission: Park permit. Park hours: 8 a.m.–10 p.m. Address: The park is located in Fillmore County, about halfway between Spring Valley and Preston. The entrance is 4 miles south of U.S. Highway 16 on Fillmore County Highway 5, and 2 miles east on Fillmore County 12. Phone: (507) 352-5111.

★★ **Harmony**—A town of around 1,000, Harmony serves as an agricultural and business hub in the region, as well as the gateway for tours of nearby Amish farmsteads. This is the place to buy handcrafted Amish furniture and other products. Horse-drawn buggies are common on Harmony streets: The grocery even has a hitching rail. The town is 13 miles south of Lanesboro, via State 16 and U.S. 52. Phone: (800) 247-MINN or (507) 886-2469. Guided Amish tours include **Michel's Amish Tours**, 45 Main Ave. N., with 2½- to three-hour tours for $23: A guide joins you in your car, (507) 886-5392. **Amish Country Tours**, 90 2nd Ave. N.W., (507) 886-2303 or 886-2577, gives a similar two-hour tour for $22, plus an $8 minibus tour. All require reservations. You'll stop at Amish farms, where goods for sale range from jams and honey to quilts and furniture. The guides explain Amish customs and offer historical and anecdotal details. It is courteous to refrain from taking pictures of Amish people. You can also tour the Amish farm country independently by driving east of town on State 44 and turning north onto the first gravel road. Then drive country roads at random, watching for farms with windmills, no electric service, horse-drawn field machinery, and huge gardens. **Village Depot & School** sells Amish furniture, quilts, and other goods at 90 2nd Ave. N.W. in Harmony and is the base for Amish Country Tours. Phone: (507) 886-2409.

★★ **Spring Valley**—In this pleasant little town, the **Methodist Church Museum** occupies an 1876 National Historic Registry church attended by Laura Ingalls Wilder and her husband, Almanzo Wilder, in 1890 and 1891. Two floors of exhibits include religious and pioneer artifacts and memorabilia, such as a wooden coffin with a glass viewing window—used for victims of contagious disease. Across the street, at 220 W. Courtland, the 1866 **Washburn-Zittleman House** contains 1870s furnishings, quilts, and toys. Admission: $3–$4 for guided tours of the museum and house. Hours: Open daily, 10 a.m.–4:30 p.m. June–August. Noon–4 p.m., weekends, September and October. Address: 221 and 220 W. Courtland St. Phone: (507) 346-7659 or (507) 346-2763. (1–1½ hours) Spring Valley is located 25 miles west of Lanesboro on State 16. Phone: (507) 346-1015.

FITNESS AND RECREATION

Biking is *the* sport in this area. Bring your bike or rent a 10-speed or 12-speed mountain bike from **Capron Hardware**, 119 Parkway Ave. N., in

Lanesboro, (800) 726-5030; rentals from $4 for one hour to $12 for one day; open daily. Call ahead to reserve. Kids' single-speed bikes and Kiddie Karts are for rent, too. At **Little River General Store**, 104 Parkway Ave. N., (507) 467-2943, bike rentals cost around $10 for two hours to $18 all day. The store rents skis and runs a bike/ski shuttle on request. There are also rental bikes at the **Village Square of Fountain**, in downtown Fountain, (507) 268-4406. You can rent bikes and canoes from **Root River Outfitters** in Lanesboro, (507) 467-3400, and canoes from **Lanesboro Canoe Rental**, (507) 467-2948. **Old Barn Resort**, (507) 467-2512, rents bikes, inner tubes, and canoes. If you plan to rent bikes or equipment in the area, call ahead for reservations.

Michael's Adventure Outfitters, (507) 467-2622, has horseback riding in Gribben Valley. The most popular bike route is the **Root River Trail,** (507) 467-2552, beginning in Fountain and ending in Rushford or vice versa. Signs direct you to trailheads at each of five towns along its length. You can also bike south 5½ miles from the Root River Trail at Isinours Junction to Preston via the new Harmony-Preston Valley Trail. The hard-surfaced country roads in the region also provide good biking. *Biking with the Wind*, a book by David Dixen, Peter Seed, and Nancy Wilson, describes several Lanesboro area routes. It's available at the Little River General Store, area bookstores, and from DSW, Inc., 906 N. 4th St., Stillwater, MN 55082. **Forestville State Park**, near Spring Grove, has 16 miles of hiking trails, 14 miles of horse-riding trails, 9 miles of snowmobile trails, and 6½ miles of ski trails; (507) 352-5111.

Beaver Creek Valley State Park, 5 miles west of Caledonia on County Highway 1 off State Highway 76, has 7½ miles of hiking trails and 4 miles of skiing trails in virgin hardwood forest. This is a scenic domain with a privately owned operating gristmill and great ridgetop trails 250 feet above pretty Beaver Creek. There are numerous fresh-water springs, and watercress grows in the creek; (507) 724-2107. The Richard Dorer Memorial Hardwood Forest, (507) 724-5264, has trails for hiking, skiing, horseback riding, and snowmobiling. Opportunities for canoeing and fly fishing abound in the spring-fed streams through-out the area and in both state parks mentioned above.

FOOD

Homemade pies memorable enough to warrant a return trip are common in these small communities. You'll find decent to good food in most

LANESBORO

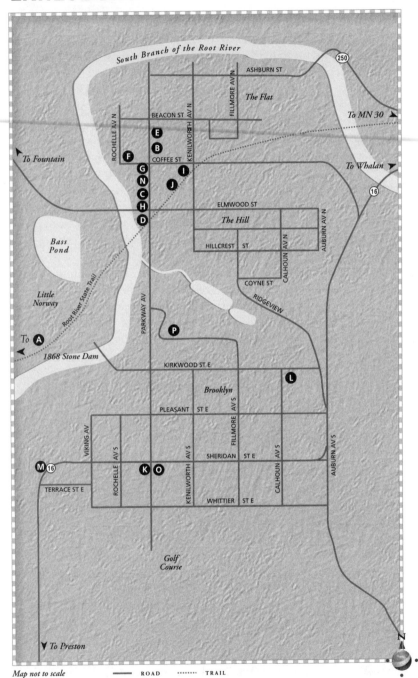

South Branch of the Root River

ASHBURN ST

250

To MN 30

The Flat

FILLMORE AV N

BEACON ST

ROCHELLE AV N

KENILWORTH AV N

To Fountain

E

B

F

COFFEE ST

To Whalan

G

I

16

N

J

C

H

ELMWOOD ST

D

The Hill

Bass
Pond

HILLCREST ST

CALHOUN AV N

AUBURN AV N

Little
Norway

COYNE ST

RIDGEVIEW

Root River State Trail

PARKWAY AV

To A

P

1868 Stone Dam

KIRKWOOD ST E

L

Brooklyn

PLEASANT ST E

FILLMORE AV S

VIKING AV

ROCHELLE AV S

SHERIDAN ST E

CALHOUN AV S

AUBURN AV S

M 16

K O

KENILWORTH AV S

TERRACE ST E

WHITTIER ST E

Golf
Course

To Preston

N

Map not to scale   ——— ROAD   ········· TRAIL

Sightseeing Highlights

- **Ⓐ** Avian Acres
- **Ⓑ** Commonweal Theatre Company
- **Ⓒ** Cornucopia Art Center and Gallery
- **Ⓓ** DNR Root River Trail Office
- **Ⓓ** Lanesboro Historical Preservation Society
- **Ⓔ** River Valley Cheese Factory
- **Ⓑ** St. Mane Theater
- **Ⓕ** Scenic Valley Winery

Food

- **Ⓖ** Das Wurst Haus
- **Ⓗ** Mrs. B's Historic Lanesboro Inn Restaurant
- **Ⓘ** Old Village Hall Restaurant and Pub
- **Ⓙ** The Picnic Basket
- **Ⓚ** The Victorian House of Lanesboro

Lodging

- **Ⓛ** The Cady Hayes House Bed & Breakfast
- **Ⓜ** Green Gables Inn
- **Ⓝ** Historic Lodge Inn
- **Ⓞ** Historic Scanlon House
- **Ⓗ** Mrs. B's Historic Lanesboro Inn

Camping

- **Ⓟ** Sylvan Park

Note: Items with the same letter are located in the same place or area.

towns, and in several Lanesboro restaurants, creative gourmet cuisine. Jean Claude Venant, the French chef/co-proprietor of the **Victorian House of Lanesboro**, serves exquisitely seasoned lamb and as perfect a tomato bisque as I've encountered. If you ask, Venant will relate the funny story about how he came to live and exercise his culinary talents in a small town in Minnesota. The house-turned-restaurant has stained glass, antiques, and lots of charm. A full dinner including dessert costs $19.95–$22.95, 709 Parkway Ave. S., (507) 467-3457. Reservations only. Open Wednesday–Sunday from 5:30 p.m. year round. **Das Wurst Haus**, in the heart of downtown, (507) 467-2902, features owners Art and Jan Fabian's smoked sausage, homemade root beer, and music by their live polka band; **Old Village Hall Restaurant and Pub**, 111 Coffee St., (507) 457-2962, serves creative lunch and dinner dishes, including fresh rainbow trout grilled with lemon, sage, and olive oil, and pastas, from from $7.95–$15.95. The restaurant has a deck on the Root River Trail. **Mrs. B's Historic Lanesboro Inn Restaurant**, 101 Parkway, (507) 467-2154, uses local produce and meats. You may dine on Gorgonzola cheese tart and roast turkey breast with sweet onion and cranberry chutney or pepper-crusted pork loin stuffed with prunes and apricots. A five-course meal is served at 7 p.m. for a set price of $22.95, Wednesday–Sunday. A three-course meal at 6 p.m. is offered Wednesday–Friday and Sunday for $16.95. By reservation only. The **Picnic Basket**, 100 Parkway Ave. N. in Lanesboro, (507) 467-2977, will fix one for you, filling it with fruit, sandwiches, freshly baked cookies, and such. The **Old Barn Resort**, on the Root River Trail, 3 miles north of Preston on County 17, then east for 1 mile, (800) 552-2512 or (507) 467-2512, has a large dining room and traditional Midwestern fare for $5–$14. At the **Branding Iron**, in Preston, (507) 765-3388, the hilltop dining room has sweeping views of the town and countryside and offers a prime rib, steak, chicken, and chops menu with a salad bar. In Whalan, the **Overland Inn**, (507) 467-2623 or 467-3321, wins raves for its pies; try a slice of caramel apple pie. Rushford eateries include the **Mill Street Inn**, 100 W. Jessie St., (507) 864-2929. In Harmony, **Country Bread Basket**, 350 Main Ave. N., (507) 886-6277, is a good breakfast and lunch place.

LODGING

There are bed and breakfasts everywhere, in every price range and variety. You can stay downtown in Lanesboro at **Mrs. B's Historic Lanesboro Inn**, 101 Parkway Ave. N., (507) 467-2154 or (800) 657-4710, and sleep in a room with a cozy sleigh or four-poster bed, a decanter of sherry, and other thoughtful touches; rates are $58 and $68 weekdays, $85 or $95 weekends and holidays. Rates at **Carrolton Country Inn**, out in the country near Lanesboro, (507) 467-2257, start at $60 midweek and $80 on weekends for bed and breakfast accommodations. At **Historic Lodge Inn**, 105½ Parkway Ave. N., Lanesboro, (507) 467-2257, $60–$75, rooms include a continental breakfast. **Historic Scanlon House**, 708 Parkway Ave. S., (800) 944-2158, has rooms for $65–$130, a full breakfast, and bike rentals. The **Cady Hayes House Bed & Breakfast**, at 500 Calhoun Ave., (507) 467-2621, offers rooms in a century-old Queen Anne–style house for $75–$105. **Wenneson Hotel** in Peterson, on the Root River Trail, at 425 Prospect, (507) 875-2587, built in 1904, charges from $50 (midweek, no breakfast) to $65 (weekend, continental breakfast). **Besta's Hus**, 520 New St., Whalen, (507) 467-2630, serves a full breakfast on antique china. Rates range from $45–$120. At **Meadows Inn B & B**, 900 Pine Meadow Lane, Rushford, (507) 864-2378, you'll get a full breakfast and "dressed up" rooms for $75–$115. In Wykoff, the **Historic Wykoff Jail Haus**, at 219 N. Main, (507) 352-4205, offers jail-cell lodging for two for $55, which includes a nearby-café breakfast voucher. Motels include the **Country Lodge Motel** at 525 Main Ave. North in Harmony, (507) 886-2515—a delight, with rooms from $36.95–$74.95 There's also the **AmericInn Motel**, (800) 634-3444, in Stewartville, with rooms from $43–$54, and **Green Gables Inn**, 303 W. Sheridan, Highway 16W, Lanesboro, (800) 818-4225, with rooms from $45–$65.

CAMPING

Public and private campgrounds fill quickly in summer and early fall. **Beaver Creek Valley State Park**, 5 miles west of Caledonia on County Road 1 off State Highway 76, (507) 724-2107, has 42 drive-in sites, showers, vault toilets, and 16 electric and six walk-in sites. **Forestville State Park**, 4 miles south of State 16 on Fillmore County 5 and 2 miles east on Fillmore County 12, (507) 352-5111, offers 73 drive-in campsites with showers and flush toilets and 23 sites with electricity. **Sylvan Park**, a city park in Lanesboro off Parkway Avenue, (507) 467-3722, has 40 sites with hookups and water, 60 tent sites, and showers, from $6–$12; no reservations. The **Old Barn Resort, Hostel and Campground**, north of Preston via County 17, with 200 sites (120 RV sites plus tent campsites) and 51 hostel beds, has showers, a dining room, gift shop, and pool; rates

are $12–$23.50; (507) 467-2512 or (800) 552-2512. At **DunRomin'
Park**, 4½ miles south of Caledonia on Highway 76, (800) 822-2514, there
are 106 campsites, some with electricity, plus tent sites, flush toilets, free
hot showers, and a heated pool, with base rates of $16–$20 for two adults,
$2 per child 2 through 18. **Supersaw Valley Campground**, 3.2 miles
north of Spring Grove on County 4, then 2½ miles west on County 19,
(507) 498-5880, has 100 sites, electricity and water or full hookups, as
well as tent sites, a swimming pool, and hiking trails for $16–$20 for two
adults, each additional person $1–$3. **Maple Springs**, next to Forestville
State Park, south of Wykoff, (507) 352-2056, has electric hookups and
primitive sites.

NIGHTLIFE AND SPECIAL EVENTS

Whenever you come to the Bluff Country, there's likely to be a festival.
The Root River Trail Towns sponsor **Sykkle Tur**, a Root River Trail
bike tour the third weekend in May (Box 398, Lanesboro, MN 55949).
Lanesboro has **Art in the Park** on Father's Day and **Buffalo Bill Days**
the first weekend in July, (800) 944-2670. Historic Forestville celebrates
Independence Day—1896 Flavor, (507) 765-2785. There's the
Fillmore County Fair in Preston in July, (507) 765-2100, and **Western
Days** in Chatfield in August, (507) 867-3966. In September, Wykoff
holds its **German Fall Festival**, (507) 352-4205, and Harmony cele-
brates with **Fall Foliage Fest**, (800) 247-MINN or (507) 886-2469.
The **Commonweal Theatre Company** in Lanesboro has performances from May–December, (800) 657-7025. Past performances have
included mysteries such as *Mousetrap*, the comedy *The Nerd*, and the
tragedy *Medea*. Tickets run around $5–$10, or you can go to **Who
Haunts Here?** to hear "true" ghost stories told by master storyteller
Duke Addicks at the Sons of Norway Lodge at 8 p.m. on Saturday,
August– October. Addicks has been investigating ghostly happenings in
the Root River region since 1990 and is a regional historian and interpretive naturalist. Admission: $3 per person, maximum of $10 per family. Address: Parkway Avenue between Elmwood and Kirkwood Streets
in Lanesboro. Phone: Duke Addicks, (507) 467-2621. (About 1 hour)

Scenic Route: County Road 4 from Spring Grove to Houston

While almost every drive in this part of Minnesota turns out to be scenic, one of my favorites is County Road 4, a partly paved, partly gravel road leading from Spring Grove to Houston. I discovered it one afternoon when I was taking the long way back from Harmony to Lanesboro. To get to Spring Grove from Harmony, take State Highway 44 east about 20 miles. If you have time, stop in downtown Spring Grove and browse the Ballard House's three floors of antiques and local memorabilia, plus a small ice-cream parlor and restaurant. Then go north on County 4. You'll pass a 125-year-old church with a black steeple and the few buildings in the town of Black Hammer. The road winds along a bluff with views of farms; nearby lie the Winnebago Indian Catacombs of Yucatan. You'll pass Yucatan and arrive in Houston (about 20 minutes in all), ending up on State Highway 16, 29 miles east of Lanesboro. You can follow State 16 to Lanesboro or catch State 76 and go south about 8 miles to visit Beaver Creek

COUNTY ROAD 4

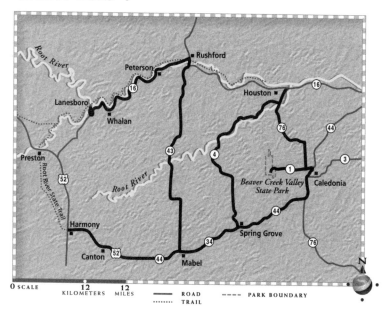

Valley State Park, picnic on the banks of Beaver Creek, and hike wooded trails. Still in the mood for exploring? Then go south for 2 miles from the park entrance on State 76 and head west on State 44 to Mabel, about 15 miles (you'll pass through Spring Grove again on the way). In South Mabel, stop at the Steam Engine Museum to view old tractors and equipment, then take State 43 north through a peaceful, lush green valley in which the tiny town of Choice is located—indeed, a choice location. You'll follow State 43 for 22 miles to Rushford Village, where you'll connect with State 16 again. From there, it's about 14 miles via State 16 southwest to Lanesboro. ◪

8
THE GREAT RIVER ROAD
OF MINNESOTA AND WISCONSIN

Marked by green-and-white pilot's wheel signs, Minnesota's U.S. Highway 61 and Wisconsin's State Highway 35 are among the most scenic of the 3,000-mile Great River Road–designated highways that follow the Mississippi River to the Gulf of Mexico. Highways 35 and 61 climb and wind to the top of steep, wooded river bluffs, affording panoramic river views, then dip down to hug the river's banks. The Mississippi River Valley and the river occupy the heart of the unglaciated region, where meltwaters cut deep gorges and river channels in sandstone and limestone.

Just as the two states have distinct personalities, so do their river roads. The Wisconsin side is less developed, with river hamlets scattered here and there; the Minnesota side is notable for its string of river towns—some sleepy and serene, others alive with activity—separated by breathtaking river views. This guide covers a selected handful of attractions on both sides of the river between Minnesota's La Crescent and Red Wing. There are river crossings at La Crescent, Minnesota/La Crosse, Wisconsin; Winona, Minnesota; Wabasha, Minnesota/Nelson, Wisconsin; and Red Wing. You can drive north on one state's Great River Road and then cross the Mississippi to go south on the other state's side. Or you can zigzag back and forth, driving portions of each state's Great River Road. ◣

GREAT RIVER ROAD

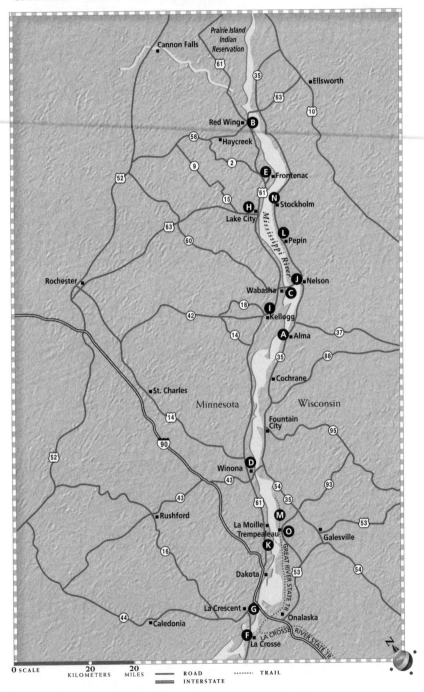

Prairie Island
Indian
Reservation

Cannon Falls

(61)

(35)

Ellsworth

(63)

(10)

Red Wing ■ **B**

(58) ■ Haycreek

(9)   (2)

(52)

E ■ Frontenac

(61)

(15)   **N** ■ Stockholm

H ■
Lake City

(63)

(60)

L
■ Pepin

Rochester ■

J ■ Nelson

Wabasha ■ ■ **C**

(18)

(42)   **I**
■ Kellogg

(14)   **A** ■ Alma   (37)

(35)   (88)

■ Cochrane

■ St. Charles

Minnesota   Wisconsin

(14)   Fountain
City

(90)   (95)

(52)

D
Winona ■

(43)   (54)   (93)

(43)

■ Rushford   **M**
(53)

La Moille ■   **O**
Trempealeau ■   ■ Galesville

(16)   **K**

Dakota ■   (53)   (54)

La Crescent ■   **G**

(44)   Onalaska

■ Caledonia

F
■ La Crosse

Mississippi River

GREAT RIVER STATE TR.

LA CROSSE RIVER STATE TR.

N

0 SCALE   20   20
KILOMETERS   MILES   ROAD ———   ·······TRAIL
———INTERSTATE

Sightseeing Highlights

(A) Alma

(B) Barn Bluff

(A) Buena Vista Park

(C) Eagle Observatory

(D) F. Rohrer Rose Garden

(E) Frontenac State Park

(D) Garvin Heights Park

(B) Goodhue County Museum

(F) Heilman Brewery

(G) La Crescent

(F) La Crosse

(F) *La Crosse Queen*

(H) Lake City

(I) L.A.R.K. Toys and the Meadowlark Shops

(D) Latsch Island and Beach houseboat community

(J) Nelson

(J) Nelson Cheese Factory

(K) O.L. Kipp State Park

(L) Pepin

(L) Pepin Historical Museum

(M) Perrot State Park

(B) Pottery Place Outlet Center

(B) Red Wing

(B) Red Wing Stoneware Company

(A) Rieck's Lake Park

(N) Stockholm

(N) Stockholm Institute Museum

(B) Swarthout Museum

(B) T.B. Sheldon Auditorium Theatre

(O) Three Walking Tours of Red Wing Architecture

(M) Trempealeau

(M) Trempealeau National Wildlife Refuge

(C) Wabasha

(H) Wild Wings

(D) Winona

(D) Winona Armory/County Historical Society Museum

Note: Items with the same letter are located in the same place or area.

A PERFECT DAY ON THE GREAT RIVER ROAD

Start in La Crescent and drive the scenic Apple Blossom Highway. Head north to Winona. Do the downtown walking tour and visit the Armory Museum. Cross the river and drive to Trempealeau to visit Perrot State Park and Trempealeau National Wildlife Refuge. Drive north to Nelson and treat yourself to Nelson Cheese Factory ice cream, then cross the river and check into the historic Anderson House in Wabasha. Explore the quaint town, dine on the inn's Pennsylvania Dutch cooking, then drift off to sleep in an antique bed with a purring cat curled up at your feet.

SIGHTSEEING HIGHLIGHTS

★★★ **La Crescent, Minnesota, Apple Blossom Drive**—See Scenic Drive at the end of the chapter.

★★★ **Red Wing, Minnesota**—Surrounded by limestone bluffs, the river city at the foot of Barn Bluff is named for Chief Red Wing, who used red-dyed swans wings in his headdress—hence the red wing symbol on Red Wing shoes and Red Wing pottery. On a bluff above the city, **Goodhue County Museum** exhibits Red Wing pottery, a diorama of Chief Red Wing's Dakota village, Dakota artifacts, and more. Admission: $2, under 16 free. Hours: 10 a.m.–5 p.m. Tuesday– Friday, 1–5 p.m. Saturday and Sunday. Closed Monday and holidays. Address: 1166 Oak St. Phone: (612) 388-6024. (½–2 hours)

Performing arts and events happen at **T.B. Sheldon Auditorium Theatre**, a grandly restored historic theater. Catch the free multimedia show and tour at 1 p.m. Thursday, Friday, and Saturday during summer, Saturday only the rest of year. Address: Third St. at East Ave. Phone: (800) 899-5759 or (612) 388-2806. (1 hour)

The best way to get to know the city is by walking. Follow the **Three Walking Tours of Red Wing Architecture** put out by the Red Wing Heritage Preservation Commission, (612) 388-6734. Each self-guided tour takes about 45 minutes. In the old pottery district, the **Pottery Place Outlet Center** on Highway 61, Withers Drive exit, occupies the renovated original Red Wing pottery factory. **Red Wing Stoneware Company** makes Red Wing stoneware and has a viewing window, 1 p.m. tours on weekdays, and a salesroom open daily 10 a.m.– 5 p.m, 4909 Moundview Dr., (612) 388-4610. But you haven't really done Red Wing until you've hiked up **Barn Bluff**, at East 5th Street, in the footsteps of Henry David Thoreau, who walked here and recorded the plant life. A hiking trail leads to the summit (1–2 hours). And yes, you can buy Red Wing shoes, boots, and work shoes in Riverfront Centre at the Red Wing Shoe Store, 314 Main; (612) 388-6233.

✩✩✩ **Trempealeau, Wisconsin**—You can walk the historic district downtown, then go to **Perrot State Park**, the site of French explorer Nicholas Perrot's 1665 trading post, for panoramic views from the top of 500-foot bluffs. There are burial/ceremonial mounds in the park and views of Trempealeau Mountain from the swimming and camping area. Admission: Park sticker. Hours: 6 a.m–11 p.m. daily. Address: Trempealeau is on Highway 35, north and west of Onalaska and north of I-90. The park is northwest of Trempealeau: follow First Street 3½ miles. Phone: (608) 534-6409. **Trempealeau National Wildlife Refuge** is 4 miles north of Perrot State Park and offers a 5-mile auto tour, half-mile nature trail, an observation deck over looking the marsh, and a wheelchair-accessible interpretive prairie trail. Watch for bald eagles, ducks, geese, heron, egrets, and white-tailed deer. Admission: Free. Address: 4 miles north of Perrot State Park. Hours: Daylight hours year-round. Phone: (608) 539-2311.

✩✩✩ **Wabasha, Minnesota**—In this venerable river city, most of the brick buildings downtown date prior to 1900. Once home to fur traders, the city's economic history includes lumber, milling, and boat-building. An historic downtown walking-tour booklet is available at the city library, 168 Allegheny Ave., (612) 565-3927 or call the Chamber of Commerce, (800) 565-4158. At **L.A.R.K. Toys and the Meadowlark Shops**, wood-carvers create basswood animals for an immense carousel and handcrafted wooden toys which are sold throughout the United States. Owner Dan Kreofsky started carving toys in his garage back in 1983, a passion that grew into a successful business. Admission: Free. Hours: Monday–Friday, 9 a.m.–5 p.m.; Saturday and Sunday, 10 a.m.– 5 p.m. Address: Lark Lane, Kellogg. Just north of the junction of Highway 61 and 42, turn on County 18 and Lark Lane. Phone: (507) 767-3387.

At the **Eagle Observatory**, bundle up and watch for the 50 to 75 bald eagles that winter in the Wabasha/Reads Landing area, where an inflowing river current creates open water in winter. Admission: Free. Hours: Staffed by trained volunteers November–December, Sunday,

1–3 p.m. unless it's below 10 degrees Fahrenheit or raining. Address: Wabasha's City Deck off Hwy. 60E, on the river bank. Phone: (800) 565-4158.

☆☆ **Alma**—All of Alma—two streets wide and 7 miles long—is a historic district. There are several restored historic bed and breakfasts, terraced rock gardens and stairs connecting streets, antique shops, a viewing tower at Lock and Dam #4, and a museum on Second Street, open weekends May through October. You can get a good view of the lock, dam, dike, river islands, and the Upper and Lower Wiggle Waggle Sloughs from **Buena Vista Park**, off County Highway E from State 35 in Alma. Migrating tundra swans by the thousands stop to feed at **Rieck's Lake Park** on their fall migration, mid-October through early November. Bald eagles winter here, and blue herons and egrets live here in the summer. The park is on the east side of State 35 on Buffalo Slough, just north of Alma. North of Alma on State 35, **Pepin** overlooks Lake Pepin, a 22-mile-long lake in the Mississippi, and is the birthplace of Laura Ingalls Wilder. A log cabin has been erected at her birth site, 7 miles from Pepin on County Road CC. Stop at the **Pepin Historical Museum** for local history and Wilder memorabilia. Admission: Donation. Hours: Mid-May–mid-October, 10 a.m.–5 p.m. daily. Address: 306 3rd St. Phone: (715) 442-3161. (½ hour)

☆☆ **Stockholm**—An artist's community now dwells in the well-preserved buildings of western Wisconsin's oldest Swedish settlement, population around 100. The 1867 Merchants Hotel has been restored, and the **Stockholm Institute Museum** in the old post office displays Swedish settlers' memorabilia, open Wednesday afternoon, from spring through fall. (¼ hour)

☆☆ **Winona**—Between 500-foot high bluffs and the Mississippi River, this city of 25,000 presents an architecturally intriguing face—elaborate Victorian mansions and quaint houses, church spires and domes, and imposing business district edifices including a Richardsonian Romanesque courthouse and a Beaux Arts Exchange Building. Hike the trails in **Garvin Heights Park** for a grand view of the city and river. Go south on Huff Street, past Hwy. 14/61. The 1915 **Winona Armory,** housing the **Winona County Historical Society Museum,** looks like a brick fortress. It holds a stained-glass exhibit, carriages, wagons, sleighs, and local historical displays. Admission: $1–$3, under 7 free. Hours:

Open Monday–Friday, 9 a.m.–5 p.m.; Saturday and Sunday, noon–4 p.m. Closed weekends in January and February (½–¾ hour). Address: 160 Johnson St. Phone: (507) 454-2723 or (800) 657-4972. On the funky side, visit **Latsch Island and Beach houseboat community,** where permanent houseboat-dwellers reside across the river's main channel from downtown. Take Hwy. 54 toward Wisconsin and turn off onto the island. To see more than 1,000 plants in bloom, go to **F. Rohrer Rose Garden**, east of the band shell in Lake Park, between Huff Street and Mankato Avenue. Near Winona, in **O.L. Kipp State Park**, blackberries are ripe for picking in August. King's Bluff Nature Trail leads through prairie to a scenic overlook in the 3,000-acre park with blufftop views and a stand of twisted white cedar. Admission: Park sticker. Hours: 8 a.m.–10 p.m. Address: 16 miles southeast of Winona on Highways 14/61. Phone: (507) 643-6849.

✴ **La Crosse**—The *La Crosse Queen* sternwheeler gives river rides and weekend dinner cruises, (608) 784-2893 or (608) 784-8253. **Heilman Brewery**, easily identified by its giant six-pack at 1111 S. 3rd St., offers hourly tours and tasting (1 hour). Admission: Free. Hours: 10 a.m.–4 p.m., Monday–Saturday; Sunday, 11 a.m.–3 p.m. In winter, 10 a.m–3 p.m., closed Sunday. Phone: (800) 433-BEER or (608) 782-BEER. **Swarthout Museum** preserves local history at 112 Main St. Admission: Donation. Hours: Tuesday–Friday, 10 a.m.–5 p.m.; Saturday and Sunday, 1–5 p.m. Phone: (608) 782-1980. Closed Sunday Memorial Day–Labor Day. (½–1 hour)

✴ **Nelson**—The drive from Alma to Nelson is especially scenic. Tour the **Nelson Cheese Factory**, located on State 35, sample the cheese, and treat yourself to one of their generous ice-cream cones. If you haven't experienced Wisconsin cheese curds, this is the place to try them. Admission: Free. Hours: Open daily, 9 a.m.–5 p.m. Phone: (715) 673-4725.

✴ **Lake City**—On wide blue Lake Pepin, in 1922, Ralph Samuelson lashed boards to his feet, got a motorboat to pull him, and discovered waterskiing. You'll find a large marina, golf, yacht excursions, and charters. For a printed Historic Walking Tour guide, contact the Chamber of Commerce, (800) 369-4123. Take time to stop at **Wild Wings** gallery and catalog showroom, featuring wildlife art, sculpture, and carvings. Admission: Free. Hours: Monday through Saturday, 9 a.m.–6 p.m.,

Sunday 11 a.m.–5 p.m. Address: 2 miles south of Lake City on Highway 61. Phone: (800) 248-7312.

Nearby, in **Frontenac State Park**, the Havana Ridge Sites date from the Hopewellian Indian culture (400 B.C. to A.D. 300). The picturesque park has highlands, lowlands, and 15 miles of hiking trails. Admission: Park permit. Hours: 8 a.m.–10 p.m. Address: On U.S. 61, 10 miles southeast of Red Wing on Lake Pepin. Phone: (612) 345-3401.

FITNESS AND RECREATION

Head for the plentiful state parks to hike, ski, and bike; or jog and walk in the town and city parks. Winona has a 5-mile walking/biking path around Lake Winona. And Red Wing's walking tours are exercise! Near Red Wing, the **Cannon Valley Trail** is a 19.7-mile recreational trail for biking, skiing, hiking, in-line skating, and skateboarding; a $2 wheel pass or ski pass is required, except for wheelchair users and pedestrians. Access the trail in Cannon Falls on State Hwy. 19: West of Red Wing, take State 19 west from U.S. 61; the trail is about 17 miles away.

Two Wisconsin state bicycle trails cross in La Crosse: the **Great River State Trail**, (608) 534-6409, running north to Trempealeau and Perrot State Park, and **La Crosse River State Trail**, (608) 337-4775, going east along the La Crosse River to Sparta. You can explore the river via **Great River Houseboat Rentals**, 1009 E. Main St., Wabasha, (612) 565-3376; play 18 holes of golf at **Mount Frontenac Golf Course** on Hwy. 61, (612) 348-5826; or, in winter, go downhill skiing at **Mt. Frontenac**, (612) 345-3506 or (800)488-5826. Red Wing's **Ole Miss Marina**, Bay Point Park, (612) 388-8643, has electricity, water, security, and showers. In Lake City, (800) 369-4123, the marina moors 600 boats with shower facilities, electricity, and water on all docks; a launching ramp; crane; and night security. There are also boat charters, yacht cruises, and fish-cleaning facilities.

FOOD

Walleye fried in a secret batter is the big seller at Winona's **Hot Fish Shop**, 965 Mankato Ave., (507) 452-5002, with meals from $7.50–$14.95. Caesar salads and homebaked French bread are specialties at **Finn & Sawyers**, on Levee Park Drive, Winona, (507) 452-3104, with views of the river's main channel; dinner costs $13.50–$16.95.

Natural Habitat Coffee House, 451 Huff St., Winona, (507) 452-7020, serves gourmet coffee and espresso, soups, salads, and vegetarian food. Wabasha's **Anderson House**, 333 W. Main, (800) 535-5467, serves Pennsylvania Dutch fare from $7–$15—try the chicken and dumplings, double Dutch fudge pie, or breakfast scrapple. In Stockholm, the **Stockholm Café**, 151 Highway 35, (715) 442-5162, features catfish cheeks, Swedish potato sausage, and other regional delicacies ($4–$10). Open for lunch Friday–Monday; dinner Friday and Saturday. The **Historic Trempealeau Hotel**, (608) 534-6898, dates to the 1800s and has large salads, homemade bread, and desserts, and good vegetarian walnut burgers, $5–$11. Between Trempealeau and Perrot State Park, **Ed Sullivan's**, on the Mississippi on Sullivan Road, (608) 534-7775, has river views, an Irish theme, brown-bread muffins, and lots of fish, steamed or batter-fried, from $8.25–$14.50. **Port of Red Wing Restaurant**, in Red Wing's historic, classy St. James Hotel, 406 Main St., (612) 388-2846 or (800) 252-1875, serves well-prepared food in the $17–$22 range. There's outdoor summer dining in the hotel's more casual **Veranda Restaurant**. **Liberty's Restaurant and Lounge** is a lively gathering place on 3rd and Plum Streets, Red Wing, (612) 388-8877, with meals from $5.50–$15.

LODGING

The **St. James Hotel**, 406 Main St., Red Wing, (800) 252-1875, has antique-furnished rooms, the morning newspaper and coffee at your door, and rates from $75–$155. The **Candlelight Inn**, 818 W. 3rd, Red Wing, (612) 388-8034, pampers guests; rates are $85–$135. Wabasha's, **Anderson House**, 333 W. Main St., (800) 535-5467, has antique furnishings, a cat for your room, and rates from $50–$125. Reserve the cat, as well as the room. Near Lake City, **Evergreen Knoll Acres** is a country bed and breakfast cottage adjacent to a dairy farm, (612) 345-2257 or (507) 753-2795, with rooms from $89–$169. In Winona, the **Carriage House Bed & Breakfast**, 420 Main Street, (507) 452-8256, is an authentic three-story carriage house. Rates from $70–$95. Motels include the **Days Inn**, West Highway 14/61, Winona, (800) 325-2525; **Sterling Motel**, 1450 Gilmore Ave., Winona, (800) 452-1235, $30–$55; and **Sonic Motel**, Highways 93 and 54, Galesville, near Trempealeau, (608) 582-2281, $36.95–$40.95. The **Historic Trempealeau Hotel**, 150 Main St., Trempealeau, (608) 534-6898, a European-style small hotel, has spartan furnishings and a bath down the hall—no frills but

GREAT RIVER ROAD

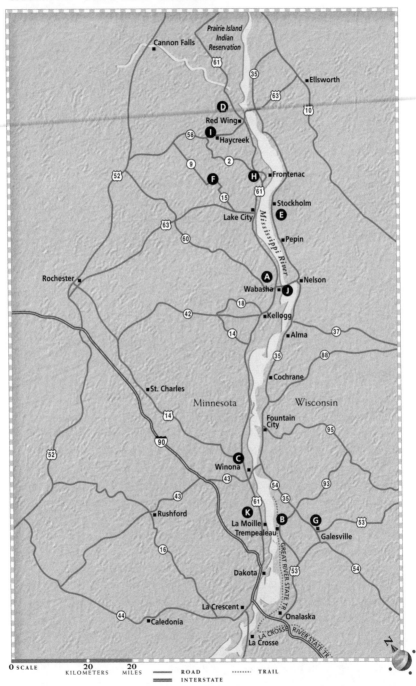

Prairie Island Indian Reservation

Cannon Falls

61

35

63

Ellsworth

10

D

Red Wing

58 **I** Haycreek

9 2

52

F **H** Frontenac

15 61

E Stockholm

Lake City

63

60

Pepin

Rochester

A Nelson

Wabasha **J**

18

42 Kellogg

14 Alma 37

35 88

Cochrane

St. Charles

Minnesota Wisconsin

14 Fountain City

90 95

52

C

Winona

43

54 93

43 61 35

Rushford

K **B** **G** 53

16 La Moille Galesville

Trempealeau

GREAT RIVER STATE TR

Dakota 53 54

La Crescent

44 Caledonia Onalaska

LA CROSSE RIVER STATE TR

La Crosse

N

0 SCALE   **20**   **20**
KILOMETERS   MILES   ——— ROAD   ········ TRAIL
            ▭▭▭ INTERSTATE

Food

Ⓐ Anderson House

Ⓑ Ed Sullivan's

Ⓒ Finn & Sawyers

Ⓑ Historic Trempealeau Hotel

Ⓒ Hot Fish Shop

Ⓓ Liberty's Restaurant and Lounge

Ⓒ Natural Habitat Coffee House

Ⓓ Port of Red Wing Restaurant

Ⓔ Stockholm Café

Ⓓ Veranda Restaurant

Lodging

Ⓐ Anderson House

Ⓓ Candlelight Inn

Ⓒ Carriage House Bed & Breakfast

Ⓒ Days Inn

Ⓕ Evergreen Knoll Acres

Ⓑ Historic Trempealeau Hotel

Ⓓ St. James Hotel

Ⓖ Sonic Motel

Ⓒ Sterling Motel

Camping

Ⓗ Frontenac State Park

Ⓘ Hay Creek Valley Campground

Ⓑ Perrot State Park

Ⓙ Pioneer Campsite

Ⓚ Winona KOA

Note: Items with the same letter are located in the same town or area.

very clean. Be aware that an active railroad track hugs the riverbank nearby. Rooms are $30–$35.

CAMPING

Perrot State Park, near Trempealeau, (608) 534-6409, has 96 sites, 36 with electricity, showers, a nature center, and 6.2 miles of hiking trails. **Frontenac State Park**, (612) 345-3401, 7 miles northwest of Lake City, MN, on Hwy. 61/63, right 1 mile on County Road 2, has 58 drive-in sites, 19 with electricity hookups, showers, and flush toilets. Reservations advised. **Winona KOA**, 6 miles southeast of Winona, on Hwy. 14/61, (507) 454-2851, has 70 sites, 60 hookups, outdoor pool, free hot showers, hiking trails, weekend activities, April 15–October 31. **Hay Creek Valley Campground**, 6 miles south of Red Wing, on Hwy. 58, (612) 388-3998, has 100 sites, electricity/water, flush toilets, and laundry for $13.50–$15. **Pioneer Campsite**, Wabasha (follow Hwy. 61 to Pioneer Trail south of Wabasha or north of Kellogg, then follow signs; 612-565-2242), has 200 sites, full and partial hookups, showers, activities, and a pool for $10–$14.

NIGHTLIFE AND SPECIAL EVENTS

Festivals include **Water Ski Days** at Lake City in June, (800) 369-4123; **Riverboat Days Festival** in Wabasha in July, (800) 565-4158; **Mark Twain Festival,** Labor Day weekend in Alma, (608) 685-3330; and **Polish Heritage Days** in May and **Steamboat Days** on the July 4 weekend in Winona, (800) 657-4972. The **Red Wing Collectors Society** auctions, sells, and swaps Red Wing pottery the second weekend in July, (800) 498-3444. Near Red Wing, the Prairie Island Dakota Community invites the public to the **Prairie Island Contest Wacipi** (powwow) the second weekend in July, (612) 385-0083 or (800) 883-8496.

Nightlife varies from community to community. Check local papers and tourism brochures for listings of current shows and concerts. Winona has **band concerts** in Lake Park every Wednesday evening, June through August, 8 p.m. Wabasha has a **"Meet Me Under the Bridge" summer concert series** at 7 p.m. on Fridays in Heritage Square Park. Red Wing publishes *Applause*, a free tabloid listing arts and entertainment, (800) 498-3444. **The Sheldon Theatre** hosts a year-round calendar of events, including a Sheldon Pops Series; (612) 388-2806 or (800) 899-5759.

Scenic Route: Apple Blossom Drive

La Crescent, Minnesota, claims an 8-mile drive of spectacular beauty through orchards on the bluffs above the Mississippi: The Apple Blossom Drive. For the best in blossoms, make the drive around the Mother's Day weekend. Late September brings views of trees hung heavy with red fruit. Pull off the road to fully enjoy the view—you'll see horses and cattle grazing in lush green pastures backdropped by fruit trees, with the meandering Mississippi River visible in the distance. It's a rural Midwest still-life that's brought me back many times.

If you are coming from the Bluff Country, follow State Highway 16 east from Lanesboro. It will bring you to La Crescent. Go west on North 4th Street heading into the town, turn north on Elm Street/County Highway 29 which becomes the Apple Blossom Drive. To get back to Highway 61, at the junction with County Road 12, turn east (right); 12 leads you to U.S. Highway 61. To cross the river into La Crosse, take U.S. 61 south and follow it east across the river.

APPLE BLOSSOM DRIVE

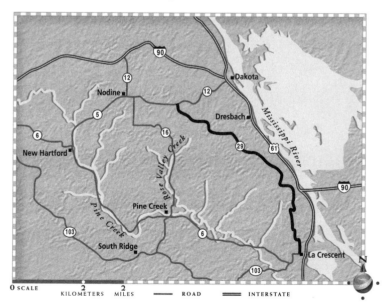

If you happen to be here in mid-September, you might catch festivities related to La Crescent's annual **Apple Festival**, (800) 926-9480). It's worth a stop. Some of the orchards offer tours, and Apple Fest officials wearing red blazers greet visitors at the beer tent next to the midway. Other tents sell freshly baked apple pies—homemade sugar-sprinkled tan crusts peaked high over mounds of cinnamon-laced fruit, just out of the ovens of La Crescent's best cooks. And, of course, there are apples. Roadside markets and stands brim with baskets and baskets of crisp, juicy, tart, or sweet apples to buy—the perfect travel snack. ◼

9

WISCONSIN'S INDIANHEAD COUNTRY

Northwestern Wisconsin's Indianhead Country embraces forested ridges and valleys cut through by rivers and streams, gently rolling farmlands, and lakes of all sizes. The region's lakes and rivers are noted for good fishing and for their scenic beauty, appreciated by the folks who frequent its resorts and pleasant towns. Thankfully, Indianhead has escaped heavy tourism; even the resort areas retain a community identity. Artists and rugged individualists squirrel away here, carving, firing their kilns, and painting—deliberately choosing to live away from the mainstream society. This chapter highlights a handful of smaller communities in the Indianhead region that fit nicely into a circle tour starting in Rice Lake and heading northeast to Birchwood; north to Stone Lake; west to Spooner; south to Shell Lake, Barronett and Cumberland; and finally east to Rice Lake.

You can arrive here from the Minnesota/Wisconsin border via various routes. If you are coming from Red Wing, take U.S. Highway 63 for 74 miles to Turtle Lake. Go east on U.S 8 for 20 miles to U.S. 53. Follow U.S. 53 about 9 miles north to Rice Lake. An enjoyable route from the Twin Cities follows I-35W or I-35E north to U.S. 8 at Forest Lake. Take U.S. 8 east to Taylors Falls/Interstate Park, cross the Mississippi to St. Croix Falls, and continue on U.S. 8 for about 36 miles to U.S. 53. Go north to Rice Lake. ◼

INDIANHEAD COUNTRY

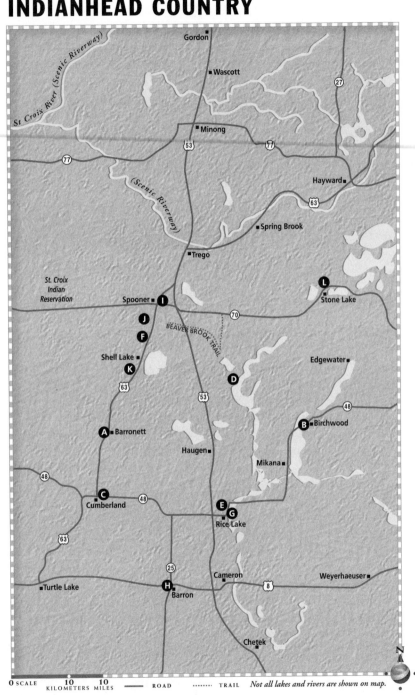

St Croix River (Scenic Riverway)

Gordon

Wascott

27

Minong

53

77

77

Hayward

(Scenic Riverway)

63

Spring Brook

Trego

St. Croix
Indian
Reservation

Spooner I

70

L
Stone Lake

J

BEAVER BROOK TRAIL

F

Shell Lake

Edgewater

K

63

D

53

48

A Barronett

B Birchwood

Haugen

48

Mikana

48

C
Cumberland

48

E
G
Rice Lake

63

25

Cameron

Weyerhaeuser

Turtle Lake

H
Barron

8

Chetek

N

0 SCALE   10   10
KILOMETERS MILES ——— ROAD ········ TRAIL *Not all lakes and rivers are shown on map.*

Sightseeing Highlights

Ⓐ Barronett

Ⓑ Birchwood

Ⓐ Brickyard Pottery and Glassworks

Ⓐ Carousel Creations

Ⓒ Cumberland

Ⓓ Hunt Hill Audubon Sanctuary

Ⓒ Louie's Finer Meats

Ⓔ Miller's Cheese House

Ⓕ Museum of Woodcarving

Ⓖ Nutmeg

Ⓐ Odden's Norsk Husflid

Ⓗ Pioneer Village Museum

Ⓖ Portals to the Past

Ⓘ Railroad Memories Museum

Ⓖ Rice Lake

Ⓙ Schaefer Apiaries

Ⓚ Shell Lake

Ⓘ Spooner

Ⓛ Stone Lake

Ⓔ Tuscobia Cheese

Ⓚ Washburn County Historical Museum

Note: Items with the same letter are located in the same place or area.

A PERFECT DAY IN INDIANHEAD COUNTRY

Start the day early with breakfast at Maxine's or the Coffee Cup Café in Rice Lake. Pick up Wisconsin cheeses and accompaniments at Miller's Cheese House or Tuscobia Cheese, pack a knapsack with food and water, and head for the Blue Hills. Hike the trail leading from Murphy Dam to Tagalong Golf Resort. Stop for a picnic lunch and hike back to your car. Browse a few antique shops in Rice Lake. Eat dinner at Lehman's Supper Club and go to the Red Barn for Hardscrabble

Players summer theater or, if it's Thursday, catch the free concert in Rice Lake City Park.

SIGHTSEEING HIGHLIGHTS

★★★ **Rice Lake**—A bustling lakeside town of 8,000, Rice Lake got its start when the Knapp, Stout and Company logging firm built a dam on the site of a wild-rice bed. The Red Cedar River flows through Rice Lake and is locally praised for outstanding bass fishing. Near Rice Lake, you can visit **Hunt Hill Audubon Sanctuary** in the Sarona/Long Lake area, a 400-acre sanctuary with a mature maple, basswood, and oak forest; groves of venerable pines; meadows; black spruce and tamarack bogs; and two lakes. Sundew and pitcher plants grow in Dory's Bog. There are nature trails and environmental education programs. Admission: Donation. Hours: Daily, dawn until dusk. Address: Follow U.S. 53 north from Rice Lake, go east .7 mile on County Highway D to the "T" at Pavlas Lake. Turn left on County Highway P, go .2 mile, then right 3.4 miles on Audubon Road. Phone: (715) 635-6543. (1 hour or more)

The area's **Pioneer Village Museum** has 21 furnished pioneer buildings, a machinery building, three display buildings, and a hall with display cases. Admission: Donation. Hours: Open Thursday, Saturday, and Sunday, 1–5 p.m., June 1–Labor Day. Address: 1½ miles west of Cameron, on Museum Road and County Highway W. Cameron is about 8 miles south of Rice Lake via U.S. 53. (½–1 hour) At the edge of town, **Miller's Cheese House** carries 70 varieties of Wisconsin cheese, plus honey, fudge, rag rugs, and more. Address: 1 mile north of Rice Lake on Highway 48. Phone: (715) 234-4144. At **Tuscobia Cheese**, you can walk into the chilly "cold room" of this 1906 former cheese factory to sample slices cut from wheels of a variety of cheeses. Address: About 3 miles north of Rice Lake. Take U.S. 53 or County Highway SS north, then go west on 26th Avenue. Phone: (715) 234-2506. Interesting area antique shops include **Portals to the Past**, 613 N. Main St., (715) 234-7530; and **Nutmeg**, 120 W. Messenger, (715) 234-4840.

★★★ **Shell Lake/Barronett**—An avenue of pines escorts U.S. 63 travelers along the 5 miles south from Spooner to **Shell Lake**, a city of 1,200 on a 2,588-acre lake. The town started out as a trading post on the lake in 1879, followed by the establishment of a lumber company, and later, a boat factory. In 1895, the sale of cut-over lands brought farming to the community. The tiny hamlet of **Barronett** lies 9 miles south of Shell Lake on Highway 63, with a high concentration of artisans and a surprisingly creative supper-club restaurant. People come from around the world to the **Museum of Woodcarving** on Highway 63 near Shell Lake. This one-of-a-kind museum exhibits life-size wooden figures carved by the late Joseph T. Barta, showing the life of Christ. Admission: $2–$3.50, under 5 free. Hours: Open 9 a.m.–6 p.m daily from May–October. Phone: (715) 468-7100. (1½–2 hours) For area history, including logging equipment and boats from the boat company, visit **Washburn County Historical Museum,** in an 1888 church at 200 W. Second St., Shell Lake. Admission: Free. Hours: Open Memorial Day–Labor Day, Wednesday–Saturday, 10 a.m. to 4 p.m.; (715) 468-2982. (½–¾ hours) **Schaefer Apiaries** sells Wisconsin honey, maple syrup, and beeswax candles, and has free beekeeping equipment, 3–4 miles south of Spooner on Highway 63, (715) 468-7484.

Don't miss **Carousel Creations,** where Ron Helstern carves carousel animals complete with his trademark heart; his wife, Sue Helstern, does the painting. There's a glassed-in viewing room in the studio on Hwy. 63 in Barronett; (715) 822-4189. Their carousel horses also cavort next door in the Carousel Café. Across the street, a troll grins outside **Odden's Norsk Husflid**. The store sells Norwegian Bunads and imported Scandinavian specialties such as wool sweaters and handknit caps and scarves, and is the showroom for Norsk Woodwork's hand-carved furniture, including *kubbestul* chairs carved out of solid pieces of basswood. Open daily, except from January through March, when the store is open Monday, Friday, and Saturday; (715) 822-8747 or (715) 468-7624. In a renovated 1921 brick school, **Brickyard Pottery and Glassworks** showcases the work of husband and wife potter Brian Dosch and artist Mary Dosch, along with the work of other regional artists. The building has a pottery studio, a glass studio, and a sales gallery, 1 mile north of Barronett, just west of Highway 63. Hours: 10 a.m.–5 p.m. daily, except noon–4 p.m. Sunday, Memorial Day–Labor Day and from Thanksgiving–December; Wednesday–Saturday in April; other months, by chance or appointment. Phone: (715) 468-7341.

★★ **Birchwood/Stone Lake**—Quiet little **Birchwood** lies northeast of Rice Lake about 18 miles via State Highway 48. Long, shop-lined Main Street leads to Birch Lane Inn on Little Birch Lake at one end and The Porch at the other. At The Porch, you can sip a cappuccino on the wrap-around porch or order a Reuben pizza or a hearty sandwich—the menu is imaginative, the food is great, and musicians sometimes play on the porch. Then browse the eclectic wares in the knotty-pine building: imported gourmet condiments, Mary Engelbreit cards, handmade regional crafts, and fun clothing. Phone: (715) 354-7087. Stroll over to Murly's Sports Hut, the ultimate mom-and-pop resort-area shop. You'll find everything from minnows and tackle to moccasins and shirts. Shops and people are the attractions in a town refreshingly short on upscale entertainment. Then head to **Stone Lake** via the prettiest route. Take County Road D west to a "T" intersection, turn right (north) on County M, and pass Long Lake. At County B, turn right (east). It will meld into State Highway 70, which you'll follow northeast into Stone Lake (about 15 to 20 miles). With a population of some 300, Stone Lake courts a distinctly different resort community. Instead of a funky sports shop, you'll find quality antiques in quaint shops, a café or two, and a store specializing in custom-designed settings for precious gems and diamonds.

✯✯ **Spooner**—Richly endowed with water, the Spooner area splashes in 300 lakes and unspoiled Namekagon River, part of the St. Croix National Scenic Riverway. Bass, walleye, and muskie fishing bring droves of anglers; canoeing, tubing and other water-based activities also take center stage. Abundant waterfowl translate into upland and big-game hunting. There's also winter skiing and snowmobiling. **Railroad Memories Museum** appropriately occupies the old C&NW depot, once the largest depot in northern Wisconsin. Displays include original passenger train cars, uniforms, hand tools, switch lights, watches, a model railroad display, and a video. Friendly retired railroad buffs lead the tours. Admission: 50 cents–$2, under 6 free. Hours: Open 10 a.m.–5 p.m daily from Memorial Day–Labor Day; weekends through mid-October. Address: Front Street behind the post office. Phone: (715) 635-2752 or (715) 635-3325. (1–1½ hours)

✯ **Cumberland**—Surrounded by water, Cumberland (population 2,163) bills itself as "Island City." You'll find a delightful, unhurried atmosphere and walkable downtown streets with fun shops—it's quasi-tourist but small-town enough to be charming. The noon whistle still blows in this town, and **Louie's Finer Meats** sells a remarkable variety of sausages made on the premises from the market's own recipes—from hot and spicy Cajun sausage to award-winning *cotto* salami and Wisconsin sausage. There are also meat loaves, salads, and pickles—plus Wisconsin products such as honey and wild rice, cherry mustard, and other condiments. Sausage samples are available if you can't make up your mind. Address: U.S. Hwy. 63N in Cumberland. Phone: (715) 822-4728.

FITNESS AND RECREATION

Hike the **Blue Hills Ice Age Trail** east of Rice Lake in the undeveloped, hilly, and well-forested Blue Hills, teeming with goldfinches and all manner of wildlife, including herons on the ponds and deer at dusk. To get there, follow County Highway C out of town about 15 minutes, and you'll see forested highlands in the distance, appearing a hazy blue. County C turns into County Road O when you enter Rusk County; at an elbow turn north, O joins County F. Follow County F/O north to Murphy Dam. Leave your car and hike the trail north to Red Cedar Lake and Tagalong golf course/resort. It's a 3½- to four-hour hike, so bring water and trail food. Call Rusk County Information Center, (800) 535-RUSK, for detailed maps of the region. **Tuscobia State Trail**, longest of the state trails at 74 miles, winds through portions of Barron, Washburn, Sawyer, and Price Counties. A 12-mile section of the trail from Tuscobia to Birchwood is part of the Ice Age Scenic Trail and leads through mostly open farmland with a few pothole lakes. Along the trail, monarch butterflies flit above pink clover and sweet-scented wild roses. To walk or bike a segment of the cinder trail from the Rice Lake Area, follow County Highway SS north from State 48. Drive out of town a few miles and watch for the Tuscobia Trail sign; (715) 634-6513 or (715) 635-2101. Other hiking/cross-country ski trails include **Beaver Brook**, south of Spooner, off Highway 53; **Nordic Woods**, east of Spooner, off Highway 70; and **College Street Park** in Spooner. **Hay Lake Ranch Riding Stable** has horseback riding from $15 for one hour to $50 all day, north of Spooner, off Highway 63 and County Road F; (715) 766-2305. For downhill skiing, drive to **Christie Mountain Ski Area**, 18 miles east of Rice Lake in the Blue Hills; (800) 373-SNOW for ski conditions or (715) 868-7800. Golf courses include **Tagalong Golf Course**, nine holes, patterned after St. Andrew's Golf Course in Scotland, on Red Cedar Lake, (800) 657-4843; 18-hole **Cumberland Golf Course**, 2 miles west of town, just off Highway 48 (follow signs), (715) 822-4333; and **Butternut Hills Golf Course** in Sarona/Long Lake, with 18 holes, (715) 635-8563. **Bulik's Amusement Center**, one-half mile north of Spooner on U.S. Highway 63, has waterslides, golf, a go-kart track, picnic area, and more; (715) 635-7111.

FOOD

Lehman's Supper Club & Cocktail Lounge, 2911 S. Main in Rice Lake, across from Cedar Mall, closed Monday, (715) 234-9911, in operation since 1934, features hand-cut steaks, hot popovers, and homemade soups. **Maxine's Family Restaurant**, 1721 S. Main, (715) 234-1662, Rice Lake, is a pleasant restaurant with good buckwheat pancakes. Go to **Bresler's Ice Cream & Yogurt**, 2410 S. Main, (715) 234-3011, in Rice Lake for sundaes, malts, fudge, and quaint ice-cream parlor atmosphere. **Maximilian Inn**, on Highways 27/70 in Stone Lake, (715) 865-2080, specializes in veal dishes and Continental-American cuisine for $10–$17. In Barronett, **Spanky's Supper Club**, on Highway 63, (715) 822-2475, is a real find. Behind the unassuming exterior is a fine restaurant with a menu including filet mignon, walleye, and raspberry braised chicken breast. Wonderful cheesecake is served with a dollop of whipped cream. Prices range from $4.95 to $27.95. Also in Barronett, the **Carousel Café**, on Highway 63, has soups, sandwiches, breakfasts, and light meals, plus heavenly chocolate cream pie—all inexpensively priced. The **Coffee Cup Café**, (715) 822-3858, in downtown Cumberland, has four tables, seats 18, and opens at 4:30 a.m. for early risers. Go there for good-natured banter between local customers, lunch platters for $4 and under, and luscious blueberry pie. You can't miss the **Tower House**, an 1882 mansion on main street in Cumberland, (715) 822-4515. It's a family dining place with Italian specialties and decent food for under $15 in the former home of a lumberman and banker. For gourmet dining, go to **Stout's Restaurant** near Mikana, (715) 354-3646. Or try the **5 O'Clock Club**, (715) 822-2924, 2¼ miles north of Cumberland, off Highway 63.

LODGING

Canoe Bay Inn & Cottages, (800) 568-1995 or (715) 924-4594, on 280 acres of hardwood forest near Chetek, has been rated "one of the Midwest's top country inns" by the *Chicago Sun-Times*. Owners/ innkeepers Dan and Lisa Dobrowolski pay careful attention to detail— from the room furnishings to the menu's breakfast croissants, egg soufflés and other gourmet dishes. Rates range from $115–$195 with $20 off Sunday–Thursday and extended-stay discounts. **Stout's Lodge, Island of the Happy Days**, was lumber-wealth heir Frank Stout's family retreat, built with red cedar logs in 1903. There are perennial flower beds, hiking trails, and meals based on vegetables and herbs from the resort gardens. Rates range from $88–$159. The lodge is 1 mile north of Mikana via State Highway 48, (715) 354-3646. At the **Super 8 Motel**, double rooms range from $65.88–$70.88; 2401 S. Main, Rice Lake, (800) 800-8000 or (715) 234-6956. **Currier's Lakeview Resort Motel**, 2010 E. Sawyer St., on County Road C in Rice Lake, is a Swiss chalet–style motel in a pleasant location, with rates from $49–$81; (800) 433-5253 or (715) 234-7474. The **Lake House Bed and Breakfast**, (715) 865-6803, N5793 Division Ave., Stone Lake, has four rooms and a full breakfast for $55–$75. The **Stout Trout Bed & Breakfast** near Springbrook, (715) 466-2790, has rooms for $65 on a quiet lake with adjacent woods, berry-picking, hiking, boating, and biking; free use of boats and bicycles. The **Rectory Bed and Breakfast**, 1575 Second Ave., Cumberland, (715) 822-3151, in a 1905 rectory, has an extensive library and rooms furnished with antiques; rates are $55–$65. **Aqua Vista Resort/Motel**, Highway 63N and County Road B, Shell Lake, (715) 468-2256 or (800) 889-2256, has rooms from $45–$100. At **Island Inn Motel**, Highway 63N, Cumberland, (715) 822-8540, rates are $45.95–$64.95. **American Budget Inn**, 101 Maple St., Spooner, (800) 356-8018, has a 24-hour pool, whirlpool, and sauna and double rooms from $57–$62.

CAMPING

Highland Park Campground is 2½ miles west of Spooner on State Highway 70, then .4 mile on Carlton Road.; (715) 635-2462. There are 45 sites, 19 with full hookups, 12 with electricity/water, seven with electricity, and seven grassy tent sites. It's on Cyclone Lake, with a sandy beach and rental boats. Open May 1–September 30; rates $12–$18. **Shell Lake Municipal Campground**, on Shell Lake, has a swimming beach, 40 sites with electrical hookups and water, and showers for $13.50. Reservations welcome: (715) 468-7846 or (715) 468-7679 off-season. **Bay Park Resort & Campground/Good Sampark** has 70 wooded campsites, 24 full hookups, 37 with electricity/water, showers, and tent camping from $15–$19, in Trego, (715) 635-2840. **Rice Lake-Haugen KOA**, (715) 234-2360, is ten minutes north of Rice Lake on Highway 53, on Devil's Lake. The campground has 104 sites, 37 with full hookups, 46 with water and electricity, and 15 with no hookups, showers, a swimming pool, hiking trails, and boat and canoe rentals; rates range from $17–$41.50.

INDIANHEAD COUNTRY

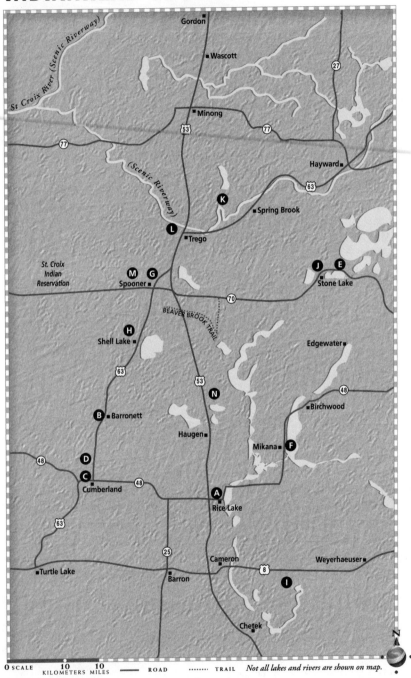

St Croix River (Scenic Riverway)

Gordon

Wascott

27

Minong

53

77

77

Hayward

(Scenic Riverway)

63

K

Spring Brook

L

Trego

St. Croix
Indian
Reservation

M G

Spooner

J   E

Stone Lake

70

BEAVER BROOK TRAIL

H

Shell Lake

Edgewater

63

48

53

N

B Barronett

Birchwood

Haugen

Mikana F

D

4B

C

Cumberland

48

A

Rice Lake

63

25

Cameron

Weyerhaeuser

Turtle Lake

Barron

8

I

Chetek

N

O SCALE   10   10
KILOMETERS   MILES   ROAD   .... TRAIL   *Not all lakes and rivers are shown on map.*

Food

- Ⓐ 5 O'Clock Club
- Ⓑ Bresler's Ice Cream & Yogurt
- Ⓒ Carousel Café
- Ⓓ Coffee Cup Café
- Ⓑ Lehman's Supper Club & Cocktail Lounge
- Ⓔ Maximilian Inn
- Ⓑ Maxine's Family Restaurant
- Ⓒ Spanky's Supper Club
- Ⓕ Stout's Restaurant
- Ⓓ The Tower House

Lodging

- Ⓖ American Budget Inn
- Ⓗ Aqua Vista Resort/ Motel
- Ⓘ Canoe Bay Inn & Cottages
- Ⓑ Currier's Lakeview Resort Motel
- Ⓐ Island Inn Motel
- Ⓙ The Lake House Bed and Breakfast
- Ⓓ The Rectory Bed and Breakfast
- Ⓕ Stout's Lodge, Island of the Happy Days
- Ⓚ The Stout Trout Bed & Breakfast
- Ⓑ Super 8 Motel

Camping

- Ⓛ Bay Park Resort & Campground/Good Sampark
- Ⓜ Highland Park Campground
- Ⓝ Rice Lake-Haugen KOA
- Ⓗ Shell Lake Municipal Campground

Note: Items with the same letter are located in the same place or area.

NIGHTLIFE AND SPECIAL EVENTS

Red Barn Theatre, a 1904 barn in Rice Lake, is home to the Hardscrabble Players and hosts summer-stock theater productions, 2 miles east of Rice Lake on State Highway 48; (715) 234-8301. **Music in the Parks** sponsors Thursday 7:30 p.m. free concerts in the band shell in Rice Lake City Park, June through August; (800) 523-6318. At the **Cranberry Festival** in Stone Lake, the first weekend in October, contestants race down Stone Lake's steep hill in cranberry crates. You can see cranberries being harvested in the bogs; watch a parade; eat cranberry-laced ice cream, pancakes, or crandogs; and, naturally, buy cranberries by the pound. (715) 865-3461. Spooner celebrates **Railroad Days** in mid-June, (800) 367-3306. The **Spooner Rodeo** happens in mid-July with a rodeo parade and competition, chicken barbecue, and cowboy church service. Tickets cost $4–$10; reserved seats $5–$12; Friday-only family pass, $10–$20; (800) 367-3306. **Indianhead Arts Center** at the University of Wisconsin-Shell Lake, (715) 468-2414, has a full summer concert schedule ranging from jazz and symphony concerts to keyboard and horn recitals. **Town and Country Days** in Shell Lake, held in September, is a five-day celebration with a street dance, sailboat regatta, parade, chainsaw woodcarving, a horse pull, a play, and musical concerts; (715) 468-4477. There's even a **Rutabaga Festival** in Cumberland the weekend before Labor Day weekend, with a carnival, food, and name bands; (715) 822-3378.

10

BAYFIELD AND MADELINE ISLAND

On a forested Lake Superior peninsula, the quaint coastal town of Bayfield sits across a deep-water harbor from Madeline Island, the largest in the chain of 22 Apostle Islands. The area tolerates—and welcomes—a boisterous influx of summer tourists but somehow maintains its relaxed, laid-back attitude.

Madeline Island Ferry Line transports people and cars back and forth between Bayfield and Madeline Island. Since the mid-1800s, tourists have been coming to Bayfield and Madeline Island—first by steamboat and later by car. On the island are sea caves to explore via canoe or kayak, 1½ miles of sand beach, an historical museum, a few shops and lodging places, and a smattering of restaurants. You can unwind, hike, bike, picnic, and camp in Big Bay State Park or the town of LaPointe's Big Bay Island/Town Park.

Madeline Island and Bayfield are part of the Apostle Islands National Lakeshore, which encompasses 21 of the islands and 12 miles of mainland shoreline. Sailing, biking, fishing, and kayaking are popular, with rentals and charters available. You can explore the island on north and south shore drives and via County Highway H. Other Apostle Islands are accessible by water: tours and a water-taxi service are available. ◩

BAYFIELD AND MADELINE ISLAND

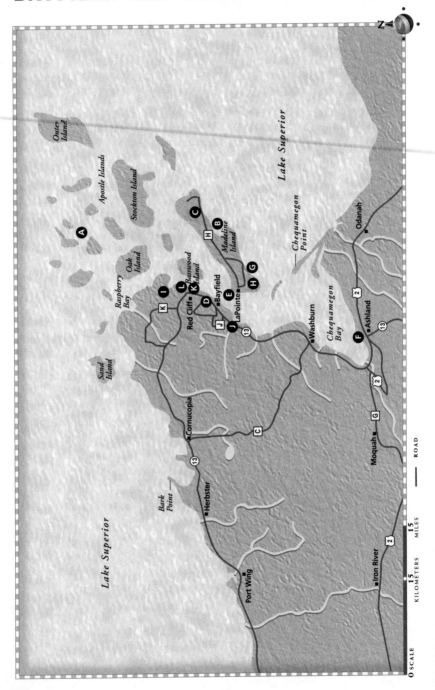

Sightseeing Highlights

A Apostle Islands National Lakeshore

B Big Bay Island/Town Park

B Big Bay State Park

C The Cheese House

D Farmers Market and Apple Orchards

E Madeline Island Historical Museum

Food

F Ashland Depot

G The Clubhouse on Madeline Island

E Grandpa Tony's and Espresso

H The Inn on Madeline Island

Lodging

E Madeline Island Motel

I Thimbleberry Inn

E Woods Manor

Camping

J Apostle Islands View

B Big Bay Island/Town Park

B Big Bay State Park

K Dalrymple Campground

L Red Cliff/Buffalo Bay Campground and Marina

Note: Items with the same letter are located in the same place or area.

A PERFECT DAY IN BAYFIELD AND MADELINE ISLAND

Arrive in Bayfield, eat breakfast amid the flamingoes at Maggie's, then take a ferry to Madeline Island. Rent a kayak or canoe and paddle Big Bay, explore sea caves, then visit the Madeline Island Historical Museum. After a hike in Big Bay State Park, dine at the Inn on Madeline Island, watch the boats come in, and catch the sunset show. Do a little beach walking before heading for one of the best bargains in town: the well-tended Madeline Island Motel. Or pitch a tent in the island's city or state park campground and sleep under the star-filled night sky.

SIGHTSEEING HIGHLIGHTS

★★★ **Apostle Islands National Lakeshore**—Park rangers at the Headquarters Visitor Center will guide you in planning your activities. They offer interpretive programs; maintain visitor's centers on Little Sand Bay and Stockton Island; and offer tours of Raspberry Island Lighthouse (lighthouse and buildings), Manitou Fish Camp (a historic commercial fishing operation), and Hokenson Brothers Fishery on Little Sand Bay (tours of buildings, tools, and techniques used in a family-operated commercial fishery). Headquarters hours vary slightly, depending on when you visit: Late April–late May, 8 a.m–4:30 p.m. daily; late-May–early September, until 6 p.m. daily; early September–late October, until 5 p.m daily; late October–late May, 8 a.m.–4:30 p.m. Monday–Friday.

Private companies offer numerous tours and cruises, from sailing charters with instruction provided to narrated cruises, plus water-taxi service and inner-island shuttles, fishing charters, kayaking expeditions with instruction provided, and lighthouse cruises. Among the companies offering such services are the long-established **Apostle Islands Cruise Service,** with a range of options including a narrated grand tour of all 22 Apostle Islands, and taxi and shuttle service, (715) 779-3925 or (800) 323-7619; **Trek and Trail,** with guided kayak trips, sailing, biking, fly-fishing, and dogsledding, (800) 354-TREK; **Catchun-Sun** Charter's 3½-hour rides twice daily on a classic sailing yacht, (715) 779-3111, located at the Bayfield city dock; and **Schooner *Ananda*,** in Bayfield, with sailing trips on a 56-foot schooner, (800) 300-7770 or (715) 779-5774.

If your sea legs are shaky, **Madeline Island Bus Tours** in LaPointe offers narrated Madeline Island tours visiting historic sites, Indian burial grounds, and Big Bay State Park, mid-June–September. You can board the bus a half-block from the ferry landing. Tours are offered two to three times daily, $3.75–$6.75, under 6 free; (715) 747-2051. (It is advisable to call ahead for reservations.) Or you can rent a bike or a moped and tour on your own. **(Moped Dave's) Motion To Go** rents mopeds, mountain bikes, and more in the "big blue building" located a half block from the island's ferry dock, (715) 747-6585.

Most tours and cruises operate from late-May or June through early September or October. Apostle Islands National Lakeshore Headquarters Visitor Center is located in the old county courthouse in Bayfield on Washington Avenue, (715) 779-3397. To get to and from Madeline Island requires a 20-minute ferry ride between downtown Bayfield and downtown LaPointe. **Madeline Island Ferry Line** runs from 6 or 7 a.m.–1 a.m. from late June–early September, with a slightly reduced schedule the rest of the season between ice breakup and freeze-up. One-way rates range from $1.50 (for a bike)–$8 (motor home) per vehicle and $1.75–$3 per passenger, under 6 free; (715) 747-2051 or (715) 747-6801.

★★★ **Big Bay Island/Town Park**—Operated by the town of LaPointe, the park is 7 miles east of LaPointe, across the bay from the Big Bay State Park. You'll find a footbridge across the lagoon, a sandy beach, fishing and canoeing in the lagoon, and rustic campsites. Canoes, paddle- and rowboats can be rented near the town park from Bog Lake Outfitters for $7.50 per hour, $25 for a half day, and $35 for a full day. From Big Bay, you can paddle or row south to Long Island, an elongated comma-shaped strip of land facing Chequamegon Bay, for blueberry-picking or fishing for smallmouth bass in the warm, shallow waters. The only building on Long Island is a lighthouse, now electronically operated. (1–3 hours or more)

★★★ **Madeline Island Historical Museum**—Displays track three centuries of Madeline Island history—from ancient Ojibwa culture, fur trade, and missionaries to logging and maritime industries. Watch the 25-minute multimedia show for colorful historical details. Admission: $1.25–$3. Hours: Open late-May–early October; 9 a.m.–5 p.m. from early May–mid-July, until 8 p.m. through late August, 10 a.m.–5 p.m. late August–early October. Address: One block from the ferry dock in La Pointe, 3 miles offshore from the city of Bayfield. Phone: (715) 747-2415. (1–2 hours)

You can do a little historical "sleuthing" on your own, too. An old Indian cemetery/burial ground is located five blocks to the right of the ferry landing, behind the Madeline Island Yacht Club. It's overgrown, returning to its natural state in accord with Ojibwa wishes, but visitors are welcome to walk quietly among the old tombstones.

★★ **Art and Art Galleries**—Painters, writers, photographers, and other artists gravitate to this scenic region. Fine galleries display and sell their works, much of it devoted to capturing the essence of the island and mainland, from lighthouses to shoreline and woods. **Woods Hall Craft Shop** is noted for handwoven rugs, handcrafted jewelry, pottery, and "rock people." The shop displays and sells the work of 50 craftspeople, as well as providing a loom room, mud room and kiln, and wood shop where artisans work. Admission: Free. Hours: Memorial Day–Apple Fest, 10 a.m.–4 p.m. Monday–Saturday; 11 a.m. to 2 p.m. Sunday. Address: Three blocks south of the ferry landing, next to St. John's Church in LaPointe. Phone: (715) 747-3943. **Eckel's Pottery** sells handcrafted stoneware and porcelain. Admission: Free. Hours: Year-round, daily. Address: Highway 13, Bayfield. Phone: (715) 779-5617.

✯✯ Big Bay State Park—Wisconsin's northernmost state park includes sandstone bluffs with hollowed-out caves, more than 5 miles of hiking trails, picnic areas, and a sandy beach running about 1½ miles along Lake Superior. White-tailed deer live here, as do eagles. There are 60 primitive campsites. Admission: Park sticker. Hours: 6 a.m.– 11 p.m. daily. Address: Madeline Island, access from County Road H. Phone: (715) 779-3346 and (715) 747-6425. The park does accept camping reservations.

✯✯ The Booth Cooperage Museum—In this working barrel factory/museum, you can watch barrels being made and learn about the history and art of barrel-making. Admission: Free. Hours: Memorial Day–early October, 10 a.m.–5 p.m., daily. Address: Across from the ferry dock in Bayfield. Phone: (715) 779-3400. (½–1 hour)

✯✯ The Cheese House—This is one of those places reflective of the islanders' independent character. In a small, pristinely white-painted building, one of the island's rugged individualists sells specialty cheeses, snacks, and candy. Address: 1 mile past Big Bay Town Park on Big Bay Road. Phone: Call Madeline Island Chamber of Commerce for information; (715) 747-2801.

✯ Farmers Market and Apple Orchards—The Farmers Market is held Saturday's from 8 a.m.–noon in Maggie's restaurant parking lot, at the corner of Manypenny and 4th Street in Bayfield, starting in mid-June. The area is dotted with apple orchards—more than 15— many selling strawberries, raspberries, cherries, and blueberries, as well. To go orchard-hopping, follow County Road I west from the Bayfield ferry dock, then turn right on County Road J. There are other orchard routes, too; see the *Bayfield Scene* visitor's guide, available from the Bayfield Chamber of Commerce, (800) 447-4094, for a map and complete listing.

FITNESS AND RECREATION

You can hike and bike in Big Bay State Park and Big Bay Island Park. Go sailing, fishing, canoeing, kayaking, and swimming. There's **Mt. Ashwabay Ski Area,** with 11 downhill runs and 40 km of cross-country trails for winter visitors, (715) 779-3227. ATV trails and snowmobile trails abound throughout Bayfield County: call (800)

GRAND-FUN for maps. Bayfield also has a pool and recreation facility with swimming, whirlpool, and racquetball, (715) 779-3201. The **Madeline Island Golf Course**, on Madeline Island just south of the ferry landing, is an 18-hole Robert Trent Jones–designed Scottish links-style course, (715) 747-3212. **Roberta's Sport Fishing** provides all gear and light tackle for sportfishing, (715) 779-5744 in summer, or call (612) 462-8866 from November through March.

FOOD

You have many foods and price ranges to choose from here—from fine, award-winning restaurants to the funky and unusual. You'll find most dinners fall in the $8–$18 range. There are exceptions, however, such as renowned **Old Rittenhouse Inn**, 301 Rittenhouse Ave. in Bayfield, (715) 779-5111, serving wonderful chilled fruit soups and a hot Burgundy raspberry soup to die for. The cuisine is gourmet—local ingredients with a French touch—and dinner is a set price of $37.50. A place to go for very special events is the **Clubhouse on Madeline Island**, overlooking the Madeline Island Golf Club and Yacht Club south of the ferry dock, (715) 747-2612 in summer, (715) 779-5010 winter—expensive, gourmet, creative, and noted for an outstanding wine list. The redone **Bayfield Inn**, 20 Rittenhouse Ave. in Bayfield, (715) 779-3363, has a wonderful New England–style dining room. **Greunke's Restaurant**, 17 Rittenhouse Ave., Bayfield, (715) 779-5480, serves excellent food amid 1940s nostalgia, memorabilia, and antiques. Bayfield fruit desserts are a specialty, along with Lake Superior whitefish, all for moderate prices. At **Maggie's**, 257 Manypenny Ave., Bayfield, (715) 779-5641, pink flamingoes are everywhere, a train runs along a ledge below the ceiling tooting and whistling, and you can order heavenly fresh strawberry daiquiris and the area delicacy—whitefish livers. You'll find good black beans and rice here, and meals from $5–$17. **Grandpa Tony's and Espresso**, one-half block from the ferry on Main Street in LaPointe, (715) 747-3911, has deli foods, gourmet coffee, and great salads and bread. The **Inn on Madeline Island**, four blocks south of the ferry landing, (715) 747-6315, has good food and great sunset views. **Ashland Depot**, 400 3rd Ave. W. in nearby Ashland, (715) 682-4200, has a nice atmosphere, good prime rib and whitefish, meals from $9–$28, and a dock for parking your boat if you come by water.

BAYFIELD

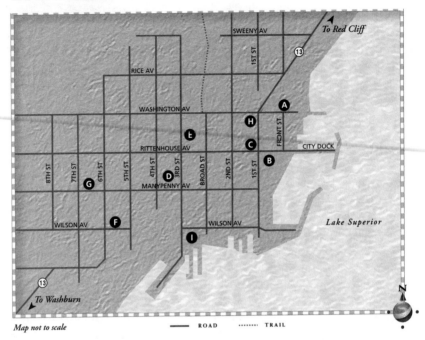

Map not to scale — ROAD ······· TRAIL

Sightseeing Highlights

A The Booth Cooperage Museum

Food

B Bayfield Inn

C Greunke's Restaurant

D Maggie's

E Old Rittenhouse Inn

Lodging

F Bayfield Cottage

B Bayfield Inn

G The Cooper Hill House

C Greunke's First Street Inn

H Harbor's Edge Motel

E Old Rittenhouse Inn

I Reiten Boatyard Condominiums

Note: Items with the same letter are located in the same town or area.

LODGING

The area offers an interesting variety of lodging options. **Old Ritten-house Inn**, 301 Rittenhouse Ave., (715) 779-5111, furnishes guest rooms with antiques in a restored 1890s Victorian mansion. You'll find working fireplaces in the rooms, Jacuzzis, and rates from $99–$229. The **Cooper Hill House**, 33 S. 6th St., Bayfield, (715) 779-5060, a bed and breakfast in an 1888 historic home, has quilts and country-American ambiance, with rooms for $67–$80. At **Greunke's First Street Inn**, 17 Rittenhouse Ave., Bayfield, (800) 245-3072 or (715) 779-5480, guests enjoy a full breakfast and antique-filled rooms in a historic inn with rates from $40–$75. The **Madeline Island Motel**, two blocks east of the ferry landing in LaPointe, (715) 747-3000, is a pleasant, well-kept motel with beautiful gardens. Rates range from $56.95 to $61.95. On the Bayfield waterfront, **Reiten Boatyard Condominiums**, (800) 842-1199, occupies the site of the old Halvor Reiten Boatyard. The bright and airy studios and suites range from $55–$105. **Harbor's Edge Motel**, 33 N. Front St. in Bayfield, (715) 779-3962, offers accommodations for $45–$92. **Bayfield Inn**, 20 Rittenhouse Ave., (715) 779-3363, is on the Bayfield waterfront, with moderately priced rooms from $30–$60. **Thimbleberry Inn**, (715) 779-5757, in Bayfield, is on the Lake Superior shore, with island views, fireplaces, and rooms from $75–$115. **Bayfield Cottage**, 140 6th St. in Bayfield, (715) 779-5904 or (612) 476-4364, has a full kitchen and will accept pets; rates start at $69. **Woods Manor**, 2½ miles from the ferry landing in LaPointe, (715) 747-3102, is a bed and breakfast with a tennis court, bikes, sauna, canoes, and a sandy beach on the lake. Rates are $94–$114.

CAMPING

You can backcountry camp on the Apostle Islands with a permit from the Apostle Islands National Lakeshore headquarters. Write: Apostle Islands National Lakeshore, Rt. 1, Box 4, Bayfield, WI 54814; (715) 779-3397. **Big Bay State Park**, (715) 779-3346 or 747-6425, has 60 campsites, no electricity, showers, backpacking, a wheelchair-accessible picnic area and camp area, swimming, boating, 6.6 miles of hiking trails, 3½ miles of ski trails, and winter camping. **Big Bay Island/Town Park**, across the bay from the state park, has a sandy beach, 45 rustic camp-sites for tents or RVs, a few sites with electricity; no reservations are accepted. Rates are $9 per night; (715) 747-2801. **Apostle Islands**

View, (715) 779-5524, a half-mile south of Bayfield, on Highway 13 and County Road J (follow the signs), is a private campground with 56 sites, pay showers, 30 with electric/water hookups, 11 full hookups, a separate tenting area, open Memorial Day weekend until October 10. Rates are $12–$19. **Dalrymple Campground**, 1 mile north of Bayfield on Highway 13, (715) 779-5712, has 30 rustic tent and RV sites, open mid-May–mid-October. **Red Cliff/Buffalo Bay Campground and Marina**, 3 miles north of Bayfield on Hwy. 13, (715) 779-3743 between 10 a.m. and 2 p.m., offers 42 sites, some with water and electricity, hot showers, and transient boat slips for $10–$14. No reservations.

NIGHTLIFE AND SPECIAL EVENTS

Under a huge canvas tent, "the Carnegie Hall of tent shows"—the **Lake Superior Big Top Chautauqua**—hosts a variety of entertainment including concerts, public radio programs, and musicals about the Apostle Islands region on 65 summer evenings. In the Spirit of Summer programs started in Chautauqua, New York, in 1874. The Lake Superior Chautauqua celebrity guests have included Emmylou Harris and Garrison Keillor. Admission: Varies with event. Hours: Mid-June–Labor Day, Tuesday–Saturday, 8:15 p.m. Address: 3 miles south of Bayfield on Mt. Ashwabay. Phone: (715) 373-5552. The **Bayfield Festival of the Arts** in late July showcases the work of local metal-smiths, potters, painters, weavers, and woodworkers. It's held in Memorial Park and/or the waterfront pavilion along the town dock in Bayfield; (800) 447-4094. **Red Cliff's Annual Pow Wow** draws visitors to the Red Cliff Tribal Grounds on July 4; (715) 779-3700.

Other July Fourth celebrations include **Fireworks in Bayfield Harbor** and Madeline Island's **Annual Parade and Fireworks**. The mid-June **Inland Sea Symposium** has on-water events at the Red Cliff Chippewa Reservation Tribal Grounds, (715) 779-3700, classes on kayak techniques for all levels including beginners, and special family programs. The Bayfield **Wooden Boat and Maritime Heritage Fest** in mid-August and the **Annual Apple Festival** in early October are great fun. Call the Bayfield Chamber of Commerce, (800) 447-4094, for information on these and other festivals. For gaming action, the **Isle Vista Casino**, 3 miles north of Bayfield on Hwy. 13, (715) 779-3712, is open daily from 10 a.m.–1 p.m. Check the current *Bayfield Scene* publication, available from the chamber at the above number, for other happenings.

11

WISCONSIN'S NORTH WOODS

W isconsin's North Woods, in the state's northern midsection, has a colorful history. About 62 miles southeast of Bayfield (via State Highway 13 and U.S. Highway 2) lies Hurley, a once-bawdy and brawling town in mining and logging country. (For a scenic route to Hurley, see the Scenic Route at the end of this chapter.) Hard-drinking, rough-edged miners and loggers gave the town a reputation as one of the toughest places on earth. During Prohibition, 200 thinly disguised saloons in Hurley were frequented by big-name gangsters. South of Hurley 30-some miles, in Manitowish Waters, bullet holes remain in the windows of Little Bohemia Lodge, just off U.S. 51 on Little Star Lake, remnants of a 1934 John Dillinger–FBI gun battle.

Before all this, in 1745, the Lac du Flambeau band of Chippewa established a permanent settlement on the banks of Lac du Flambeau. Named by French explorers who saw the Chippewa fishing by torch-light from birch-bark canoes, the lake and town bearing the same name (about 15 miles southeast of Manitowish on State Hwy. 47) are at the center of the contemporary Lac du Flambeau Indian Reservation. Area forests and lakes make the area popular for skiing, hunting, fishing, snowmobiling, camping, and boating. Just 13 miles southeast of Lac du Flambeau, Minocqua sits at one end of the Bearskin State Trail. The 222,000-acre Northern Highland–American Legion State Forest bor-ders Minocqua and neighboring Woodruff. ◼

NORTH WOODS REGION

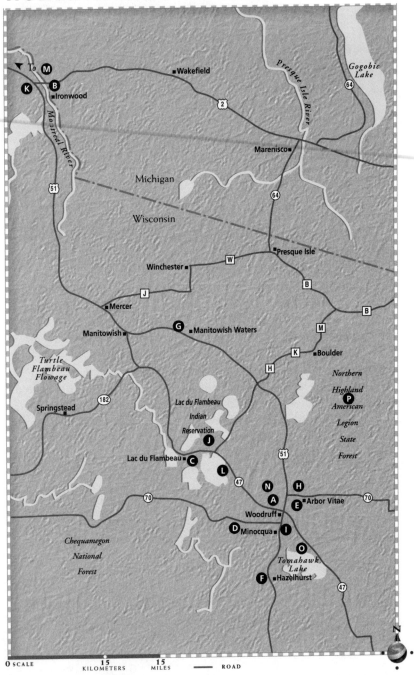

To

Ironwood

■Wakefield

Presque Isle River

Gogobic Lake

64

2

Montreal River

51

Marenisco■

Michigan

64

Wisconsin

■Presque Isle

Winchester ■   W

B

J

B

■Mercer

■Manitowish Waters

M

Manitowish ■

K   ■Boulder

Turtle Flambeau Flowage

H

Northern

Highland

182

Lac du Flambeau

American

Springstead ■

Indian

Reservation

Legion

State

Forest

Lac du Flambeau ■

51

47

70

■Arbor Vitae

Woodruff ■

Chequamegon

Minocqua ■

National

Forest

Tomahawk Lake

■Hazelhurst

47

N

0 SCALE   15   15
         KILOMETERS   MILES   ━━━ ROAD

Sightseeing Highlights

Ⓐ Dr. Kate Pelham Newcomb Museum
Ⓑ Iron County Historical Museum
Ⓒ Lac du Flambeau Chippewa Museum and Cultural Center
Ⓒ Lac du Flambeau Fish Hatchery
Ⓓ Northwoods Wildlife Center
Ⓐ Scheer's Lumberjack Show
Ⓔ Woodruff State Fish Hatchery

Food

Ⓕ Jacobi's
Ⓖ Little Bohemia Restaurant
Ⓐ Lula's Deli & Ice Cream
Ⓔ Ma Bailey's Supper Club
Ⓐ Paul Bunyan's Cook Shanty
Ⓗ The Plantation Supper Club
Ⓘ Polecat and Lace
Ⓐ S.A. Loons
Ⓘ Spangs Italian Restaurant

Lodging

Ⓘ The Beacons of Minocqua
Ⓘ Best Western Lakeview Motor Lodge
Ⓘ Cross Trails Motor Lodge and Family Restaurant
Ⓙ Dillman's Sand Lake Lodge
Ⓚ Eagle Bluff Condo Rentals
Ⓛ Fence Lake Lodge Resort
Ⓒ Lake of the Torches Casino Hotel
Ⓘ The Pointe Resort Hotel and Conference Center
Ⓘ Super 8 Motel

Camping

Ⓜ Copper Falls State Park
Ⓝ Fox Fire Campground
Ⓞ Indian Shores
Ⓒ Lac du Flambeau Tribal Camprground
Ⓟ Northern Highland–American Legion State Forest

Note: Items with the same letter are located in the same place or area.

A PERFECT DAY IN WISCONSIN'S NORTH WOODS

Start the day with breakfast at Paul Bunyan's Cook Shanty, between Minocqua and Woodruff on Highway 51, then head for Northern Highland–American Legion State Forest for some serious hiking or biking. Have a trailside picnic, then visit the Dr. Kate Pelham Newcomb Museum in Woodruff. Before leaving Woodruff, grab an ice-cream treat at Lula's, then drive to Lac du Flambeau to visit the Chippewa Museum and check out the action at the hatchery trout pond. Go to Hazelhurst and treat yourself to dinner at Jacobi's followed by a Northern Lights Playhouse production.

SIGHTSEEING HIGHLIGHTS

★★★ **Dr. Kate Pelham Newcomb Museum**—This delightful museum tells the story of Woodruff's "Angel on Snowshoes," a doctor who reached her North Woods–country patients by snowshoe and snowplow. Displays include photos, her medical equipment, snowshoes, and a recount of the heartwarming million-penny collection launched by schoolchildren to help Dr. Kate build a hospital. TV's Ralph Edwards heard about Dr. Kate and brought attention to her dedicated work on his *This Is Your Life* program. Donations came and the hospital got built. Admission: Donation. Hours: Second Monday in June–Labor Day, Monday–Friday, 11 a.m.–4 p.m. Address: 923 Second Ave. in Woodruff. Phone: (715) 356-6896. (½–1 hour)

★★★ **Iron County Historical Museum**—"I've been making rugs at the museum for 18 years—and they sell out quick," relates rug-maker Lilian Kostac. You probably won't see Kostac unless there's a special event at the museum, which preserves colorful logging and mining history in Hurley's National Historic Registry courthouse. Kostac comes in early to work at a loom weaving rugs to be displayed and sold at the museum. The museum has working looms from the nineteenth century, the old courthouse clock, and cultural artifacts. Admission: Free. Hours: Year-round, Monday, Wednesday, Friday, and Saturday, 10 a.m.–2 p.m. Address: 303 Iron St. in Hurley. Phone: (715) 561-2244. (½–1 hour)

★★★ **Lac du Flambeau Chippewa Museum and Cultural Center**— Featuring Chippewa (Ojibwa) customs, traditions and arts, the museum includes an excellent collection of Native American artifacts, including a

100-year-old dugout canoe and a four-seasons diorama. Guides offer daily tours; there are also demonstration workshops. Admission: $1–$2, under 5 free. Hours: May 1–October, 10 a.m.–4 p.m. daily, until 7 p.m. on powwow nights. November–April, 10 a.m.–2 p.m., Tuesday–Thursday. Address: Downtown Lac du Flambeau, 603 Peace Pipe. Phone: (715) 588-3333. (½–1 hour)

★★ **Lac du Flambeau Fish Hatchery**—This state-of-the-art hatchery raises more than 30 million walleye, muskie, and northern pike yearly. You can fish for trout in a hatchery fishing pond, no license required. Admission: Free. Fee for trout fishing. Hours: Open Memorial Day–Labor Day, 7 a.m.–3:30 p.m., trout pond 9 a.m.–dusk. Address: Highway 47N. Phone: (715) 588-9603. (½ hour)

★★ **Northwoods Wildlife Center**— At this wildlife hospital and rehab facility, injured wildlife are cared for and returned to the wild. Tours walk past baby animals being fed in the nursery and follow outdoor trails to see permanently disabled animals including a golden eagle and hawk. Admission: $2 tour fee. Hours: Memorial Day–Labor Day, Monday–Saturday, 10 a.m.–4 p.m.; winter hours, 10 a.m.–2 p.m. Tours every half-hour during summer. The center offers impromptu tours in winter. Address: Off Highway 70W, across from Trig's shopping center, 8683 Blumstein Rd., Minocqua. Phone: (715) 356-7400. (½ hour–1 hour)

★ **Scheer's Lumberjack Show**—On Highway 47 in Woodruff, you'll learn about life in the lumberjack era at lakeside shows. Admission: $4–$7. Hours: Tuesday, Thursday, and Saturday, 7:30 p.m.; an occasional Thursday matinee. Address: Highway 47, Woodruff. Phone: (715) 356-4050. (1 hour)

★ **Woodruff State Fish Hatchery**—This hatchery produces muskie fingerlings as well as northern pike and walleye. Catch the guided tour at 11 a.m. to learn about how the hatchery works. Admission: Free. Hours: Memorial–Labor Day, 8 a.m.–4 p.m., Monday–Friday. Closed holidays. Address: 8770 County Road J, Woodruff. (715) 356-5211. (¾–1 hour)

FITNESS AND RECREATION

Outdoor recreation is the backbone of this region. **Northern Highland–American Legion State Forest**, (715) 356-5211, offers hiking and nature trails, fishing, swimming, picnicking, winter recreation, back-packing, and canoe campsites. The forest's **Madeline Trail** southeast of Woodruff leads through 9½ miles of rolling terrain; while aspen and birch shade 2.2-mile **Schlect Trail**, 1¼ miles south of Minocqua. There are also 10-mile **Raven Trail**, 7-mile **McNaughton Trail**, and **Bearskin State Trail**, (715) 385-2727—all within 18.3 miles of wilderness south from Minocqua—and other nondesignated trails. These add up to hundreds of miles of hiking, biking, and cross-country skiing. Snowmobile trails are plentiful, too. **Copper Falls State Park**, (715) 274-5123, contains 7 miles of hiking and off-road biking trails and 13.7 miles of ski trails on 2,483 acres. **Lac du Flambeau Tribal Campground and Marina**, (715) 558-3303, ext. 331 (ask for Russ Wolfe), has boat and motor rentals for $30–$35 per day and canoe rentals for $10 a day. If you're intent on catching that really big one, **Greg Biggs Guide Service**, (715) 385-2611, specializes in trophy muskie and walleye. Golfers can play three courses, including a championship, 18-hole course at **Pinewood Country Club**, (715) 282-5500. **Circle M Corral Family Fun Park** specializes in recreational fun with a water slide, go-karts, train rides and such, 10295 Highway 70 W, Minocqua, open mid-May–mid-October; (715) 356-4441. For more information, call (800) 44-NORTH.

FOOD

The garlic-stuffed tenderloin with cognac mustard sauce ($17.95) warrants applause at **Jacobi's**, (715) 356-5591, 9820 Cedar Falls Rd., a quarter-mile west of the Amoco station in Hazelhurst, open at 4:30 p.m.; dinners cost $12–$24. Sauteed veal and chicken dishes are specialties at **Polecat and Lace**, (715) 356-3335, 427 Oneida St., Minocqua, with dinners from $12–$15. Meaty and tender barbecued ribs bring riblovers to the **Plantation Supper Club**, (715) 356-9000, 1½ miles north of Woodruff at the junction of Highways 51 and 70E, in Arbor Vitae, with meals from $12–$18. You'll eat family-style at long tables and drink from tin cups at **Paul Bunyan's Cook Shanty**, (715) 356-6270, on Highway 51 between Minocqua and Woodruff, open May through September: all-you-can-eat breakfast costs $6.50, dinner from $7.95–$9.95. For casual, fun dining go to **S.A. Loons**, (715) 356-1700, on Highway 51N in Woodruff, or to **Spangs Italian Restaurant**, (715) 356-4401, in downtown Minocqua. Try **Lula's Deli & Ice Cream**, (715) 358-2200, Highway 51N in Woodruff, for homemade soups, salads, sandwiches, or breakfast. At **Little Bohemia Restaurant**, (715) 543-8433, in

Manitowish Waters, you can view the John Dillinger-FBI bullet holes as you dine. Liver dumpling soup (Saturday only) and roast duck are specialties; the restaurant closes in winter. To rub elbows with more of the region's shady past, go to **Ma Bailey's Supper Club**, (715) 356-6133, Highway 51 to Highway J, 2 miles east to Woodruff Rd. The former bordello was a gangsters' favorite.

LODGING

At **Dillman's Sand Lake Lodge**, selected by *Changing Times* as one of America's best family vacation values, cabin No. 5 was gangster Baby Face Nelson's hideout. The resort on White Sand Lake, (715) 588-3143, has tennis courts, activities, sand beaches, and water sports; cabins average $50. Opened in 1996, **Lake of the Torches Casino Hotel**, (800) 25-TORCH, on Highway 47 in Lac du Flambeau, carries out a North Woods theme. **Fence Lake Lodge Resort**, 12919 Frying Pan Camp Lane, (715) 588-3255, offers log suites with whirlpools and fireplaces on the Flambeau Chain of Lakes for $70–$205. The **Beacons of Minocqua**, 8250 Northern Road, (800) 236-3225, rents upscale vacation condominiums and has a wide range of activities, $95–$150. Rooms at the **Super 8 Motel** on Highways 51 and 70W in Minocqua, (800) 800-8000, range from $42–$68. **Best Western Lakeview Motor Lodge**, 311 Park St. and Highways 51 in Minocqua, (800) 852-1021, has a $47–$99 range. **Eagle Bluff Condo Rentals**, 990 10th Ave. N. in Hurley, (800) 336-0973, has rooms from $45– $235. The **Pointe Resort Hotel and Conference Center**, on Highway 51 in Minocqua, (715) 356-4431, has attractive rooms and condo-suites for $49–$179. Also in Minocqua, **Cross Trails Motor Lodge and Family Restaurant**, 8644 Highway 5N, (800) 841-5261, offers comfortable lodging from $30–$69.

CAMPING

Lac du Flambeau Tribal Campground, on Highway 47N across from the fish hatchery in Lac du Flambeau, (715) 588-3303, ext. 33 (ask for Russ Wolfe), has 72 paved sites with water and electricity, 17 with full hookups, tent camping, and free showers for $13. There are 55 sites, 13 with electricity, and no showers at **Copper Falls State Park**, off Highway 169 north of Mellen, (715) 274-5123. **Northern Highland– American Legion State Forest**, mostly north and east of Minocqua and Woodruff, (715) 356-5211, offers family backpacking and canoe campsites, a total of 886 sites with some shower facilities. Bring your fishing gear to take advantage of the abundance of lakes in the forest and binoculars to spot eagles, osprey, and hawks. Check with the Woodruff DNR headquarters for canoe route and hiking trail maps and summer programs. Private campgrounds include **Indian Shores**, off Highway 47E in Woodruff, (715) 356-5552, its own community with 210 wooded RV sites, 205 with electricity, 70 with sewer, showers, a rec room, swimming pool, store, boat rentals, and more. Rates are around $19–$25. At **Fox Fire Campground**, 11180 Fox Fire Rd., Arbor Vitae, (715) 356-6470, 56 of 90 sites have full hookups, 15 have electricity, and 21 have no hookups. Tent areas are separate; there are rental boats and paddleboats, pay showers, and a swimming beach. Rates are in the $14–$18 range.

NIGHTLIFE AND SPECIAL EVENTS

Ceremonial dancers present authentic Chippewa dances at the **Lac du Flambeau Indian Bowl Pow Wow**, County Road D, Indian Bowl, downtown Lac du Flambeau. The powwow takes place Tuesday evenings, from the third Tuesday in June through the fourth Tuesday in August; ceremonial dances are at 7 p.m. Admission is $2–$4, under 5 free (1 hour or more). (715) 588-3333. **Lake of the Torches Casino** has gaming and dining, daily, 24 hours; (800) 25-TORCH. **Bear River Pow Wow** takes place at Bear River Pow Wow grounds on Old Indian Village Road, the second weekend in July; (715) 588-3333. (1 hour to all day) Two **Annual Native American Artist Shows**, one in July and one in August, feature authentic cultural and contemporary Native American art—painting, carving, birch-bark, beadwork, and yarnwork—in downtown Lac du Flambeau; (715) 588-3333. People come from near and far to attend **Northern Lights Playhouse** summer productions— seven shows weekly including Broadway hits. The playhouse is on Highway 51 in Hazelhurst, 6 miles south of Minocqua; performances are May–Labor Day at 8 p.m., September–October at 7:30 p.m., children's theater Wednesday at 11 a.m. Call for reservations and ticket prices; (715) 356-7173.

Scenic Route: To Hurley Via Copper Falls State Park

Be prepared to be surprised on this scenic route to Hurley. To find the hidden treasure—waterfalls tucked away in the woodlands—turn off U.S. Highway 2 between Ashland and Hurley onto State Highway 169. Go south 3 miles to tiny Gurney. At the south edge of Gurney, Rowe Farm Road leads west a short drive to a small park overlooking Potato River Falls. It's a pleasant place to linger awhile, and picnic facilities are available. Continue southwest on State 169 about 11 miles to Copper Falls State Park—and suddenly, you've entered a domain of canyons, streams, and waterfalls. Ominously named, Bad River courses through the park. The river's 30-foot Copper Falls plunges between tall cliffs, and 31-foot Brownstone Falls tumbles through the Bad River Gorge. Take the 7 miles of hiking trails through stands of hemlock, cedar, birch, basswood, and white pine to see the 2,483-acre park. A self-guided nature loop-trail gives you clifftop views of both falls, far above the rushing water. Other trails lead to Red Granite Falls and Murphy and Loon Lakes. You can also cross the Tyler's Forks footbridge and follow the river to sandstone ledges, or hike the segment of the North

COPPER FALLS SCENIC ROUTE

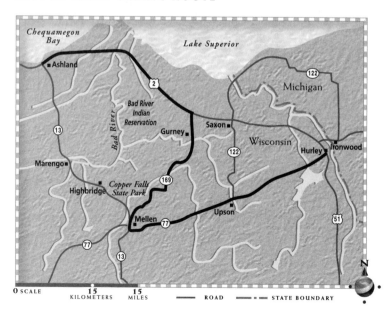

Country National Scenic Trail that runs through the park. Wildlife is plentiful, and you may encounter deer, porcupine, or pileated woodpeckers. Anglers fish the Bad River for trout; Loon Lake has a sand beach for swimming and a boat landing; a spacious picnic area with a log shelter and playground overlooks Bad River. There are also off-road bike trails, cross-country ski trails, and campsites (water and some with electricity but no showers); (715) 274-5123. To get to Hurley from the park, take State 169 south a short distance to the junction with State 13, and follow State 13 south to Mellen. Then head northeast on State 77 about 26 miles to Hurley. ◼

12
WISCONSIN'S DOOR PENINSULA

In far northeastern Wisconsin, Door Peninsula juts out into the water between the bay of Green Bay, Wisconsin, and Lake Michigan. Its mix of rugged limestone bluffs overlooking the shore, coastal fishing villages with white-painted Victorian houses, woodlands, stone fences, fields of mustard and Queen Anne's lace, and ten lighthouses gives the peninsula a New England/coastal Maine flavor beloved by locals and throngs of tourists in summer and fall.

Two counties share the peninsula, Door and Kewaunee; Door occupies the more dramatically scenic northern end of the 70-mile-long peninsula. At the tip lies "Death's Door" (Porte des Mortes), a 6-mile-wide tempestuous strait between the peninsula and Washington Island, where many ships sank. The region's rich maritime history is chronicled in a Sturgeon Bay maritime museum. To explore the top half of the peninsula, you can drive north through Sturgeon Bay—a major ship-building port on the Great Lakes—and follow State Highway 57 along the Lake Michigan side of the peninsula until it merges with State 42. Follow State 42 north to the tip of the peninsula, then after backtracking a short distance, follow 42 south along the Green Bay side. A must is the ferry ride from the tip of the peninsula to Washington Island. From there, take another ferry to Rock Island, a wooded promontory with a lighthouse and a primitive state park—the one place in the area you are likely to find genuine solitude. ◣

DOOR PENINSULA

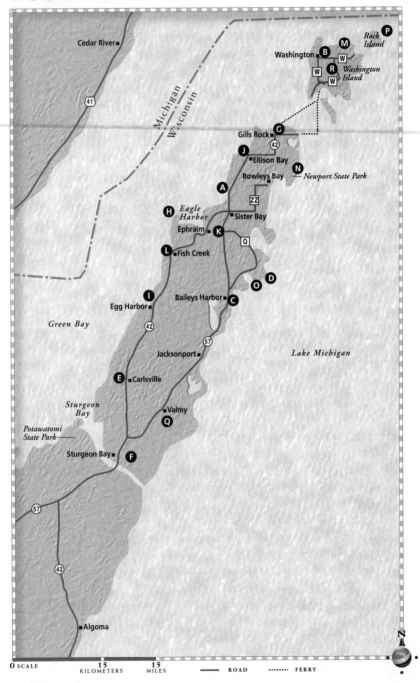

Cedar River ■

Rock Island P

M

Washington ■ **B**
W

W **R** **Washington Island**

W

Michigan
Wisconsin

41

Gills Rock ■ **G**

42

J
■ Ellison Bay

Rowleys Bay ■ **N** *Newport State Park*

A

ZZ

H *Eagle Harbor*

■ Sister Bay

Ephraim ■ **K**

Q

L ■ Fish Creek

O **D**

I Baileys Harbor ■ **C**

Egg Harbor ■

42

57

Green Bay

Jacksonport ■

Lake Michigan

E ■ Carlsville

Sturgeon Bay

■ Valmy

Potawatomi State Park —— **Q**

Sturgeon Bay ■ **F**

57

42

■ Algoma

N

O SCALE   15 KILOMETERS   15 MILES   —— ROAD   ⋯⋯⋯ FERRY

Sightseeing Highlights

Ⓐ Anderson Barn Museum

Ⓑ Arts and Nature Center

Ⓒ Bailey's Harbor

Ⓓ Cana Island Lighthouse

Ⓔ Carlsville

Ⓕ Cherryland Brewery and Pub

Ⓖ Door County Maritime Museum (Gills Rock)

Ⓕ Door County Maritime Museum (Sturgeon Bay)

Ⓗ Eagle Bluff Lighthouse

Ⓘ Egg Harbor

Ⓙ Ellison Bay

Ⓚ Ephraim

Ⓛ Fish Creek

Ⓖ Gills Rock

Ⓜ Jackson Harbor Maritime Museum

Ⓝ Newport State Park

Ⓞ Ridges Sanctuary

Ⓟ Rock Island

Ⓕ Sturgeon Bay

Ⓠ Valmy

Ⓡ Washington Island

Note: Items with the same letter are located in the same place or area.

A PERFECT DAY IN DOOR PENINSULA

Fortify yourself with breakfast and unforgettable pecan rolls at Grandma's Swedish Restaurant. Pack a backpack lunch and water bottles and drive to Northport Pier to board the Washington Island Ferry. Drive across Washington Island and catch the Rock Island Ferry, *Karfi*. Spend the day hiking and exploring Rock Island. Visit the Viking Hall and take a lunch break on the beach. Ride the two ferries back to the mainland, then stop for a fish-boil dinner (The White Gull Inn in Fish Creek is my first choice). Later in the evening go to a Peninsula Players play.

SIGHTSEEING HIGHLIGHTS

★★★ **Ellison Bay/Gills Rock/Washington Island**—At the top of the peninsula, a commercial fishing fleet is based at the seaport town of Gills Rock. Sportfishing is fantastic here, and divers can explore shipwrecks. The story of commercial fishing, shipwrecks, and navigation unfolds at **Door County Maritime Museum** at Gills Rock. Admission: 50 cents–$1. Hours: Memorial Day–Labor Day, daily 10 a.m.–4 p.m., opens at 1 p.m. Sunday; September–October, noon–4 pm., Sunday, 1–4 pm. Address: Memorial Park. Phone: (414) 854-1844 or (414) 743-5958. (½–1 hour)

Washington Island lays claim to being the oldest Icelandic community in the United States. The Washington Island Ferry will carry you and your car safely from Northport Pier near Gills Rock across Death's Door Strait to the island's Detroit Harbor. Expect a chilly, blustery ride. Fee: $16 round-trip for a car, $7 for adults, $3.50 for children 6–11. Hours: 7:15 a.m.–5:30 p.m., every half-hour in July and August; from 8 a.m.–5 p.m. May–June and September–October with a reduced schedule; year-round service. Address: Northport Pier (the end of Highway 42). Phone: Northport Pier and Restaurant, (414) 854-4146. Island Ferry Terminal: (414) 847-2546. (40 minutes)

Explore the scenic island backroads by car, on your own bike, or rent a single-speed bike at the Washington Island Ferry dock for $3 per hour.

Two open-air trams—Cherry Train, (414) 847-2039, and Viking Train, (414) 854-2972—offer 90-minute narrated island tours for $3.50–$6. Two passenger-only narrated cruises leaving from Gills Rock connect with the trams and cost $3.50–$7 round-trip. CG Richter Passenger Cruises, (414) 847-2546, operated by the Washington Ferry Line Memorial Day–Columbus Day weekend, links up with Cherry Train. The Island Clipper operates from late May to mid-October and connects with Viking Train. You can buy a package ticket for the Island Clipper and Viking Train for $7–$13, or for $11.50–$17.50 with lunch included. The Clipper also has bike rentals ($3 per hour) and moped rentals ($15–$20 per hour), (414) 854-2972. For more information, call the Washington Island Chamber of Commerce, (414) 847-2179.

On the Island, the **Jackson Harbor Maritime Museum** has indoor and outdoor maritime exhibits. Admission: $1. Hours: Memorial Day–Labor Day, 10:30 a.m.–4:30 p.m. daily. Closed Columbus Day weekend to Memorial Day weekend. Address: Jackson Harbor Road.

Phone: (414) 847-2179. (½–1 hour) You can also visit the **Arts and Nature Center** to see the work of island artists and take nature hikes and art classes. Admission: 50 cents–$1. Hours: Open mid-June–mid-September, 10:30 a.m.–4:30 p.m. After Labor Day, 11 a.m.–3 p.m. Address: Corner of Main Road and Jackson Harbor. Phone: (414) 847-2657 or (414) 847-2025. (½ hour)

★★★ **Newport State Park**—East of Ellison Bay, this 2,200-acre wooded, rugged, and mostly undeveloped park overlooks the Lake Michigan shoreline and contains 28 miles of hiking trails through remnant boreal forest and virgin white pine. The park has a naturalist program and guided hikes. Follow the European Bay trail for views of Pilot Island Lighthouse. In the park, hikers may encounter the foundations of old logging camps and lilac bushes marking the former settlement of Newport. You'll find wild strawberries in early summer. Admission: State park sticker. Hours: Open all year. Address: 475 County NP, Ellison Bay. Take Highway 42 and Newport Road. Phone: (414) 854-2500. (2 hours–all day)

★★★ **Rock Island**—All of the island is contained in the 912-acre Rock Island State Park. No motorized vehicles are allowed. To get here from the peninsula, go to Washington Island via the Washington Island Ferry, drive across the island, and catch the Rock Island Ferry from Jackson Harbor on Washington Island. Or leave your car on the mainland and rent a bike on Washington Island to ride to Jackson Harbor. A day on the island removes you from the tourist traffic of popular Door County. Attractions include 9½ miles of hiking trails, a sand beach, cliff carvings, a lighthouse on the north shore, campsites, and the stone Viking Hall boathouse and other buildings built by Icelanders in the early 1900s, when inventor Chester Thorardson owned the island. The craggy island reminded him of his native Iceland. The boathouse now houses the park's nature center. It's wise to reserve ferry space and campsites in advance. Admission: Ferry fee. Hours: Open May–December. Address: Rock Island lies off the northeast shore of Washington Island. The park office is located on Washington Island at the Jackson Harbor state dock. To request information, write to: Rock Island State Park, Washington Island, WI 54246, or call (414) 847-2235. (3 hours or more)

Karfi, the Rock Island Ferry, departs Washington Island from Jackson Harbor for Rock Island. The ferry fee replaces the state park

car fee, hence the name "Karfi": Round trip, $4–$8. Hours: Every
hour July–September, 10 a.m.–4 p.m. daily. From late-May–June and
early September–early October, departure times are 10:30 a.m., 1, and
3:30 p.m. daily, with additional trips on weekends and Memorial Day.
Address: Jackson Harbor, Washington Island. Phone: (414) 847-2252.
(15 minutes)

★★ **Bailey's Harbor**—On the shores of Lake Michigan north of
Jacksonport, wetlands and wilderness surround Bailey's Harbor.
Privately owned **Ridges Sanctuary** offers bird-watching and guided
hikes originating from the headquarters of the 900-acre wildflower preserve, which contains rare plant communities and 23 species of orchids
native to Wisconsin. Admission: $1–$2. Hours: Trails open dawn to
dusk year round. Nature center open 9 a.m.–4 p.m., Memorial
Day–mid-October; Monday–Saturday, tours at 9:30 a.m. and 1:30 p.m.
Address: Highway 57N. Phone: (414) 839-2802. (1–2 hours)
    Northeast of Bailey's Harbor stands the 1869 **Cana Island
Lighthouse.** Follow Cana Island Road. You can reach the lighthouse by
a causeway when the lake is low, or by wading. Admission to the
grounds (the lighthouse is not open): $1–$2. Hours: 10 a.m.–5 p.m.,
May–October. Parking is limited.

★★ **Fish Creek**—The entrance to Peninsula State Park lies a short way
from the heart of this historic village noted for its professional summer
theater. The 3,763-acre park has 20 miles of hiking trails, a nature center with guided tours, and a 9-mile bikeway. Sunset Trail passes **Eagle
Bluff Lighthouse,** built in 1868, now restored, furnished, and open for
summer tours. Park Admission: Sticker. Eagle Lighthouse, 50 cents–$1.
Hours: State Park hours are 6 a.m.–11 p.m. Some campsites here are
open for winter camping. Lighthouse hours: 10 a.m.–4:30 p.m.,
Memorial Day–Labor Day, with tours every half hour or less. Address:
Between Fish Creek and Ephraim on Highway 42. Park phone: (414)
868-3258. This scenic park is extremely popular and crowded; make
reservations as early as possible.

★★ **Sturgeon Bay**—This city of 9,000 people is one of the largest
Great Lakes shipbuilding ports. Its **Door County Maritime Museum**
features shipbuilding history and maritime trades. Admission: 50
cents–$1. Hours: Memorial Day–Labor Day, 9 a.m.–6 p.m.; closes at
4 p.m. September–mid-October. Weekends, 10 a.m.–4 p.m from mid-

to late October. Address: 101 Florida St. Phone: (414) 743-8139 or
(414) 743-5958. (½–1 hour)

Cherryland Brewery & Pub is at the west end of downtown in
an old railroad station: You can watch the brewer at work while you
sample the beer. Hours: 11 a.m.–9 p.m. daily. Address: 341 N. 3rd Ave.
Phone: (414) 743-1945.

Door County Museum has exhibits on local history. Admission:
Donation. Hours: May through October, 10 a.m.–4:30 p.m. daily.
Address: 18 N. 4th Ave. Phone: (414) 743-5809. (½ hour)

✷ **Egg Harbor/Carlsville**—Orchards thrive on Door Peninsula. You'll
see cherry and apple trees in blossom in mid- to late May. Come summer and early fall, plump strawberries, tart cherries, and ruby-red
apples fill produce stands on Highway 42 between Egg Harbor and Fish
Creek. Door Peninsula Winery at Carlsville, south of Egg Harbor, produces wines from locally grown cherries, apples, cranberries, and plums.
Stop for a tour and tasting. Admission: $1. Hours: Year round. 9 a.m.–
6 p.m daily, June–October; until 5 p.m. November–May. Address: 5806
Highway 42. Phone: (414) 743-7431. (1 hour)

✷ **Ephraim**—Memorable for tiers of white wooden houses and
churches overlooking Eagle Harbor on the Green Bay side of the
peninsula, this picturesque hamlet was founded in 1853 by Moravians
who came here from Norway. It's a favored spot for windsurfing and
sailing. If you're yearning to try either, Ephraim Sailing and Windsurfing Center offers lessons and rentals at South Shore Pier, (414)
854-4336. The town is also the northern entrance to Peninsula State
Park. Ephraim's history is preserved at **Anderson Barn Museum,** a
barn with a square silo, open during the resort season. There's also a
restored and furnished pioneer school and country store. Call Ephraim
Information Center for details, May–October, (414) 854-4989.

✷ **Valmy**—Northeast of Valmy, between Lake Michigan and Clark
Lake, 90-foot sand dunes are the main attraction in 863-acre
Whitefish Dunes State Park. There are 13 miles of hiking trails, a
sand beach, and in the northeastern section cliffs rise 20 feet above the
shoreline. Admission: Park sticker. Hours: Day use only. Address: East
on Clark Lake Road off Highway 57. Phone: (414) 823-2400. At the
northern end of the park, waves boom against undercut limestone
cliffs at Cave Point County Park. This side of the peninsula is wilder

than the Green Bay side, and the park has few visitors in early morning or late afternoon.

FITNESS AND RECREATION

Diverse recreational options include fishing charters, such as **Eagle Harbor Charters** (promising trophy trout and salmon fishing) at South Shore Pier in Ephraim, (414) 854-4324 or (414) 854-4667, and **Lynn's Charter Fishing** (with a zoologist as your guide) at Bailey's Harbor Yacht Club, (414) 854-5109. There are sailing cruises, horse stables, boat rentals, scuba diving (**Shoreline Resort Charters** at Gills Rock/ Ellison Bay 414-854-2606), and parasailing (**Wisconsin Water Wings** in Ephraim, 414-854-9000). You can hike in any of the five Door County state parks, bike in most of them, and golf on seven courses. **Peninsula Golf Course** in Peninsula State Park, (414) 868-5791, is majestically situated above Green Bay. Bike rental shops are plentiful: **Bailey's Harbor Yacht Club Resort** in Bailey's Harbor, (414) 839-2336, rents six-speeds for up to a full day, and kid carts for $5–$15. A 100-mile **Backroad Bicycle Route** traverses the fields and forests between small towns; pick up a map from the Door County Chamber of Commerce on State Highways 42 and 57, just south of Sturgeon Bay, (414) 743-4456, or in any village information center.

FOOD

Fish boil is a Door County tradition handed down from Scandinavian settlers and lumberjacks and served nearly everywhere. Whitefish steaks, potatoes, and onions are boiled in an open pot over an outdoor fire. The meal is served along with melted butter and, if you're lucky, a slab of fresh cherry pie. Dinner rates are a moderate $8–$13 in most restaurants, with a few costing up to $20; reservations are recommended. **The Viking**, on Highway 42 in Ellison Bay, (414) 854-2998, serves fish boil nightly, also steaks and seafood. In Sister Bay, goats graze on the roof of **Al Johnson's Restaurant**, (414) 854-2626, a good breakfast spot with Swedish pancakes. At **Elquists Door County Market**, Highway 42 and Townline Road in Ephraim, (414) 854-2552, you can buy deli sandwiches, salads, and cherry pie, and rent a bicycle, too. The pecan rolls have been rated best in the state at **Grandma's Swedish Restaurant** at Wagon Trail Resort, Restaurant and Conference Center on Rowleys Bay at 1041 Highway ZZ, (800) 99-WAGON. There's also a nightly

Swedish smorgasbord. The **Inn at Cedar Crossing**, 336 Louisiana St., Sturgeon Bay, (414) 743-4200 or 743-4249, gets raves for its cherry pie and other homemade fare. **Square Rigger Galley**, 6332 Highway 57, on the lakeshore in Jacksonport, (414) 823-2408, has a nightly fishboil and breakfast daily July through August. The **White Gull Inn**, Main Street in Fish Creek, (414) 868-3517, serves fish boil Wednesday, Friday, Saturday, and Sunday evenings, $14.75, and wonderful food in general, $13.95–$19.95.

LODGING

Choosing among the fine lodging places is the hard part. Among the best bed and breakfasts/inns is historic **White Gull Inn**, a country inn at 4225 Main St. in Fish Creek, (414) 868-3517, with inn rooms and cottages for $90–$175. There's also the **Whistling Swan Inn**, 4192 Main St. in Fish Creek, (414) 868-3442, with rooms from $98–$140. You'll find excellent lodging in Sturgeon Bay at the **White Lace Inn**, 16 North 5th Ave., with rooms from $48–$158, (414) 743-1105; the **Scoffield House Bed and Breakfast**, 908 Michigan St., (414) 743-7727, $69–$190; and **Inn at Cedar Crossing**, 336 Louisiana St., $79–$138, (414) 743-4200. In Rowleys Bay, **Wagon Trail Resort**, 1041 Highway ZZ, (800) 99-WAGON, has lodge rooms and rental homes from $109–$275. In Ephraim, **Eagle Harbor Inn**, 9914 Water St., (414) 854-2121, is a nine-room inn with five guest cottages and rates from $79–$156; and **French Country Inn**, 3052 Spruce Lane, (414) 854-4001, has seven guest rooms in a 1912 summer cottage, two with private baths, for $57–$84. Area motels include **Grand View Motel**, Highway 42S, Ellison Bay, (800) 258-8208, with rooms from $48–$75, and **Findlay's Holiday Inn** with a Scandinavian theme, Detroit Harbor, Washington Island, (414) 847-2526, rooms from $60–$100 daily, $450–$650 weekly. Reserve in advance.

CAMPING

State parks offer public camping. **Potawatomi State Park** on Sturgeon Bay has 1,231 acres, 125 sites, 25 with electricity, and showers. The Ice Age National Trail starts here. From the city of Sturgeon Bay, take Highway 42/57 south, go north on County Road S, west on County C, and turn right on Park Road; (414) 746-2890. **Peninsula State Park** has 469 sites, 100 with electricity, and showers; **Newport State Park**

DOOR PENINSULA

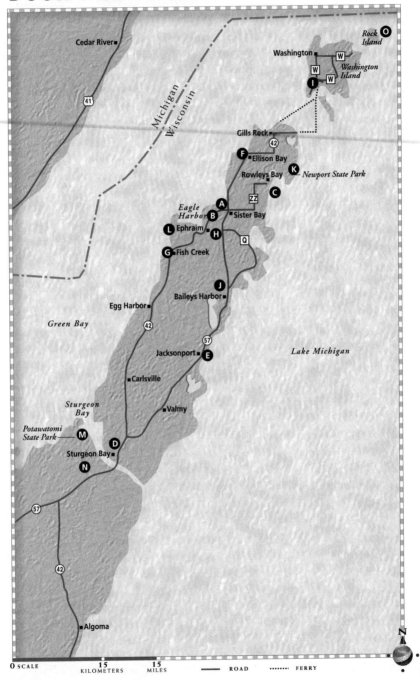

Cedar River■

Michigan
Wisconsin

41

Rock
Island O

Washington■ W
                    Washington
            W   Island
    I   W

Gills Rock■

42

F
    ■Ellison Bay

Rowleys Bay■   K
                          Newport State Park

                    C
            ZZ
A
    B
        ■Sister Bay
Eagle
Harbor
L ■Ephraim
        H
            Q
G ■Fish Creek

            J
Egg Harbor■   Baileys Harbor■

Green Bay
        42

            57
Jacksonport■ E

    ■Carlsville

Sturgeon
Bay   ■Valmy

Potawatomi
State Park— M
            D
Sturgeon Bay■
        N

    57

42

    ■Algoma

Lake Michigan

N

Food

- **Ⓐ** Al Johnson's Restaurant
- **Ⓑ** Elquists Door County Market
- **Ⓒ** Grandma's Swedish Restaurant
- **Ⓓ** Inn at Cedar Crossing
- **Ⓔ** Square Rigger Galley
- **Ⓕ** The Viking
- **Ⓖ** The White Gull Inn

Lodging

- **Ⓗ** Eagle Harbor Inn
- **Ⓘ** Findlay's Holiday Inn
- **Ⓗ** French Country Inn
- **Ⓕ** Grand View Motel
- **Ⓓ** Inn at Cedar Crossing
- **Ⓓ** The Scofield House Bed and Breakfast
- **Ⓒ** Wagon Trail Resort
- **Ⓖ** Whistling Swan Inn
- **Ⓖ** White Gull Inn
- **Ⓓ** The White Lace Inn

Camping

- **Ⓙ** Bailey's Grove Travel Park & Campground
- **Ⓚ** Newport State Park
- **Ⓛ** Peninsula State Park
- **Ⓜ** Potawatomi State Park
- **Ⓝ** Quiet Woods North Camping Resort
- **Ⓞ** Rock Island State Park
- **Ⓒ** Wagon Trail Campground

Note: Items with the same letter are located in the same town or area.

has 16 sites, no electricity, and no showers; **Rock Island State Park** has 40 backpacking sites, no electricity or showers. (See Sightseeing Highlights for details on these parks.) Private campgrounds include **Wagon Trail Campground**, 1190 Highway ZZ, 6 miles northeast of Sister Bay on County ZZ, (414) 854-4818, with 140 sites, 12 full hookups, 93 with water and electricity, and 35 with no hookups, free showers, and a separate tent area. Rates are about $17–$29. **Bailey's Grove Travel Park & Campground**, left on County Road F from Bailey's Harbor, (414) 839-2559, has 68 shaded sites and a grassy tent area with trees, showers, and electricity. Rates are about $17–$24. **Quiet Woods North Camping Resort**, (800) 9-TO-CAMP, about 2 miles southwest of Sturgeon Bay off County Road C, has 260 mostly wooded sites—25 full hookup, 204 water and electricity, and 32 no hookup—a swimming pool, and showers. Rates are about $19–$27.

NIGHTLIFE AND SPECIAL EVENTS

Birch Creek Music Center, a noted music academy east of Egg Harbor, hosts summer evening concerts in a barn; (414) 868-3763. **The Peninsula Players**, a venerable and respected professional resident theater company, perform plays and musicals in a bayside pavilion Tuesday through Sunday evenings; (414) 868-3287. Annual events include a May **Door County Lighthouse Walk** (414) 743-5958, and Ephraim's June **Fyr-Bal** Scandinavian festival, (414) 854-4989.

13
LAKE WINNEBAGO, HORICON MARSH, AND THE KETTLE MORAINE

Lake Winnebago's 215-square-mile glacially crafted bed makes it the largest lake in Wisconsin. Lake Michigan and Lake Superior, both Great Lakes, aren't contenders since Wisconsin shares their shorelines with other states. Winnebago, inland from Lake Michigan about 35 miles and 60 miles northwest of Milwaukee, measures 28 miles long, 10 miles wide, and a shallow 20 feet deep. Fed by the Fox and Wolf Rivers, the lake attracted a variety of Native American tribes, including Fox, Menominee, Winnebago, Macouten, Ottawa, and Sauk. A settlement named for Menominee Chief Oshkosh grew into the city of Oshkosh. Its 55,000 or so residents populate Lake Winnebago's west shore. In the 1870s, Oshkosh took on the nickname of "Sawdust City" when lumber-era mills on the Fox River transformed it into the largest wood-manufacturing city in the country.

Today only a handful of mills remain, and the city's contemporary claim to fame lies in overalls: first, the heavy-duty bibbed variety and, more recently, upscale kids' duds labeled Oshkosh B'Gosh. Oshkosh has a lovely lakeside park, as does Fond du Lac, a city of nearly 38,000, 21 miles south of Oshkosh on the southern end of Lake Winnebago. Both cities abound in water sports activities and have interesting historic buildings. Fond du Lac's location makes it a handy base for outings to waterfowl haven Horicon Marsh and the Kettle Moraine State Forest's Northern Unit. ◼

LAKE WINNEBAGO REGION

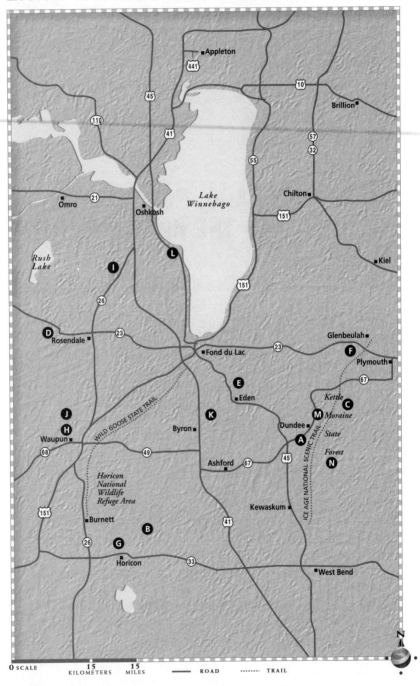

Appleton
441
45
110
Brillion
41
57
32
55
Chilton
Lake
Winnebago
151
Omro
21
Oshkosh
Rush
Lake
L
I
Kiel
26
151
D
23
Rosendale
Glenbeulah
23
F
Fond du Lac
Plymouth
67
E
Kettle
Eden
C
K
Moraine
J
M
H
Byron
Dundee
State
Waupun
A
68
49
Forest
Ashford
67
45
N
Horicon
National
Wildlife
Refuge Area
Kewaskum
151
Burnett
B
26
G
41
Horicon
33
West Bend

WILD GOOSE STATE TRAIL
ICE AGE NATIONAL SCENIC TRAIL

N

0 SCALE
15
KILOMETERS
15
MILES
—— ROAD   ·········· TRAIL

Sightseeing Highlights

- **Ⓐ** Henry S. Reuss Ice Age Visitor Center
- **Ⓑ** Horicon Marsh
- **Ⓑ** Horicon Marsh Wildlife Area
- **Ⓑ** Horicon National Wildlife Refuge
- **Ⓒ** Kettle Moraine State Forest Northern Unit
- **Ⓓ** Larsen's Ranch Clydesdales
- **Ⓔ** Silver Wheel Manor Museum and Shoppes
- **Ⓕ** Wade House Stagecoach Inn and Wesley Jung Carriage Museum

Food

- **Ⓖ** The Ice Cream Station

Lodging

- **Ⓗ** The Rose Ivy Inn

Camping

- **Ⓘ** Circle R Campground
- **Ⓙ** Fond du Lac County Park
- **Ⓚ** Fond du Lac KOA Kampground
- **Ⓛ** Kalbus' Country Harbor
- **Ⓒ** Kettle Moraine State Forest
- **Ⓜ** Long Lake Recreation Area
- **Ⓝ** Mauthe Lake Recreation Area

Note: Items with the same letter are located in the same town or area.

A PERFECT DAY IN LAKE WINNEBAGO, HORICON MARSH, AND THE KETTLE MORAINE

Head out to Horicon Marsh to glimpse some of the thousands of geese, egrets, herons, and other migratory and resident water-loving birds. Then set off for the Kettle Moraine State Forest; bring hiking boots, a camera, and a picnic lunch. Visit the Ice Age Center to bone up on moraine characteristics, then hike the wooded trails and eat lunch under a tree. Drive to Greenbush to tour the historic Wade House Stagecoach

Inn and Wesley Jung Carriage Museum, built in 1850, then head back to Fond du Lac for a lakeside stroll and dinner at the elegant Rosewood Dining Room.

SIGHTSEEING HIGHLIGHTS

★★★ **Experimental Aviation Association (EAA) Air Adventure Museum**—In Oshkosh, the EAA Museum preserves aviation history and has the world's largest private aircraft collection. The Eagle Hangar features WW II displays. There are five theaters, photo and art galleries, and docents to answer questions. Held near the museum, the annual **EAA Fly-In Convention** is a major aviation event, with educational forums, workshops, seminars, evening programs, and 15,000 airplanes, from antiques to homebuilts and ultralights. Aerobic performers give daily air shows. The seven-day convention is usually the last weekend in July and first week in August. Museum admission: $5.50–$7, under 8 free. Hours: Monday–Saturday, 8:30 a.m.–5 p.m.; Sunday, 11 a.m.–5 p.m. Closed major holidays. Address: 3000 Poberezny Drive, East of U.S. Highway 41, off State Highway 44/26. Phone: (414) 426-4818. (1–2 hours)

★★★ **Horicon Marsh**—The northern two-thirds of this 31,904-acre marsh is the federal **Horicon National Wildlife Refuge**; the southern third is the **Horicon Marsh Wildlife Area**, under the auspices of the Wisconsin State DNR. Skirting the western edge of the marsh, 34-mile Wild Goose State Trail, (414) 929-3135, is open to hikers, bikers, cross-country skiers, and snowmobilers. Thousands of migrating geese stop at the marsh in spring and fall. There are trails leading into the marsh and weekend interpretive programs in May and mid-September through October. Stop at the main DNR Headquarters office on Highway 28, about 2 miles north of Horicon, for views of the marsh and hiking and program information. The DNR Field Headquarters on N. Palmatory Street in Horicon has marked trails, parking, and public restrooms. (Take State Highway 28 to Horicon, turn right on State 33 at the edge of town, go one block, and turn right on N. Palmatory Street. The Field Headquarters are at the top of the hill.) You can also tour the marsh on a pontoon boat run by Blue Heron Tours, (414) 485-2942 or (414) 485-4663, located on State Hwy. 33 at Blue Heron Landing by the bridge in Horicon. A one-hour lecture tour at 1 p.m. daily May–October costs $3.50–$7.50, under 4 free; or you can rent a canoe for $14–$21 a day and explore on your own. There are also special rookery tours. Blue Heron Tours opens at 10 a.m. DNR Headquarters hours: Monday–Friday, 7:45 a.m.–4:30 p.m. To get to DNR Headquarters from Fond du Lac, take State Highway 175 south from Fond du Lac about 20 miles to County Highway 28, and go southwest through Theresa and Maysville to the headquarters, about 11 miles. Phone: Horicon Marsh Wildlife Area, DNR: (414) 387-7860; Horicon National Wildlife Refuge, (414) 387-2658. For the informative tabloid *Horicon Marsh Visitor*, call the Horicon Chamber of Commerce, (414) 485-3200.

★★★ **Kettle Moraine State Forest Northern Unit/Henry S. Reuss Ice Age Visitor Center**—The center interprets by film and panorama the drumlins, kettles, kames, and other dramatic Northern Unit characteristics left by receding glaciers 18,000-plus years ago. You can hike trails, including the **Ice Age National Scenic Trail** that runs north/south through the northern unit. Admission: Hourly, daily, or annual park sticker. Ice Age Center hours: 8:30 a.m.–4 p.m. weekdays, 9:30 a.m.–5 p.m. weekends. Location: About 18 miles southeast of Fond du Lac: Take U.S. Highway 45 southeast, then follow State Highway 67 northeast to the center. Phone: KMF Northern Unit Headquarters, (414) 626-2116; Ice Age Center, (414) 533-8322. (Ice Age Center, ½–1 hour)

★★★ **Wade House Stagecoach Inn and Wesley Jung Carriage Museum**—At the Wade House, you'll meet the costumed innkeepers, tour the rooms, and speak with inn "patrons"—all of whom are caught up in talk about a civil war. The Wisconsin State Historical Society operates this 1850s stagecoach inn, built alongside a plank walk in the village of Greenbush. A horse-drawn carriage takes you to view more than 100 restored hand- and horse-drawn carriages at the carriage museum. Admission: $2–$5. Hours: Open May 1–October 31 daily, 9 a.m.–5 p.m. Address: Located 23 miles east of Fond du Lac, off state Highway 23 in Greenbush. Phone: (414) 526-3271. (1–2 hours)

★★ **Galloway House and Village**—In Fond du Lac, you can tour a restored 30-room Victorian mansion surrounded by 23 turn-of-the-century buildings, including the Blakely Museum, the Adams House Resource Center, a photographer's shop, and more—a National Registered Historic Landmark. Admission: $1–$4. Hours: 10 a.m.–5 p.m., Memorial Day–Labor Day. Address: 336 Old Pioneer Rd., Fond du Lac. Phone (414) 922-6390. (½–1 hour)

★★ **Paine Art Center and Arboretum**—The center occupies an impressive 1920s Tudor Revival house in Oshkosh, designed for lumber baron Nathan Paine and his wife, Jessie. In addition to period rooms, nineteenth-century French and American paintings, sculpture, Oriental rugs, and decorative arts, the center has an arboretum with six display gardens including a rose garden. Ask about musical performances and family events. Guided tours by appointment, (414) 235-6903. Admission: $2–$3, under 12 free. Open year round, Tuesday–Sunday, 11 a.m.–4 p.m.; Friday until 7 p.m. Closed Monday and some holidays. Address: 1410 Algoma Blvd. Phone: (414) 235-4530. (1 hour)

★★ **Oshkosh Public Museum**—Tiffany studios–designed interiors are preserved in a 1907 English Tudor–style mansion built for lumber baron and banker Edgar Sawyer. Displays include the Wisconsin folk art Apostles Clock and exhibits on regional history. Admission: Donations welcomed. Hours: Tuesday–Saturday, 9 a.m.–5 p.m., Sunday 1–5 p.m. Address: 1331 Algoma Blvd. Off Highway 41 on City Route Highway 21, at the intersection of Algoma Boulevard, Congress, and High Avenues. Phone: (414) 424-4731. (½–1 hour)

★ **Larsen's Ranch Clydesdales**—Larsen's ranch visits include a 90-minute guided tour, a museum, antique hitch wagons, harnesses, and a Clydesdale horse show—plus a Clydesdale foal to pet. Admission: $3–$6. Hours: May–October, Monday–Saturday. Shows at 1 p.m. Advance reservations requested. Address: Located 17 miles west of Fond du Lac. Take Highway 23W to County Road KK. Phone: (414) 748-5466. (1 hour)

★ **Oshkosh B'Gosh stores**—Based in Oshkosh since 1895, the company has two stores here—a factory outlet merchandise store and a "showcase" store with the latest in their children's collections. Factory store hours: March–January, Monday–Friday, 10 a.m.–9 p.m., Saturday until 8 p.m., Sunday 11 a.m.–6 p.m.; January–February, Monday–Thursday 10 a.m.–6 p.m., Friday and Saturday until 8 p.m., Sunday 11 a.m.–6 p.m. Address: Horizon Outlet Center, 3001 S. Washburn. (414) 426-5817. Showcase store hours: Monday–Thursday, 9:30 a.m.–6 p.m., Friday until 8 p.m., Saturday until 5 p.m. Address: 206 State St. Phone: (414) 231-4458.

★ **Silver Wheel Manor Museum and Shoppes**—If you're in search of vintage wedding gowns, there are 2,200 of them here in this "collections-

gone-wild" place featuring "rentable history." Marlene Hansen fills a
30-room mansion with her family's 87-year collection of antique furnishings, 1,000 dolls, 38 doll carriages, 300 trains, and more—and rents
out antiques for magazine and catalog photographs. Many exhibits offer
rentable or buyable items. Admission: $5–$10. Hours: April–September,
Monday, Wednesday, Friday, and Saturday, 10 a.m.–4 p.m. Address:
Located southeast of Fond du Lac. From Highway 41, follow Highway
23 east 5 miles to County Road K and go south about 1 mile. Phone:
(414) 922-1608. (1 hour or more)

FITNESS AND RECREATION

In Oshkosh, **Larsen Recreational Trail** begins on Westwind Road in
the Sunset Point area off Highway 110 and offers 20 miles of backcountry for hiking or biking. **Wild Goose State Biking and Hiking Trail**
can be accessed in Fond du Lac from Rolling Meadows Drive just south
of the intersection of Highways 41 and 151, (414) 929-3135. Families
enjoy 400-acre **Lakeside Park on Lake Winnebago** in Fond du Lac
with picnic grounds, floral displays, an amusement park, a lighthouse
with an observation deck, a miniature train, and bumperboats. There is
a petting zoo open 1–3 p.m. on weekdays and 11 a.m.–3 p.m. weekends
and holidays, from Memorial Day–Labor Day. Aqua bikes and canoe
rentals are available 11 a.m.–8:30 p.m., Monday–Saturday and 10 a.m.–
8:30 p.m. Sunday. There are five public boat launches in Oshkosh and
three in Fond du Lac. In Oshkosh, three businesses offer boat rentals:
Try **Fox River Marina** (414) 236-4220, at 501 S. Main. There are
canoe rentals at **Blue Heron Landing** on Highway 33 in Horicon,
April 1–September 30, (414) 485-2942 or (414) 485-4663. For jet-ski,
boat, and equipment rentals in Fond du Lac, try **Wisconsin Water
Sports**, Highway 151 at Winnebago Drive across from Roosevelt Park,
(414) 929-8823. With lots of water, windsurfing is popular here: **Wind
Power** has lessons and rentals Memorial Day–Labor Day on Monday,
Wednesday, and Friday at 4:30–8:30 p.m. and Saturday and Sunday
from 10 a.m.–5 p.m., across from the Roosevelt Park area at Highway
151N, 7351 Winnebago Drive in Fond du Lac; (414) 922-2550. You
can bowl at five bowling alleys in Oshkosh, four in Fond du Lac.
Among the plentiful fishing guides and charters are **4 Seasons Guide
Service** in Fond du Lac, (414) 922-6982, and **Gib's Guide Service**,
2115 Hickory Ln., Oshkosh, (414) 233-3148. Oshkosh's golf courses
include **Westhaven Golf Club**, 1400 Westhaven Dr., (414) 233-4640,

(18 holes). Fond du Lac's four courses include **Camelot Country Club Golf Course** on Highway 67, 1 mile east of Highway 41, (414) 269-4949. Both cities have a number of marinas. For more information on Fond du Lac recreation, call (800) 937-9123; for Oshkosh, (800) 876-5250.

FOOD

Dinner at most of the best restaurants here costs under $20. In addition to steak and prime rib, **Granary Restaurant**, a National Historic Site former mill at 50 W. Sixth Ave. in Oshkosh, (414) 233-3929, has a steamed vegetable platter; prices range from $7–$18. The cold strawberry soup elicits praise at **Esprit Restaurant** in the Hilton Hotel, 1 N. Main in Oshkosh, (414) 231-5000, as does Sunday brunch: Dinner prices are $9.95–$14.95. Seafood and veal are specialties at **Butch's Anchor Inn**, 225 W. 20th Ave. in Oshkosh, (414) 232-3742, with dinner from $9.95–$13.95. You'll find a formal dining atmosphere in Fond du Lac's **Rosewood Dining Room**, (414) 923-3000, 1 N. Main at Division St., in a renovated 1920s hotel that's now a Ramada Inn; dinner costs from $9–$11. The Fond du Lac **Main Exchange**, 161 S. Main, (414) 923-8181, offers casual dining in a restored turn-of-the-century tavern with steaks, sandwiches, and specialty drinks; meals are an affordable $6.95–$13. **Salty's Seafood and Spirits**, 503 N. Park Ave. in Fond du Lac, (414) 922-9940, is popular and crowded on weekends, with dinner from $8.95–$27.95. Another recommended restaurant is **Theo's Supper Club**, 24 N. Main, (414) 922-8899; meals cost $6.94–$17.95. Closed Sunday. The **Ice Cream Station**, 518 E. Lake St. in Horicon, (414) 485-2311, is a tiny ice-cream joint open May through October. The honey almond yogurt and coconut chocolate-chip ice cream—huge double dips in waffle cones—are pure bliss.

LODGING

Fond du Lac lodging includes **EconoLodge** (formerly Friendship Inn), 649 W. Johnson St., (800) 553-2666, $34–$59, with a complimentary continental breakfast; **Budgetel Inn BudgetDome**, 77 Holiday Lane, (414) 921-4000, $43–$87, also with continental breakfast; **Motel 6**, 738 W. Johnson St., Highway 23, (800) 4-MOTEL6, $23.99–$35.99; and the **Ramada Inn**, 1 N. Main St. at Division St., (800) 2-RAMADA, $56–$85, with indoor pool and whirlpool, in a historic

OSHKOSH

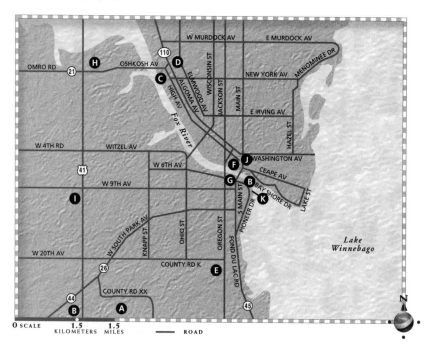

Sightseeing Highlights

Ⓐ Experimental Aviation Association (EAA) Air Adventure Museum

Ⓑ Oshkosh B'Gosh Stores

Ⓒ Oshkosh Public Museum

Ⓓ Paine Art Center and Arboretum

Food

Ⓔ Butch's Anchor Inn

Ⓕ Esprit Restaurant

Ⓖ Granary Restaurant

Lodging

Ⓗ Budgetel Motor Inn

Ⓘ Motel 6

Ⓙ Oshkosh Hilton and Convention Center

Ⓚ Pioneer Inn and Marina

FOND DU LAC

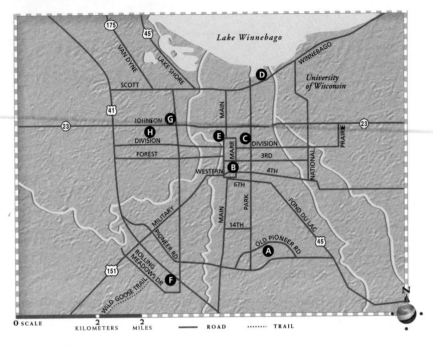

Sightseeing Highlights
Ⓐ Galloway House and Village

Food
Ⓑ Main Exchange
Ⓒ Rosewood Dining Room
Ⓓ Salty's Seafood and Spirits
Ⓔ Theo's Supper Club

Lodging
Ⓕ Budgetel Inn BudgetDome
Ⓖ EconoLodge
Ⓗ Motel 6
Ⓒ Ramada Hotel

Note: Items with the same letter are located in the same place or area.

hotel. Oshkosh choices include **Pioneer Inn and Marina**, 1000 Pioneer Dr., (800) 683-1980, where rates start at $85, and $95 buys a view of the lake; **Budgetel Motor Inn**, 1950 Omro Rd., (414) 233-4190, with doubles for $48.95; **Oshkosh Hilton and Convention Center**, downtown, (800) HILTONS, $85–$105; and **Motel 6**, 1015 S. Washburn, (414) 235-0265, $25–$31. In the surrounding area, bed and breakfasts include the **Rose Ivy Inn**, a bed and breakfast in a Victorian home, 228 S. Watertown St., Waupun, (just west of Horicon National Wildlife Refuge), (414) 324-2127 or (800) 258-5019, with rooms from $59–$79.

CAMPING

Private campgrounds in the Oshkosh area include **Circle R Campground**, 1185 Old Knapp Road (from 41 and 26 junction, exit on 26; go northeast one block to County N, then east on N to Old Knapp Rd.; go right 1½ miles). The campground is 3½ miles south of Wittman Field, (414) 235-8909, and has 110 sites with electricity (44 full hookups) from $13–$16.50. There's a grocery store, firewood, showers, and a playground. **Kalbus' Country Harbor**, 5309 Lake Rd., 7 miles south of Oshkosh, just off Highway 45 on Lake Road near Point Comfort, (414) 426-0062, has 35 tent sites, 12 sites with electricity, ten with electricity and water hookups, flush toilets, showers, boat rentals, ice, and wood for $13–$18. The **Fond du Lac KOA Kampground**, W. 5099 County Highway B, 5 miles south on U.S. 41 and 1½ miles east on County B, (414) 477-2300, has a spring-fed pond for swimming and fishing, hot showers, 75 sites, 55 with electricity and water, and 15 full hookups, from $16–$25. **Fond du Lac County Park**, on County Highway MMM off State Highway 49 in Waupun, has 38 sites, (414) 324-2769. **Kettle Moraine State Forest**, (414) 626-2116, has camping east of Dundee on Kettle Moraine Drive at **Long Lake Recreation Area**, (414) 533-8612, and at **Mauthe Lake Recreation Area**, (414) 626-4305. There's a total of 358 sites, 49 with electricity. To get to Long Lake, follow the Kettle Moraine Scenic Drive from Highway 67 and the Ice Age Center. Go east and then north on the Scenic Drive and follow signs for the Long Lake campground. To get to Mauthe Lake, follow the Scenic Drive South and watch for the Mauthe Lake Recreation Area. The Kettle Moraine North Unit has 72 miles of hiking trails, 39 miles of horse trails, 19 miles of mountain bike trails, 58 miles of snowmobile trails, and 33 miles of cross-country ski trails. (See Practical Tips chapter for fees and reservation information.)

NIGHTLIFE AND SPECIAL EVENTS

Oshkosh's 1883 **Grand Opera House** has been restored to its former glory and now hosts diverse programs, including national and international touring companies. Recent performers have included the Peking Acrobats and Jack Daniel's Original Silver Cornet Band. For information, (414) 424-2355; for ticket availability, (414) 424-2350. Oshkosh hosts **concerts in Riverside Park** Thursday evenings June through September, the **Winnebago County Fair** in August, and **Country Harvest Days** in October. In Fond du Lac, the **Buttermilk Performance Center** on South Park Avenue at Old Pioneer Road holds **open-air concerts** by the Fond du Lac Symphonic Band on Wednesdays at 7:15 p.m. and **Music Under the Stars** performances on Mondays from 7–9 p.m., mid-June–late August. For Fifties and Sixties nostalgia, there's **Jukebox Charlie's,** with a Wurlitzer jukebox, DJ dancing, and waitresses in poodle skirts, 248 N. Hickory St. in Fond du Lac, (414) 923-8185. Fond du Lac events include the **Annual Walleye Weekend Festival and Tournament** in June and a **July 4th concert and fireworks** in Lakeside Park. In Greenbush, the **Historic Wade House 1890 Country Horse Fair** takes place in June. Pick up the Fond du Lac visitor's guide for lodging and current happenings or call (800) 937-9123.

14
MILWAUKEE

The onion domes and cathedral spires of Milwaukee's gracious old churches and the eclectic mix of architectural styles bespeak a city of diverse cultures and traditions. Native Americans once occupied this spot where three rivers feed into Lake Michigan. Then came the hard-working German, British, Norwegian, and Irish immigrants, who shaped an industrial, manufacturing city. New immigrants arrived to work in the factories—Poles, Bohemians, Bavarians, Russians, Ukrainians, and others.

Today the landmark grand business structures and mansions, the ethnic working-class neighborhoods, and the elaborate churches bring texture to this city of 601,839. Settled first, the eastern section's historic structures include the Mitchell Building, at 207 E. Michigan, with lion-head keystones. North of downtown stand the industrial barons' mansions. To the south lie the old industrial area and ethnic communities.

The Milwaukee County Transit System's sightseeing tours from June through August, (414) 344-6711, are a good way to meet the city that's been called "the beer capital of the world." The only big-name active breweries in Milwaukee now are Pabst and Miller, but micro-breweries keep the tradition alive. For travel information, contact the Convention and Visitors Bureau, 510 W Kilbourne Ave., (800) 231-0903 and (414) 273-7222. ◼

MILWAUKEE

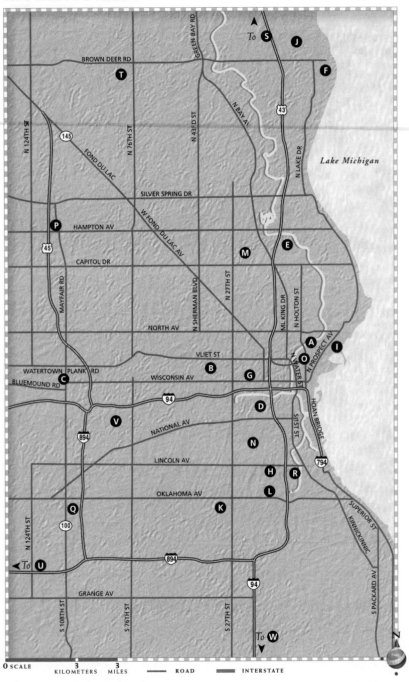

Sightseeing Highlights

Ⓐ Charles Allis Art Museum

Ⓑ Miller Brewing Company

Ⓒ Milwaukee County Zoo

Ⓓ Mitchell Park Horticultural Museum

Ⓔ Pabst Mansion

Ⓕ Schlitz Audubon Center

Ⓖ St. Joan of Arc Chapel

Ⓗ St. Josaphat's Basilica

Ⓘ Villa Terrace Decorative Arts Museum

Food

Ⓙ Chip and Py's

Ⓚ Leons

Ⓛ Mike and Anna's

Ⓜ Mr. Perkins Family Restaurant

Ⓗ Old Town Restaurant

Ⓝ Polish Crocus Restaurant and Cocktail Lounge

Ⓞ Water Street Brewery

Lodging

Ⓟ Budgetel Inn

Ⓠ Golden Key Motel

Ⓡ Marie's Bed & Breakfast

Ⓢ Stagecoach Inn Bed & Breakfast

Ⓣ Super 8 Milwaukee North

Camping

Ⓤ Kettle Moraine State Forest South Unit

Ⓥ Wisconsin State Fair RV Park

Ⓦ Yogi Bear Jellystone Camp Resort

Note: Items with the same letter are located in the same place or area.

A PERFECT DAY IN MILWAUKEE

Start the day visiting churches. View Polish-heritage St. Josaphat's
Basilica and Old St. Mary's Church dating to 1846. Tour St. Joan of Arc
Chapel and the Cathedral of St. John the Evangelist. Go to the
Milwaukee Art Museum for a look at the work of Degas, O'Keeffe, and
Picasso. Have lunch at a custard shop. Tour the elaborate Pabst
Mansion, then follow Old World Third Street to Usinger's Famous
Sausage in the old German business district. Stroll in Pere Marquette
Park to work up an appetite. Eat red cabbage and sauerbraten at
Mader's German Restaurant and top off the day with jazz at a pub.

SIGHTSEEING HIGHLIGHTS

★★★ **Churches: Cathedral of St. John the Evangelist**—This
Romanesque Greco-style church, seat of the Archdiocese of Milwaukee,
offers self-guided tours. Pick up the tour booklet in the vestibule.
Admission: Free. Hours: 9–11:30 a.m. and 1–4:30 p.m., Monday
through Friday. Address: 802 N. Jackson St. Phone: (414) 276-9814.
(¼–½ hour)

  Old St. Mary's Church—The oldest Catholic church in the city
has been a downtown landmark since 1846 and is beautifully restored.
Admission: Free. Hours: Open daily 11 a.m.–1 p.m. Pick up a brochure
on church history in the pamphlet rack. Address: 836 N. Broadway.
Phone: (414) 271-6180. (½ hour)

  St. Joan of Arc Chapel—On the Marquette University campus,
this fifteenth-century chapel built in France was reconstructed on the
campus in 1965. Admission: Free. Hours: Daily 10 a.m.–4 p.m. Closed
major holidays. Address: 14th Street and Wisconsin Avenue. Phone:
(414) 288-6873. (½ hour)

  St. Josaphat's Basilica—More than 90 years old, this National
Landmark's stained glass and murals pay tribute to Milwaukee's cultural
history and heritage. The basilica was built by Polish immigrants.
Admission: Donation. Hours: Tours at 11 a.m. Sunday: Go inside and
meet guides in the sanctuary. Address: 2336 S. 6th St., Phone: (414)
645-5623. (½–¾ hour)

★★★ **Milwaukee Art Museum**—Housed in the striking Eero
Saarinen–designed **War Memorial Building** overlooking Lake
Michigan, exhibits include significant artworks by Picasso, Georgia

O'Keeffe, Warhol, other greats, and lesser-knowns. There are also special exhibits. Admission: $2–$4, under 12 free. Hours: Open Tuesday, Wednesday, Friday, and Saturday from 10 a.m.–5 p.m., Thursday, noon–9 p.m., Sunday, noon–5 p.m. Address: 750 N. Lincoln Memorial Dr. Phone: (414) 224-3200. (1–2 hours)

✿✿✿ **Pabst Mansion**—The accurately restored Flemish Renaissance–style home built for the Pabst Brewery founder has exquisite wood, glass, and ironwork. Admission: $3–$8, under 6 free. Hours: Tours daily, 10 a.m.–3:30 p.m.; Sunday, noon–3:30 p.m. Address: 2000 W. Wisconsin Ave. Phone: (414) 931-0808. (1–2 hours)

✿✿✿ **Usinger's Famous Sausage**—This turn-of-the-century store boasts 75 varieties of sausage, as well as brats and old-world ham. Hours: Monday–Saturday, 8:30 a.m.–5 p.m. Address: 1030 N. Old World Third St. Phone: (414) 276-9100. As long as you're here, take a walk to see the vintage architecture in the old German industrial district. (¼–½ hour)

✿✿ **Charles Allis Art Museum**—An elegant 1909 Edwardian-style mansion designed for the first Allis-Chalmers Company's president, a millionaire by virtue of tractors and farm machinery, displays collections of art by Whistler, Homer, Corot, and other artists. Admission: $2. Hours: Thursday–Sunday, 1–5 p.m., Wednesday until 7 p.m. Address: 1801 North Prospect Ave. at Royal Place. Phone: (414) 278-8295. (1–2 hours)

✿✿ **Milwaukee County Zoo**—Animals here inhabit natural environments, separated by hidden moats. You can ride the zoo train, take zoomobile tours, and watch a multimedia show in the Welcome Center. The zoo has a restaurant and gift shop. Wheelchair-accessible. Admission: $5.50–$7.50, April 1 to October 31; $4–$6, rest of year; under 2 free. Stroller rental $3–$5. Hours: May 1–September 1, 9 a.m.–5 p.m., until 6 p.m. Sunday and holidays; 9 a.m.–4:30 p.m., rest of year. Parking: $5 per car. Address: 10001 W. Blue Mound Rd., ten minutes from downtown. Phone: (414) 771-3040. (4 hours)

✿✿ **Miller Brewing Company**—Tour, taste, and learn about brewing. There's also a gift shop. Admission: Free. Hours: Open year round, Monday–Saturday, 10 a.m.–3:30 p.m. Gift shop hours: 9 a.m.–4:30 p.m.

Closed Sunday and holidays. Address: 4251 W. State St. Phone: (414) 931-BEER. (1 hour)

✹ **Walking Tour**—Historic Milwaukee offers 14 tours featuring Milwaukee's early settlements, east side mansion areas, German/Polish heritage and more. Admission: $4. Hours: June 1–October 15, Saturday at 10 a.m. and 1 p.m.; Sunday at 1 p.m. Address: Starting points vary. Phone: (414) 277-7795 for a recorded list of the week's schedule. There's also a year-round **SkyWaukee Tour** through the skyways every Saturday at 1 p.m., leaving from Plankinton Arcade Bldg., 161 W. Wisconsin Ave., in the Grand Avenue Mall. No reservations needed for any tours. (½ hour)

✹ **Milwaukee Public Museum**—Natural habitat reconstructions bring the world's cultures and natural sciences to life in exhibits such as "The Streets of Milwaukee" and "Tropical Rainforest." Admission: $3.50–$5.50, under 4 free. Hours: Open 9 a.m.–5 p.m. daily. Wheelchair-accessible. Address: 800 W. Wells St. Phone: (414) 278-2700. (1–2 hours)

✹ **Mitchell Park Horticultural Museum**—Tropical and seasonal plants thrive under the conservatory's three glass domes. Admission: $1.75–$3.25. Hours: Daily, 9 a.m.–5 p.m. Wheelchair-accessible. Address: 524 S. Layton Blvd. Phone: (414) 649-9800. (¾–1 hour)

✹ **Schlitz Audubon Center**—This 225-acre lakeshore nature preserve with woodlands, meadows, bluffs, and fields has an interpretive center, natural history bookstore, and gift shop. Admission: $1–$2. Hours: Year-round, Tuesday–Sunday, 9 a.m.–5 p.m. Address: 1111 E. Brown Deer Rd., on the north lakeshore. Phone: (414) 352-2880. (1 hour or more)

✹ **Villa Terrace Decorative Arts Museum**—Decorative arts are showcased in an Italian-style villa, once a private home, overlooking Lake Michigan. Admission: $2, under 12 free. Hours: Wednesday–Sunday, 1–5 p.m. Address: 2220 N. Terrace Ave. Phone: (414) 271-3656. (½–1 hour)

Mackie Building—If you happen to be near 225 E. Michigan, visit the Grain Exchange Room on the second floor, a trade center when

Milwaukee was the largest cash grain market in the world. The building dates to 1879, with a restored Victorian Renaissance interior.

FITNESS AND RECREATION

Schlitz Audubon Center (see Sightseeing Highlights) is a wonderful place for walks, as are the 137 parks and parkways in the Milwaukee County Park System. A **bicycle trail** of 75 miles or so circles around the city. (Call 414-257-6100 for maps.) Head to a city park around Lincoln Memorial Drive for a jog with the locals. At least six companies offer Lake Michigan charter fishing, including **McKinley Marina**, 1750 N. Lincoln Memorial Dr., (414) 273-5224. The marina also has rental slips, launching ramps, and marine supplies. **McKinley Beach** on North Lincoln Memorial Drive offers swimming, water-bike rental, and boardsailing. South of McKinley Marina, **Veterans Park** has bike and skate rental and kite-flying. You'll find championship golf, including the courses at Brown Deer and Whitnall Parks, (414) 257-6100. And there's lawn bowling every afternoon and Monday, Tuesday, and Thursday evenings at Lake and Dineen Parks. Instruction and equipment are available. Call (414) 257-6100. Additionally, 34 county parks have free tennis courts.

FOOD

Food is fun in Milwaukee, whether it's gourmet or down-home. Milwaukee is surely the only city to publish a guide just for beer, Friday night fish fries, and frozen custard—three of its long-standing traditions. Of course, you'll want to sample the specialties. Frozen custard is loaded with eggs and heavy cream—alas, not for the cholesterol-conscious. Made fresh daily, it comes in countless flavors, from standard vanilla to Grand Marnier, blueberry crisp, and pineapple caramel pecan. Some custard stands publish a flavor calendar and even have a flavor hotline. Among the numerous places to indulge, **Leon's**, at 3131 S. 27th St., has been serving custard since 1942; (414) 383-1784. A Friday night fish-fry meal is usually breaded or batter-fried fish served with coleslaw, a potato (maybe baked, maybe American fries, maybe a pancake), rye bread, and butter.

For a real dip into Milwaukee cultural heritage, get your Friday night fish-fry fix at the German-heritage **Milwaukee Turner's Hall, Bar and Restaurant**, 1034 N. 4th St., (414) 273-5590. For beer, try

DOWNTOWN MILWAUKEE

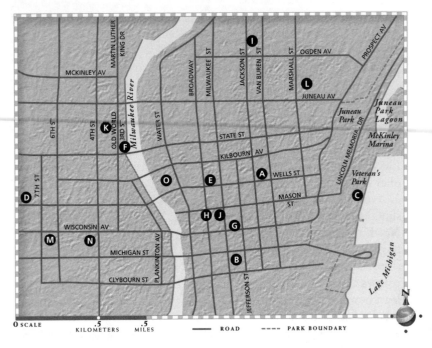

Sightseeing Highlights

A Cathedral of St. John the Evangelist

B Mackie Building

C Milwaukee Art Museum/War Memorial Building

D Milwaukee Public Museum

E Old St. Mary's Church

F Usinger's Famous Sausage

Food

G The English Room

H Grenadier's

I John Ernst

J Karl Ratzsch's Restaurant

K Mader's German Restaurant

K Milwaukee Turner's Hall, Bar and Restaurant

Lodging

L Astor Hotel

M Holiday Inn Milwaukee City Centre

N Milwaukee Hilton

O Pfister Hotel

O Wyndham Milwaukee Center

Note: Items with the same letter are located in the same place or area.

Water Street Brewery brew-pub (a watch-the-brewer-work-while-you-drink-and-eat place) at 1101 N. Water St., (414) 272-1195. You can dine formally on French Continental cuisine at **Grenadier's**, 747 N. Broadway, (414) 276-0747: Dinner from $17.95–$22.95, jacket and reservations required. **Mike and Anna's**, on the south side at 2000 S. 8th St., (414) 643-0072, is a small restaurant noted for the sweetbreads appetizer and wing of stingray called "Tilapia skate wings"; dinner $19–$26. Pfister Hotel's intimate **English Room**, 424 E. Wisconsin Ave., (414) 273-8222, is wonderful for special occasions; a dinner averages $23.50. You'll get German cuisine with all the trappings at **Mader's German Restaurant**, 1037-41 N. Old World Third St., (414) 271-3377, $15–$20; **Karl Ratzsch's Restaurant**, 320 E. Mason St., (414) 276-2720, $10–$20; and **John Ernst**, 600 E. Ogden Ave., (414) 273-1878, $15–$20 and up—all mainstays of German cooking in Milwaukee, with Ernst the oldest.

For a different ethnic adventure, try **Old Town Restaurant**, 522 W. Lincoln, (414) 672-0206, featuring well-regarded Serbian food and music on weekends, $15–$20. **Chip and Py's**, 1340 W. Towne Square Rd. on Mequon and Port Washington/County W Roads, just west of U.S. Highway 43 in Mequon, (414) 241-9589, has weekend jazz and an eclectic menu, $10–$15. **Mr. Perkins Family Restaurant**, 2001 W. Atkinson Ave., (414) 447-6660, has been cooking up homemade sweet-potato pie, fried apples, chitterlings, greens, and other Southern treats for 50 years and is easy on the budget. **Polish Crocus Restaurant and Cocktail Lounge** at 1801 S. Muskego Ave., (414) 643-6383, on Milwaukee's south side, serves inexpensive homemade Polish food including pierogi and stuffed potato dumplings.

LODGING

The **Pfister Hotel**, 424 E. Wisconsin, (414) 273-8222 or (800) 558-8222, over 100 years old, remains a grandly elegant hotel; double rooms/suites range from $160–$235. The **Astor Hotel**, 924 E. Juneau, (414) 271-4220 or (800) 558-0200, is a nice older hotel with doubles from $79–$89 and suites $96–$127. **Marie's Bed & Breakfast**, 346 E. Wilson St., (414) 483-1512, is a Victorian house in the Bay View area with a full breakfast and rooms from $58–$70. About 20 miles north of Milwaukee, **Stagecoach Inn Bed & Breakfast**, W. 61 N. 520 Washington Ave., Cedarburg, (414) 375-0208, offers rooms from $70–$105 in an 1853 historic building. The downtown **Milwaukee**

Hilton, 509 W. Wisconsin Ave., (800) 558-7708, has double and single rooms for $109. At the **Wyndham Milwaukee Center**, located in the renovated theatre district at 139 E. Kilbourne Ave., (800) WYND-HAM or (414) 276-8686, double rooms/suites cost $94–$187. Motels offering economical lodging are **Super 8 Milwaukee North**, 8698 Servite Dr., with doubles for $44–$46, (800) 800-8000; **Golden Key Motel**, 3600 S. 108th St., (414) 543-5300, with doubles about $45–$60; and **Budgetel Inn**, 5442 N. Lovers Lane Rd. (northwest area), (414) 535-1300 or (800) 428-3438, with rates starting around $39. **Holiday Inn Milwaukee City Centre**, 611 W. Wisconsin, (800) HOLIDAY, is a full-service downtown hotel, where double rooms from $89–$139 are subject to seasonal and weekend variation. Milwaukee's lodging and reservation service can help with information and reservations for major hotels or motels. Call (800) 554-1448.

CAMPING

Reservations are needed—all campgrounds near Milwaukee fill, especially on weekends. You'll find public camping at **Kettle Moraine State Forest South Unit**, about 35 to 40 miles west of Milwaukee at Eagle (take I-94 west and State 67 south). The unit has 328 campsites, 49 with electricity, showers, and 80 miles of hiking trails. (414) 594-6200. (See Practical Tips chapter for reservation/fee details.) **Wisconsin State Fair RV Park** is a closer option, although hardly scenic, at I-94 and 84th St., with 88 sites, showers, and electrical hookups. Open from April–October; (414) 266-7035. Or try **Yogi Bear Jellystone Camp Resort**, south of Milwaukee near Caledonia, (take I-94 South, exit at 7 Mile Road, then go east 2 miles and north a quarter-mile), (414) 835-2565. There are 247 sites, 51 with full hookups and 168 with electricity and showers; a swimming pool, snack bar, and more. Rates for three people are $34 per night for full hookups, $29.75 for water and electricity, and $24–$26 for tent sites. Add $2.50 to rates for holidays.

NIGHTLIFE AND SPECIAL EVENTS

Festivals happen nonstop in Milwaukee, where the Henry W. Maier Festival Park (HMFP) enjoys a prime waterfront location at 200 N. Harbor Dr., with an adjacent amphitheater handy for performances. Festivities include June's **Polish Fest** in HMFP and **Bavarian Volkfest** in Old Heidelberg Park. July and August bring **Bastille Days** in East

Town, the **Great Circus Parade** downtown, **Fiesta Italiana**, **German Fest** and **Irish Fest** in HMFP, plus **Serbian Days** at the St. Sava Cathedral grounds. In September and October, celebrations include **Oktoberfest** in Old Heidelberg Park and **Indian Summer**, a Native American cultural celebration, in HMFP.

For sports fans there's an equivalent bounty, from **Milwaukee Admirals** professional hockey at the Bradley Center (414) 227-0550 to the American League **Milwaukee Brewers'** baseball games at Milwaukee County Stadium, (414) 933-9000. The city also has the **NBA Milwaukee Bucks,** (414) 227-0500, and the **Milwaukee Wave**, a professional indoor soccer team, (414) 962-WAVE.

The **Performing Arts Center**, (414) 273-7206, or (800) 472-4458, in the heart of downtown, is home to the Florentine Opera Company, First Stage Milwaukee, the Milwaukee Ballet Company, and the Milwaukee Symphony Orchestra. Additionally, the historic Victorian Baroque **Pabst Theater**, (414) 286-3663, and the **Riverside**, (414) 224-3000, host touring Broadway shows, symphony, and popular music artists. There's also a fine repertory theater and an opera theater

center. There are, of course, lots of lively pubs and clubs in "the beer capital of the world," plus dinner cruises at **Edelweiss Cruise Dining**, (414) 272-DOCK. To find out about current happenings, call **Milwaukee's Funline of Events**, (414) 799-1177 or (800) 272-0049.

SIDE TRIP: OLD WORLD WISCONSIN

Old World Wisconsin is a must-see. On 600 acres of Kettle Moraine woods, costumed interpreters do their daily chores and re-create the life lived by immigrants in more than 50 ethnic farmhouses, barns, village homes, merchants' and craftsmen's shops. It takes a full day—better yet, two days—to experience everything on this site, operated by the Wisconsin State Historical Society. Admission: $3–$7, or buy a family season pass for $35. Hours: Open May 1–October 30, 10 a.m.–4 p.m. weekdays and 5 p.m. weekends May, June, September, and October; closes at 5 p.m. daily in July and August. Address: 1½ miles south of Eagle just off Highway 67. Eagle is 35 miles from Milwaukee. Take I-94 west to State Highway 67, then take Highway 67 south through Eagle. Phone: (414) 594-2116. (1–2 days)

15
MADISON

Picturesque Madison sits on a mile-wide isthmus between Lake Mendota to the north and Lake Monona to the south. Centered on the isthmus is the white-domed State Capitol, a scaled-down replica of our country's capitol in Washington, D.C. With a population of around 200,000, the city is home to the top-ranking University of Wisconsin and its more than 40,000 students. The university and the government bring a heady cultural milieu to the city. There is always something going on, and lodging can be scarce. Reservations are a must. The city's heart beats on State Street, a long stretch of shops, bars, and restaurants between the State Capitol and the university—great for people-watching.

Madison has nearly 200 parks as well as Cherokee Marsh, with its herons, ducks, and cranes. Since this is dairy country, you'll encounter rich ice creams, frozen custards, and cheese curds (a dairy by-product popular as an appetizer), plus German-heritage beer and bratwurst, called "brats." Madison is about 90 minutes southwest of Milwaukee via I-94. For current happenings pick up the *Isthmus* magazine, free at newsstands or visitor centers. You can also contact the Wisconsin Information Center, 123 W. Washington Ave., (608) 266-2161, and the Greater Madison Convention and Visitors Bureau, 615 E. Washington Ave., (800) 373-6376. ∎

MADISON

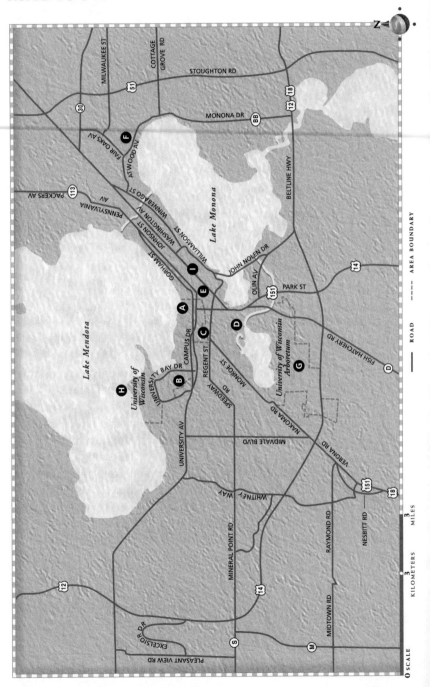

Sightseeing Highlights

Ⓐ Elvehjem Museum of Art

Ⓑ First Unitarian Society Meeting House

Ⓒ Geology Museum

Ⓓ Henry Vilas Park Zoo

Ⓔ Madison Art Center

Ⓔ Madison Children's Museum

Ⓕ Olbrich Botanical Gardens

Ⓔ State Street

Ⓖ University of Wisconsin Arboretum

Ⓗ University of Wisconsin-Madison

Ⓘ Wisconsin State Capitol

Ⓘ Wisconsin State Historical Museum

Ⓘ Wisconsin Veterans Museum

Note: Items with the same letter are located in the same place or area.

A PERFECT DAY IN MADISON

Start out with a State Capitol tour and a visit to the State Historical Museum. Stroll down State Street and check out the action at the open-air mall. Eat lunch at a State Street café or the Memorial Union Terrace on Lake Mendota. Visit the Elvehjem Museum, then hike the trails at the arboretum and go to Olbrich Botanical Gardens. Treat yourself to dinner at L'Etoile or Delaney's, catch a Madison Repertory Theatre play, and stop for a cappuccino at the 544 State Street Steep 'n' Brew.

SIGHTSEEING HIGHLIGHTS

★★★ **State Street**—State Street, that anything-goes stretch of open-air mall between the Capitol and the state university, is the best place to experience free-spirited Madison. The street holds a children's museum, galleries, cozy bookstores, eclectic shops and eateries, art vendors and street musicians, and hordes of energetic university students. Give yourself time to browse or sit on a bench and people-watch. (at least 1 hour)

★★★ **Wisconsin State Capitol**— This unusually beautiful capitol, separating Washington Avenue East and West, is the seat of government in a state that has embraced populist extremes—from progressive "Fighting" Robert LaFollette, who chalked up 5 million votes as a 1924 independent presidential candidate, to the post–World War II anti-Communist fervor of Wisconsin senator Joseph McCarthy. If you're there on Saturday, don't miss the farmer's market on Capitol Square, Saturday morning May–October, 6 a.m.–2 p.m. The Capitol has an observation platform on the dome. Daily free tour hours: Monday– Saturday from 9 a.m.–3 p.m., excluding noon, and Sunday, 1–3 p.m. Also at 4 p.m. from Memorial Day–Labor Day. Wheelchair-accessible. Phone: (608) 266-0382. (1 hour)

★★★ **Wisconsin State Historical Museum**— Located on Capitol Square, the museum displays include an excellent Native American exhibit and a hand-built clock made by Sierra Club founder John Muir when he attended the university. To reinforce study habits, the clock drops books on a student's desk at regular intervals. Admission is free. Hours: Open Tuesday–Saturday, 10 a.m.–5 p.m., Sunday, 12–5 p.m. Wheelchair-accessible. Address: 30 N. Carroll. Phone: (608) 264-6555. (½ hour)

★★ **First Unitarian Society Meeting House**—Frank Lloyd Wright designed this 1950 stone and glass church with a soaring peaked roof. (Oddly enough, a new Frank Lloyd Wright structure is being built in Madison—a civic center Wright designed in 1938. The city rejected his plan then but in the interim has changed its mind.) Admission: Suggested $3 donation. Guided tour hours: mid-May–September, 10 a.m.– 4 p.m. weekdays; Saturday, 9 a.m.–noon. Tours also by appointment. Address: 900 University Bay Dr. Phone: (608) 233-9774. (½ hour)

★★ **Olbrich Botanical Gardens**—Herb, rose, rock, and other gardens on 14 acres make this a wonderful place to stroll. A glass pyramid conservatory holds tropical plants. There's also a nice gift shop. Admission: $1 for conservatory; gardens are free. Hours: Conservatory open Monday– Saturday, 10 a.m.–4 p.m.; Sunday, until 5 p.m. Grounds open June– August, 8 a.m.–5 p.m. daily; September–May, Monday–Saturday, 9 a.m.– 5 p.m. Address: 3330 Atwood Ave. Phone: (608) 246-4550. (½–1 hour)

✯✯ **University of Wisconsin Arboretum**—The McKay Center interprets plant collections and has maps of the arboretum's more than 1,200 acres. You can visit a restored prairie, a wetland with orchids, woods with effigy mounds, and spring-fed watercress beds. Spring lilac time is glorious here. Admission: Free. Hours: Open year-round for drive-through tours, Monday–Saturday, 7 a.m.–10 p.m., Sunday 1–6 p.m. The center is open September–May, Monday–Friday, 9 a.m.–4 p.m., Saturday and Sunday, 12:30–4 p.m.; June–August, Saturday and Sunday, 11 a.m.–3 p.m. Address: 1207 Seminole Highway. Phone: (608) 263-7888. (1–2 hours)

✯✯ **University of Wisconsin-Madison**—With a lakeside setting complete with an expansive terrace and boat docks, the 1,000-acre university campus has rightly been called one of the prettiest in the country. Highlights include the **Elvehjem Museum of Art**, with a permanent collection of paintings, sculpture and decorative arts from 2300 B.C. to the present; 800 University, (608) 263-2246; free; open daily 9 a.m.–5 p.m. except holidays. Kids love the **Geology Museum**'s mastodon skeleton and limestone cave that visitors may walk through. It's free and open all year, Monday–Friday, 8:30 a.m.–4:30 p.m. and Saturday, 9 a.m.–1 p.m.; Charter and West Dayton, (608) 262-2399. In Babcock Hall, the dairy science building, a dairy store sells 12-percent-butterfat ice cream, Monday–Friday, 9:30 a.m.–5:30 p.m., and Saturday, 10 a.m.–1:30 p.m. Ice-cream cones are big sellers. To get there from University Avenue, take the Campus exit, go to Linden, and take a left at the four-way stop sign. Babcock Hall is on your left. Ice-cream cones and sundaes are also sold at Memorial Union and Union South. Call (608) 263-2400 for specifics.

✯✯ **Wisconsin Veterans Museum**—Exhibits range from the Civil War to the present, including military artifacts, full-sized aircraft, model ships, and a submarine periscope which visitors may look through. Admission: Free. Hours: Year-round, Tuesday–Saturday, 9:30 a.m.–4:30 p.m., Sunday April–September, noon–4 p.m. Address: 30 W. Mifflin St. Phone: (608) 264-6086. (½–1 hour)

✯ **Henry Vilas Park Zoo**—In a pretty park on the shores of Lake Wingra, the zoo has more than 800 animals. You'll find playgrounds, beach, and picnic areas—and free Saturday morning camel rides for kids. Admission: Free. Hours: June–Labor Day, 9:30 a.m.–8 p.m.;

September–May, 9:30 a.m.–4:45 p.m. Closed holiday afternoons.
Wheelchair-accessible. Address: 702 S. Randall St. Phone: (608)
266-4732. (1 hour or more)

✿ **Madison Art Center**— The center's local, regional and national
art displays are in a restored movie theater. Admission: Donation
suggested. Hours: Open Tuesday–Thursday, 11 a.m.–5 p.m.; Friday,
11 a.m.–9 p.m.; Saturday, 10 a.m.–5 p.m; Sunday, 1–5 p.m.
Wheelchair-accessible. Closed holidays. Address: 211 State St. Phone:
(608) 257-0158. (½–1 hour)

✿ **Madison Children's Museum**— This is a hands-on museum for
kids. Admission: $3, under 2 free. Hours: Open Tuesday–Saturday,
10 a.m.–5 p.m.; Sunday, 1–5 p.m. Closed holidays. Address: 100 State
St. Phone: (608) 256-6445. (½–1 hour)

FITNESS AND RECREATION

Lots of people bike here, so bike paths are numerous, and busy streets
have bike lanes. Madison bike and road maps are available from the
Convention and Visitors Bureau, (800) 373-6376. You can rent bikes
from **Budget Bicycle**, near the lakes and arboretum at 1230 Regent,
(608) 251-8413; rates are $7 per day, $21 a week. Tandem rentals are
$10–$30 a day. Try the bicycle trail around Lake Monona that
includes Olbrich Botanical Gardens. Walking is great fun here. The
city has interesting architecture, plus good coffee shops and bookstores to explore along the way. The several public golf courses
include the Robert Trent Jones–designed **University Ridge Golf
Course**, (608) 845-7700. Hike in the arboretum or in the city's 3,500
acres of parks. There are several downhill ski areas within an hour's
drive or less.

FOOD

A Madison favorite is **Ella's Deli & Ice Cream Parlor** at 2902 E.
Washington Ave., (608) 241-5291, an old-fashioned kosher deli with
corned beef and great hot fudge sundaes. **Smoky's Club**, 3005
University Ave., (608) 233-2120, around for over 40 years, is a
Wisconsin tradition, serving steaks you'll never forget and meals around
$13–$18. Smoky's is crowded and noisy, with Wisconsin memorabilia

hanging everywhere—University of Wisconsin football slogans and signs and such. It's a bit of a trip to dine here; the wait is long on weekends, and it's not low-fat fare. Closed Tuesday and Sunday. At **Delaney's Charcoal Steaks**, 449 Grand Canyon, (608) 833-7337, on the west side, the steaks equal those at Smoky's Club without the chaotic atmosphere. Menus are seasonal at **L'Etoile**, 25 N. Pinckney St., on Capitol Square, (608) 251-0500. You can get goat cheese and garlic baked in a squash blossom come summer; dinner costs $45–$50 per person. "The place to take your aunt when she comes to visit" is how an acquaintance describes **Quivey's Grove**, 6261 Nesbitt Rd., (608) 273-4900, where you can eat lamb shank or trout in the quilt-decorated dining rooms of an 1850s fieldstone mansion for $14–$24. It's on a 4-acre estate located 2 miles south of the Beltline Highway off U.S. 151/18; prices are moderate to high. Try the **Arthouse Café**, 2827 Atwood Ave., (608) 242-7151, for fresh trout entrees, art on the walls, an espresso bar, and live music from blues to jazz. Lunch costs $8–$9; dinner, about $13. **Terrazzo's**, 1421 Regent, (608) 257-9499, serves wood-fired pizza and pastas—somewhat trendy good food for $7–$11. For home-style Italian food, go to **Antonio's**, near an old Italian neighborhood at 1109 Park St., (608) 251-1412; closed Sunday and Monday. You can also dine economically at the University's **Memorial Union**, on Lake Mendota at Park and Langdon; expect fast-food fare cafeteria-style and a chance to mingle with profs and students. **Coyote Capers**, 1201 Williamson St., on the near-east side of town, (608) 251-1313, has a creative menu and great salads; dinner runs about $25.

LODGING

The exquisite **Mansion Hill Inn**, 424 N. Pinckney St., (608) 255-3999 or (800) 798-9070, has complimentary valet parking and afternoon refreshments in the parlor. Guests find the opulence of a small European hotel in this 1858 Romanesque Revival–style mansion: Rates range from $80–$270. **Collins House Bed and Breakfast**, 704 E. Gorham St., (608) 255-4230, is a National Historic Register Prairie School house with a library, home-baked breads, and specialties including Swedish oatmeal pancakes. Rates are $59-$99. In a historic 1924 building, the **Canterbury Bookstore, Coffee House, and Inn**, 315 W. Gorham at State, (608) 258-8899 or (800) 838-3850, has rooms named for *Canterbury Tales* travelers and decorated in that theme. Guests enjoy book readings, Sunday storytelling, and live music. Rates are from

MADISON

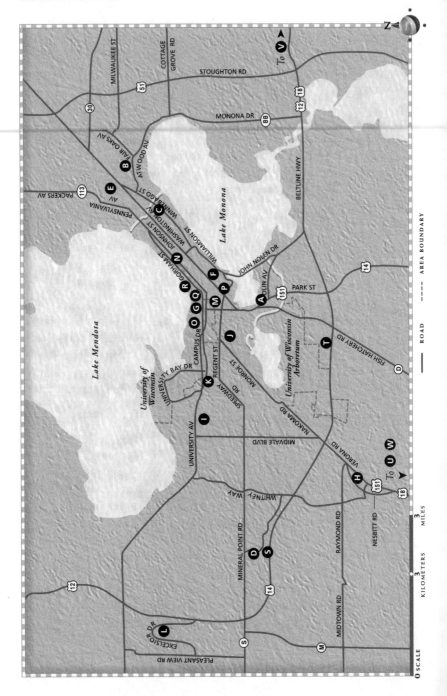

Food

- **Ⓐ** Antonio's
- **Ⓑ** Arthouse Café
- **Ⓒ** Coyote Capers
- **Ⓓ** Delaney's Charcoal Steaks
- **Ⓔ** Ella's Deli & Ice Cream Parlor
- **Ⓕ** L'Etoile
- **Ⓖ** Memorial Union
- **Ⓗ** Quivey's Grove
- **Ⓘ** Smoky's Club
- **Ⓙ** Terrazzo's

Lodging

- **Ⓚ** Best Western/The Inn Towner
- **Ⓛ** Budgetel Inn Budgetdome
- **Ⓜ** Canterbury Bookstore, Coffee House, and Inn
- **Ⓝ** Collins House Bed and Breakfast
- **Ⓞ** Ivy Inn Hotel
- **Ⓟ** The Madison Concourse Hotel and Governors Club
- **Ⓠ** The Madison Inn
- **Ⓡ** Mansion Hill Inn
- **Ⓢ** Radisson Inn of Madison
- **Ⓣ** Super 8 Motel

Camping

- **Ⓤ** Blue Mound State Park
- **Ⓥ** Lake Kegonsa State Park
- **Ⓦ** Tom's Campground

$100–$255. In the **Madison Concourse Hotel and Governors Club**,
1 W. Dayton, (608) 257-6000 or (800) 356-8293, the club occupies the
top two floors with views of the Capitol and a complimentary bar and
breakfast area. Rates from $89–$109; $119–$225 for Governors
Club. Motels include the **Madison Inn**, 601 Langdon, (608) 257-4391,
$50–$79; **Radisson Inn of Madison**, 517 Grand Canyon Dr., (608)
833-0100 or (800) 333-3333, $71–$119; **Super 8 Motel**, 1602 W.
Beltline Highway, (800) 800-8000 or (608) 258-8882, $54–$67; **Best
Western/The Inn Towner**, 2424 University Ave., (800) 258-8321,
$75–$125; the **Budgetel Inn Budgetdome**, 8102 Excelsior Dr.,
(800) 428-3438, a hotel with sauna, whirlpool, and indoor pool; doubles
$70–$95; and **Ivy Inn Hotel**, 2355 University Ave., (608) 233-9717,
$58–$65.

CAMPING

Blue Mound State Park is about 30 miles west of Madison near the
town of Blue Mounds, off U.S. Highway 151/18; (608) 437-5711. The
park has 78 sites, four with electricity, and showers. **Lake Kegonsa
State Park**, southeast of Madison near Stoughton, (608) 873-9695, has
80 campsites with showers but no electricity. **Tom's Campground** is
west of Madison off Highway 151/18, 6 miles east of Dodgeville. Take
County Road BB south from 151/18, then go left 700 feet on State 191.
There are 96 sites, 50 with electricity, a tent area, and pay showers.
Rates from $8–$16; (608) 935-5446.

NIGHTLIFE AND SPECIAL EVENTS

The **Madison Civic Center**, housed along with the Art Center in a
restored movie theater at 211 State St., hosts the **Madison Symphony
Orchestra**'s September–May season, (608) 257-3734; the **Madison
Opera** in the Civic Center's Oscar Mayer Theatre, (608) 238-8085;
and the **Madison Repertory Theatre**, year-round, (608) 266-9055.
Broadway shows appear here, as do big-name entertainers (also at the
University's Union Theater, 608-262-2201). The **UW Memorial
Union Terrace** overlooking Lake Mendota has musical entertainment
(usually LOUD) on the terrace at various times, (608) 265-3000. This
is a pleasant place to sit and read by the lake when the musicians aren't
playing. The university also has music and theater productions, (608)
262-1500 and 263-1900, and UW Badger football and hockey games at

the **Camp Randall Sports Complex**, (608) 262-1440. You can catch **Capitol City Ski Team** free waterskiing shows Sunday at 7:30 p.m. from Memorial Day–Labor Day at Brittingham Park on Lake Monona, southwest of Capitol Square. Special events include **Art Fair on the Square**, usually the weekend after the Fourth of July, from 10 a.m.–6 p.m. Saturday, until 5 p.m. on Sunday, with artists from all over the world, (608) 257-0158. There's a concurrent **Art Fair off the Square** a couple of blocks away, with a more casual and "crafty" orientation, (608) 798-4811. The first Saturday in June, **Cows on the Concourse**, (608) 221-8698, offers a chance to milk a cow on Capitol Square, courtesy of the University of Wisconsin farms. (The state's capital has dairy barns near the heart of the city.) The third week in July, agriculture grabs the limelight at the **Dane County Fair**, (608) 267-4600.

SIDE TRIP: BARABOO

If you have time, visit Baraboo. A fun route is I-90/94 north from Madison to State Highway 60. Take State 60 west through Lodi to the juncture with State 188. Go south a quarter-mile on 188 to historic **Wollersheim Winery** for tours and tasting, (608) 643-6515. Then follow State 188 north to Merrimac and ride the free ferryboat across the Wisconsin River (24 hours a day from mid-April–November).

Take State 78 west and 113 north into Baraboo, to colorful **Circus World Museum** at 426 Water St., (608) 356-8341 or (608) 356-0800, and tour the original headquarters of the old Ringling Bros. Circus. The 50-acre grounds hold gaudy circus wagons and circus exhibits; there are demonstrations, a circus parade, and performances from 9 a.m.– 6 p.m., early May–early September, $5.95–$11.95, under 3 free. (3–5 hours) The museum, exhibit hall, and visitor's center are open daily year-round except holidays, 9 a.m.–5 p.m; Sunday, open at 11 a.m. Admission is $2.50–$4.95. (1 hour)

About 5 miles north of Baraboo, you can visit **Mid-Continent Railway Museum** via State Highway 136 west, then County Road PF south to North Freedom. Steam engines offer 50-minute rides from mid-May–Labor Day at 10:30 a.m., 12:30, 2, and 3:30 p.m. Museum hours are 9:30 a.m.–5 p.m.; also open weekends through mid-October. Admission is $4.50–$8, under 3 free. A snow-train ride the third weekend in February costs from $5.50–$18.50; (608) 522-4261. (1½–2 hours)

Another Baraboo attraction is the **International Crane Foundation**, where naturalists work to save seven endangered crane species. The center has a multimedia exhibit, gift shop, and guided or self-guided tours for $2.50–$5, under 5 free, open daily 9 a.m.–5 p.m., May–October; (608) 356-9462. Travel north on U.S. Highway 12 to Shady Lane Road. (1 hour)

One of the state's extremely popular vacation spots, **Wisconsin Dells**, is 54 miles north of Madison via I-90/94. A frenzy of tourist shops, water parks, shows, and games detracts significantly from the original attraction, the Wisconsin River's tall sandstone cliffs and rock formations. You can see the latter on Dells Boat Tours' narrated rides; (608) 253-1561. Call (800) 22-DELLS or the Wisconsin Dells Visitor and Convention Bureau, (608) 254-4636, to order a travel guide.

16
THE HIDDEN VALLEYS
OF SOUTHWESTERN WISCONSIN

About 45 minutes northwest of Madison, just south of the wide Wisconsin River, two men built distinctly different houses in a breathtakingly lovely green valley near Spring Green. One of those men, famed architect Frank Lloyd Wright, was born here in 1867, kept returning, and chose the Wyoming Valley as the site for Taliesin, his "organic" architecture home of native limestone and sandstone. At Hillside School on the 600-acre Taliesin estate are the blocks given to Wright as a toddler by his mother, who wanted him to become an architect. Those wooden blocks evidently worked.

One can only wonder what might have influenced the other man, Alex Jordan, to build a house on top of a chimney of rock and then fill it with the weird and the strange. On the other hand, there's no doubt about why Norwegian immigrants chose to farm unglaciated southwestern Wisconsin's rumpled landscape of hardwood-forested ravines and valleys near Mount Horeb; it looks like Norway. This region nurtures unusual creativity. American Players Theatre performs Shakespeare in the woods a few miles from dairy barns; Global View sells Asian and African clothing and art in a country barn; and Barry Levenson opted out of a job as state assistant attorney general to start a Mount Horeb museum devoted to mustard. ◣

SOUTHWESTERN WISCONSIN

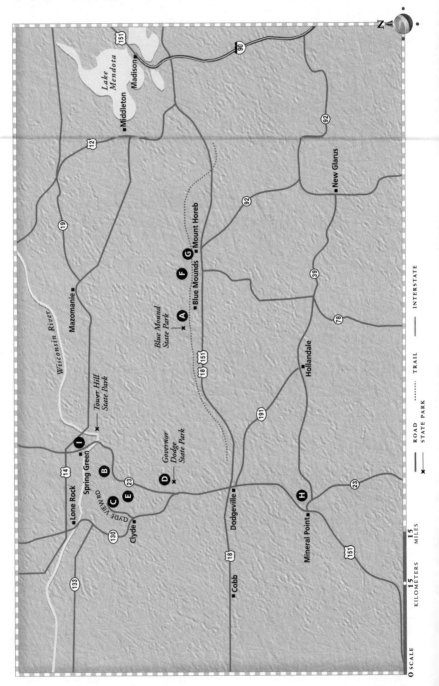

Sightseeing Highlights

A Cave of the Mounds

B Frank Lloyd Wright's Taliesin and Hillside School

C Global View

D Governor Dodge State Park

E House on the Rock

F Little Norway

G Mount Horeb

G The Mount Horeb Historical Museum

G The Mount Horeb Mustard Museum

H Pendarvis

I Wisconsin Artists Showcase and Jura Silverman Gallery

Note: Items with the same letter are located in the same place or area.

A PERFECT DAY IN WISCONSIN'S HIDDEN VALLEYS

Breakfast in Mount Horeb at Schubert's Old Fashioned Café-Bakery and stock up on their incomparable Swedish rye bread. Visit the Mustard Museum and Little Norway. Drive to Taliesin. On the way, pull off on the State Highway 23 scenic overlook to glimpse the House on the Rock. Tour Hillside School—or tour Wright's house if you can part with $35. Take an afternoon hike in Governor Dodge State Park. Dine at the Springs Golf Club Resort's Dining Room or picnic on cheese and fruit and that good Swedish rye on the American Players Theatre grounds before the play.

SIGHTSEEING HIGHLIGHTS

★★★ **Frank Lloyd Wright's Taliesin and Hillside School**—Taliesin, Wright's home for 50 years, sits on a hillside overlooking the Wyoming Valley. The entire 600-acre estate and the Wright-designed buildings on it—Taliesin, the Hillside School in which Wright based his Taliesin Fellowship (a training program for young architects still in operation today), Tan-y-deri House, Midway Farm, and Romeo and Juliet

Windmill—are a National Historic Landmark. Tour options: one- to four-hour tours of the buildings and grounds are offered seven days a week from May–October for $8–$50. On the low end of the price range is the hourlong Hillside School/theater/studio tour, conducted every hour seven days a week. Prices, hours, and days for other tours vary, and most require reservations. The walking, preservation, and house tours each last two hours. At the high end of the price scale, a four-hour estate tour includes the house. Tours start at the Frank Lloyd Wright Visitor Center, on State Highway 23, at the junction with County Highway C, 3 miles south of Spring Green. For details, call (608) 588-7900. (1–4 hours)

★★★ **House on the Rock**—As bizarre a creation as one is likely to encounter anywhere, the original house, built atop a 60-foot-high limestone rock tower, has been all but obscured by the proliferation of additional rooms and warehouses for the expansive exhibits. The House on the Rock is a huge complex today, requiring most of a day to explore in unhurried fashion. Inside are the personal collections of the late Alex Jordan, put on display for all to see. He also bought other people's collections, including music machines, the world's largest carousel, antique guns, hundreds of ship models, and on and on. A special Christmas season exhibit features a collection of 6,000 Santas. Jordan built the original house in the early 1940s, sculpting it to fit the towering chimney-rock's surfaces. He died in 1989, and facts about the mysteriously media-elusive Jordan are now being made available by House on the Rock staff. On the premises are restaurants and vast gardens. It all seems otherworldly and, well, more than a little strange. Admission: $3.50–$13.50, under 4 free. Hours: Open daily, 9 a.m., mid-March–late October. Last ticket sales are at 7 p.m., closing at 8 p.m. Memorial Day–Labor Day; otherwise, last ticket sales are at 6 p.m., closing at 7 p.m. A scaled-down holiday season tour from mid-November–early January, 10 a.m.–6 p.m., costs $1–$8. Closed Thanksgiving, Christmas Eve, and Christmas Day. Located on State Highway 23, between Dodgeville and Spring Green. Phone: (608) 935-3639. (3 hours–all day)

★★★ **The Mount Horeb Mustard Museum**—See what is claimed to be the world's largest collection of mustards—around 2,000 varieties. Watch a video about mustard, taste mustards until your tongue goes numb, and take some home. You have more than 400 mustards to choose from. Hours: Open 10 a.m.–5 p.m. daily. Address: 109 E. Main St., Mount Horeb. Phone: (608) 437-3986. (½ hour)

✷✷ **Global View**—It's a surprise to find a foreign bazaar in a barn out in the alfalfa-scented Wisconsin countryside. This unusual enterprise features handcrafted ritual objects, wall hangings, fabrics, and native costumes along with pictures and histories of the foreign-based artisans. If your timing is right, you can attend one of the festivals and special events hosted here, which in the past have included a chanting concert by the Gyuto Monks, creation of a sand mandala, and a celebration of Tibetan culture. Hours: Open May–October, 10 a.m.–5 p.m. daily, until 7 p.m. on Saturday. Open weekends November and December; call for hours. Admission is charged for special events. Address: 6593 Clyde Rd., between County Road C and State Highway 130, 8 miles west of Taliesin. Phone: (608) 583-5311. (½ hour or more)

✷✷ **Governor Dodge State Park**—Named for Henry Dodge, governor of the Wisconsin Territory from 1836 to 1841, this 5,029-acre park offers a chance to scramble atop the Enee Point rock formations for lovely views of the countryside, especially when fall transforms the hardwood-forested hills into a patchwork quilt of red, orange, and gold. Two hiking trails start at the Enee Point picnic area. (See Fitness and Camping sections for more details.)

✷✷ **Little Norway**—This genuine Norwegian pioneer farmstead dates from around 1856. The Norse architecture buildings include a growing sod-roofed cabin, a storage bin and other outbuildings, and the Norway Building, modeled after a twelfth-century *stavkirke* (Norwegian church) and made in Trondheim, Norway, for the 1893 World's Columbian Exposition in Chicago. The farm, originally called *Nissedahle* (Valley of the Elves), sits in a wooded valley in the foothills of the Blue Mounds. Admission: $2–$6, under 6 free. Hours: Open May–October, 9 a.m.– 5 p.m.; July and August until 7 p.m. Guided tours. The museum is on County Highway JG, off U.S. Highways 18/151, 20 miles west of Madison. Exit Cave of the Mounds Road between Mount Horeb and Blue Mounds, go right on County Highway ID a quarter-mile to Highway JG. Phone: (608) 437-8211. (1 hour)

✷✷ **Pendarvis**—When miners from the Cornwall area of England came to mine the lead in this region between 1830 and 1848, they created a Cornish village of cottages in a ravine. Because the women signaled their miner husbands to come to dinner by shaking a cloth in the doorway, the village was nicknamed Shake-Rag-Under-the-Hill.

Costumed interpreters guide tours through the historic site now called Pendarvis. At the edge of the Pendarvis parking lot, you can follow trails past crevice mines and lead miners' badger holes on the 43-acre Merry Christmas Mine site. (In fact, lead miners' badger holes—dugouts in which early miners lived—are why Wisconsin is called "the Badger State.") Admission: $2–$5 to tour the village, under 5 free. The mine trails are self-guided and free. Hours: Open May 1–October 31, 9 a.m.– 5 p.m. daily. Last tour at 4 p.m. Address: 114 Shake Rag St., Mineral Point. Mineral Point is on U.S. Highway 151 about 10 miles south of U.S. 18, 48 miles southwest of Madison. Phone: (608) 987-2122. (1 hour)

✿✿ **Cave of the Mounds**—The architect of Wisconsin's National Landmark Cave, acidic water, took centuries to sculpt delicate stalagmites, stalactites, columns, and other formations. Part of the cave was shaped by the force of an underground stream, a phenomenon which gives visitors a chance to compare the effects of both chemical action and water on sandstone. Admission: $4–$8, under 5 free. Hours: 9 a.m.– 7 p.m. Memorial Day–Labor Day; 9 a.m.–5 p.m. weekends the rest of the year. Guided tours leave every 15 minutes daily mid-March–mid-November and every hour on weekends during winter. Located 3 miles west of Mount Horeb, just off Highways 18/151 on County Highway ID. Phone: (608) 437-3038. (1 hour)

✿ **Mount Horeb**—In this Norwegian-heritage town, carved wooden trolls parade on Main Street, standing guard over the precious metals and minerals the troll creatures have buried in the ground (or so the story goes). In the **Mount Horeb Historical Museum** on the corner of Main and 2nd Streets, exhibits replicating pioneer life include an 1870s Norwegian-American home. Donation requested. Hours: 12:30–3:30 p.m. Open second and fourth Wednesday each month and Saturday from Labor Day–Memorial Day. Phone: (608) 437-3645. (½ hour)

✿ **Wisconsin Artists Showcase and Jura Silverman Gallery**—More than 100 Wisconsin artists exhibit their work in a restored 1900 cheese warehouse. Hours: 10 a.m. to 5:30 p.m.; open Wednesday–Sunday from May–December, Friday–Sunday from December–April. Address: 143 S. Washington St., Spring Green. Phone: (608) 588-7049. (½ hour)

FITNESS AND RECREATION

Head for state parks for hiking, biking, and ski trails. Some offer snow-mobile trails as well. A state permit is required; there's usually an extra fee for off-road bike trails. **Blue Mound State Park**'s 9 miles of hiking and cross-country ski trails and 5 miles of off-road bike trails pass through oak and sugar-maple forests. Climb two lookout towers for views. The park is about 25 miles west of Madison. Take U.S. Highway 151/18 to Blue Mounds and follow the signs.

Military Ridge State Trail offers 39 miles of hiking/biking on an abandoned railroad bed and can be accessed from Mount Horeb, Blue Mounds (town), near Dodgeville, and from Governor Dodge State Park. Cost: Trail fees, $3–$10, are required by all bicyclists 16 and older. Phone: (608) 935-5119. Bikers can also tour the area via routes recommended in the Spring Green visitor's guide. One route runs from the Frank Lloyd Wright Visitor Center parking lot to Governor Dodge State Park, where it hooks up with the Military Ridge State Trail. This is moderate to challenging biking with some big hills. To get the visitor's guide, call (800) 588-2042. (Ask for the 1995 guide; the subsequent guides do not include the bike routes.)

Governor Dodge State Park's 5,029 acres include 26.6 miles of hiking trails, 18 miles of ski trails, 25 miles of horse trails (extra fee), 10 miles of mountain-bike trails, and 15 miles of snowmobile trails, all graced with meadows, wooded bluffs, and ridges. You can also swim, boat, canoe, and fish in the park's scenic lakes. Winter camping is allowed. Call (608) 935-2315.

Area golf courses include the **Springs Golf Club Resort**'s 27-hole Robert Trent Jones–designed championship course. Off Highway 23 between Dodgeville and Spring Green, go east on County Highway C, then follow Golf Course Road. Call (800) 822-7774.

Doby Stables offers one-hour rides in the state park for $12 plus a $3 trail fee; rides depart on the hour except noon. Two-hour rides are at 10 a.m., 1 p.m., and 3 p.m. and cost $24 plus a $3 trail fee. There's also a 45-minute ranch ride for $10. The stables are open daily May–October, 9 a.m.–5 p.m. Across from Governor Dodge State Park on State Highway 23. For reservations, call (608) 935-5205.

FOOD

Food in this area tends to be standard Midwestern fare, with the **Springs Golf Club Resort**, (800) 822-7774, the exception. Try the

SOUTHWESTERN WISCONSIN

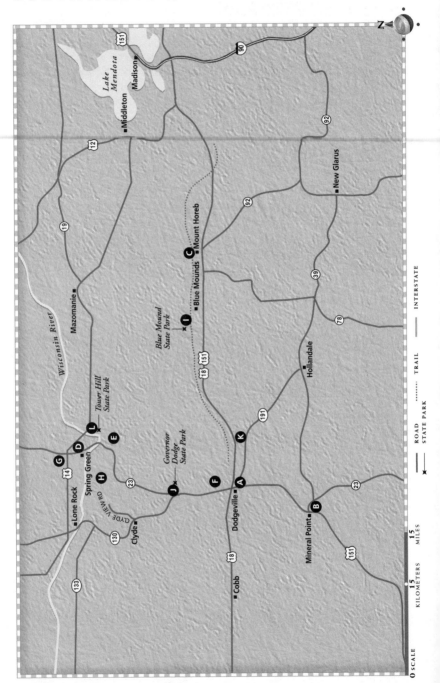

Lake Mendota

Middleton

Madison

New Glarus

Wisconsin River

Mazomanie

Blue Mound State Park

Mount Horeb

Blue Mounds

Tower Hill State Park

Hollandale

Governor Dodge State Park

Spring Green

Lone Rock

CLYDE VIEW RD

Clyde

Dodgeville

Mineral Point

Cobb

ROAD   TRAIL   INTERSTATE
STATE PARK

SCALE
0   15   MILES
0   15   KILOMETERS

Food

Ⓐ The Courthouse Inn Restaurant

Ⓑ Red Rooster Café

Ⓒ Schubert's Old Fashioned Café-Bakery

Ⓓ The Spring Green General Store

Ⓔ The Springs Golf Club Resort

Ⓕ Thym's Supper Club

Lodging

Ⓒ The H.B. Dahle House

Ⓓ Hill Street Bed and Breakfast

Ⓑ House of the Brau-Meister

Ⓒ Karakahl Inn Best Western

Ⓕ Pine Ridge Motel

Ⓖ The Prairie House Motel

Ⓖ The Round Barn

Ⓗ The Silver Star

Ⓔ The Springs Golf Club Resort

Camping

Ⓘ Blue Mound State Park

Ⓙ Governor Dodge State Park

Ⓚ Tom's Campground

Ⓛ Tower Hill State Park

Ⓖ Valley R.V. Park

Note: Items with the same letter are located in the same town or area.

mushroom strudel in the dining room but go on weekends to be sure Executive Chef Scott Finley is masterminding the kitchen. Dinner prices are in the $15–$25 range. The **Spring Green General Store**, 137 S. Albany in Spring Green, one block west of Highway 23 between Jefferson and Madison, (608) 588-7070, is a natural foods café and grocery with moderately priced homemade soups and sandwiches, weekend breakfasts, specialty beers, and, sometimes, live music. The **Courthouse Inn Restaurant,** across from the historic courthouse on Highway 23 in downtown Dodgeville, (608) 935-3663, has a generous Sunday brunch for around $7 and good food in a casual atmosphere. **Thym's Supper Club**, on State Highway 23, 1 mile north of Dodgeville, (608) 935-3344, has filet mignon for $16, pork chops, seafood, and chicken in a popular dining room. In delightfully charming (not yet too touristy) Mount Horeb, don't miss **Schubert's Old Fashioned Café-Bakery** on Main Street, serving wonderful food for breakfast, lunch, and dinner at a reasonable price, (608) 437-3393. At Mineral Point's inexpensive **Red Rooster Café**, 158 High St., (608) 987-9936, you can taste Cornish pasty and figgyhobbin.

LODGING

For luxurious resort trappings, the **Springs Golf Club Resort,** off Highway 23 and County Road C near Spring Green, (800) 822-7774, is the place to stay. Rates range from $110–$125 off-season and $165–$185 in the summer, plus a 15 percent service charge. Guests enjoy two-room suites, chocolate truffles, swimming pools, workout equipment, saunas, racquetball, tennis, and golf. The resort offers various packages. **Hill Street Bed and Breakfast**, 353 W. Hill St., Spring Green, (608) 588-7751, has seven rooms, five with private baths, in a 1904 Queen Anne Victorian house for $65–$75. The **Silver Star**, 3852 Limmex Hill Rd., out in the country south of Spring Green, west of Highway 23, (608) 935-7297, boasts its own café for European-style coffees, pastries, and entrees. The inn has nine rooms with private baths at $95–$135. Spring Green motels include the **Prairie House Motel** on U.S. Highway 14, (800) 588-2088, with spacious rooms, a recreation area, and exercise room, $42–$65 for doubles; and the **Round Barn**, on U.S. Highway 14 west of Highway 23, with doubles from $44.50–$89.50, depending on the season, (608) 588-2568.

You might want to stop at the renovated **Karakahl Inn Best Western**, 1405 Business Highway 18/151E, (608) 437-5545, Mount

Horeb, just to experience "Norwegian architecture in the Frank Lloyd Wright tradition"; doubles rates are $59–$119 for a suite. The **H.B. Dahle House**, 200 N. Second St., Mount Horeb, (608) 437-8894, is a 1908 Victorian Gothic home with two rooms and full breakfast for $95–$150. In Dodgeville, the modest, one-story mom-and-pop-run **Pine Ridge Motel**, a half-mile east of Highway 23 on County Highway YZ, is a clean, no-frills motel with rates from $35–$55, (608) 935-3386. (A plus is access to the Military Ridge State Trail across the road for your morning walk.) In Mineral Point, you can choose from ten bed and breakfasts and three motels. Try the **House of the Brau-Meister**, 254 Shake Rag St., (608) 987-2913, a Queen Anne with two guest rooms from $55–$65.

CAMPING

There is ample camping in the region, but this is a very popular summer vacation area. Campground reservations should be made early. Public campgrounds include **Blue Mound State Park**, off U.S. Highway 151/18, 1 mile northwest of Blue Mounds, (608) 437-5711. (See the Practical Tips chapter for state park fees and reservation information.) The park has 78 sites, four with electricity, and showers. **Governor Dodge State Park**, north of Dodgeville on State Highway 23, (608) 935-2315, has 267 campsites, 77 with electricity, and showers. **Tower Hill State Park**, off Highway 23 on County Road C, (608) 588-2116, has 15 sites with no electricity or showers. The main focus in the 77-acre park is an old lead-shot tower above the Minnesota River.

Private campgrounds include **Tom's Campground** near Dodgeville at 2751 County Highway BB, (608) 935-5446. From Dodgeville, go 6 miles east on U.S Highways 151/18, 2 miles south on County BB, and left 700 feet on Highway 191. There are 96 sites, 50 with electricity, six pull-throughs, pay showers, a playground, and basketball; open April–October. Rates are $14–$16 for RVs and $8–$10 for tents. At **Valley R.V. Park** in Spring Green on U.S. Highway 14, (608) 588-2717, rates are around $15 for 18 sites, 15 with full hookups, three with electricity; showers, groceries, laundry. Open three seasons.

NIGHTLIFE AND SPECIAL EVENTS

The premier area entertainment is **American Players Theatre**, a theatrical company performing Shakespeare and other classics in an outdoor amphitheater. Highly rated and professionally polished, the theater draws big crowds. Located off Highway 23, County Road C, and Golf Course Road near Spring Green. The season, mid-June through the first weekend in October, features four plays with rotating repertoire. Tickets range from $17.50–$30; (608) 588-2361 or (608) 588-7401. Last season's performances included Shakespeare's *King Henry V* and Oliver Goldsmith's *She Stoops to Conquer*. There are picnic grounds with a shelter, tables, and grills, or you can buy gourmet box lunches as well as desserts and beverages on the grounds.

Special events include the **Spring Green Arts and Crafts Fair** downtown on Jefferson Street, the last full weekend in June, (800) 588-2042; the **International Hog and Cow Calling Contest** in Dodgeville in July, (608) 935-5993; and the **Annual Mount Horeb Art Fair** in July, (608) 437-5914.

Scenic Route: Highway 33 from Reedsburg to La Crosse

For an intimate encounter with Wisconsin's Hidden Valleys countryside, take Highway 23 north from Spring Green to Reedsburg. If you're a Norman Rockwell fan, stop at the Museum of Norman Rockwell Art at 227 S. Park, open year-round, (608) 524-2123. Then follow picturesque State Highway 33 west as it twists and turns, passing through the quaint towns of Wonewoc and Hillsboro. The highway descends into a deep valley, then climbs the steep hills into wooded Wildcat Mountain State Park, (608) 337-4775, where you can hike the bluff trails to "ooh" and "ah" over sweeping vistas of forested hills and green valleys. Head for the picnic area in the northern section of the park for glimpses of the Kickapoo River far below and to hike the Old Settler's Trail (about 3 miles long). Should you decide to linger, the park offers 38 campsites with showers but no electricity. There's also a horse-trail campground. Northwest of the park, between Ontario and Cashton, highway traffic includes horses pulling

HIDDEN VALLEYS SCENIC ROUTE

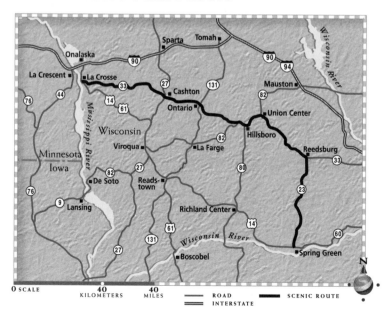

black buggies—evidence that a community of Amish live here. Wander down a few country roads, and you'll see bonneted women and barefoot children hoeing the gardens, and draft horses at work in the fields. In schoolyards during recess, long-skirted girls and black-clad boys play tag, running and laughing. Be sure to stop where signs offer goods for sale: the Amish sell maple syrup, quilts, handcrafted hickory furniture, and other wares, but not on Sundays. Leave your camera in the car—the Amish prefer not to be photographed. From Cashton, you can continue on Highway 33 west into La Crosse and connect with the Great River Road. Or follow State 27 north to I-90, which you can follow east to connect with I-94. From there, you are poised to head northwest to the Twin Cities or southeast to Madison and Milwaukee. Whichever way you go, you can feel a little smug about having driven State Highway 33, one of the Northern Heartland's prettiest roads. ◣

APPENDIX

METRIC CONVERSION CHART

1 U.S. gallon = approximately 4 liters
1 liter = about 1 quart
1 Canadian gallon = approximately 4.5 liters

1 pound = approximately ½ kilogram
1 kilogram = about 2 pounds

1 foot = approximately ⅓ meter
1 meter = about 1 yard
1 yard = a little less than a meter
1 mile = approximately 1.6 kilometers
1 kilometer = about ⅔ mile

90°F = about 30°C
20°C = approximately 70°F

Planning Map: Minnesota/Wisconsin

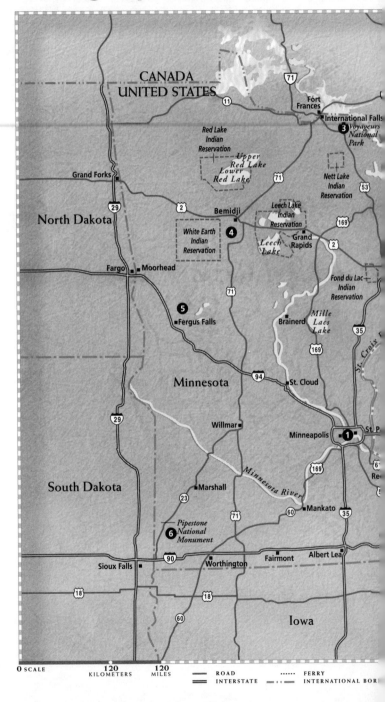

CANADA
UNITED STATES

Fort
Frances

International Falls

3 Voyageurs
National
Park

Red Lake
Indian
Reservation

Upper
Red Lake
Lower
Red Lake

Nett Lake
Indian
Reservation

Grand Forks

North Dakota

Bemidji

Leech Lake
Indian
Reservation

White Earth
Indian
Reservation

4

Leech
Lake

Grand
Rapids

Fond du Lac
Indian
Reservation

Fargo

Moorhead

5

Fergus Falls

Brainerd

Mille
Lacs
Lake

St. Croix

Minnesota

St. Cloud

Willmar

Minneapolis

St. P

South Dakota

Marshall

Minnesota River

Re

6 Pipestone
National
Monument

Mankato

Sioux Falls

Worthington

Fairmont

Albert Lea

Iowa

| 0 SCALE | 120 KILOMETERS | 120 MILES | ROAD | FERRY |
| | | | INTERSTATE | INTERNATIONAL BOR |

Not all lakes and rivers are shown on map.

INDEX

Maps Index

Other Books from John Muir Publications

Rick Steves' Books

Asia Through the Back Door, 400 pp., $17.95
Europe 101: History and Art for the Traveler, 352 pp., $17.95
Mona Winks: Self-Guided Tours of Europe's Top Museums, 432 pp., $18.95
Rick Steves' Baltics & Russia, 144 pp., $9.95
Rick Steves' Europe, 528 pp., $17.95
Rick Steves' France, Belgium & the Netherlands, 256 pp., $13.95
Rick Steves' Germany, Austria & Switzerland, 256 pp., $13.95
Rick Steves' Great Britain, 240 pp., $13.95
Rick Steves' Italy, 224 pp., $13.95
Rick Steves' Scandinavia, 192 pp., $13.95
Rick Steves' Spain & Portugal, 208 pp., $13.95
Rick Steves' Europe Through the Back Door, 480 pp., $18.95
Rick Steves' French Phrase Book, 176 pp., $5.95
Rick Steves' German Phrase Book, 176 pp., $5.95
Rick Steves' Italian Phrase Book, 176 pp., $5.95
Rick Steves' Spanish & Portugese Phrase Book, 304 pp., $6.95
Rick Steves' French/German/Italian Phrase Book, 320 pp., $7.95

A Natural Destination Series

Belize: A Natural Destination, 344 pp., $16.95
Costa Rica: A Natural Destination, 380 pp., $18.95
Guatemala: A Natural Destination, 360 pp., $16.95

City•Smart™ Guidebook Series

City•Smart Guidebook: Denver, 256 pp., $14.95
City•Smart Guidebook: Minneapolis/St. Paul, 224 pp., $14.95 (avail. 2/97)
City•Smart Guidebook: Portland, 232 pp., $14.95

Unique Travel Series

All are 112 pages and $10.95 paperback, except Georgia and Oregon.
Unique Arizona
Unique California
Unique Colorado
Unique Florida
Unique Georgia ($11.95)
Unique New England
Unique New Mexico
Unique Oregon ($9.95)
Unique Texas
Unique Washington

Travel✦Smart™ Trip Planners

All are $14.95 paperback.
American Southwest Travel✦Smart Trip Planner, 256 pp.
Colorado Travel✦Smart Trip Planner, 248 pp.
Eastern Canada Travel✦Smart Trip Planner, 272 pp.
Hawaii Travel✦Smart Trip Planner, 256 pp.
Kentucky/Tennessee Travel✦Smart Trip Planner, 248 pp.
Minnesota/Wisconsin Travel✦Smart Trip Planner, 240 pp.
New England Travel✦Smart Trip Planner, 256 pp.
Pacific Northwest Travel✦Smart Trip Planner, 240 pp.

Other Terrific Travel Titles

The 100 Best Small Art Towns in America, 256 pp., $15.95
The Big Book of Adventure Travel, 384 pp., $17.95
Indian America: A Traveler's Companion, 480 pp,, $18.95
The People's Guide to Mexico, 608 pp., $19.95
Ranch Vacations: The Complete Guide to Guest and Resort, Fly-Fishing, and Cross-Country Skiing Ranches, 528 pp., $19.95
Understanding Europeans, 272 pp., $14.95
Undiscovered Islands of the Caribbean, 336 pp., $16.95
Watch It Made in the U.S.A.: A Visitor's Guide to the Companies that Make Your Favorite Products, 328 pp., $16.95
The World Awaits, 280 pp., $16.95
The Birder's Guide to Bed and Breakfasts: U.S. and Canada, 416 pp., $17.95

Automotive Titles

The Greaseless Guide to Car Care, 272 pp., $19.95
How to Keep Your Subaru Alive, 480 pp., $21.95
How to Keep Your Toyota Pickup Alive, 392 pp., $21.95
How to Keep Your VW Alive, 464 pp., $25

Ordering Information

Please check your local bookstore for our books, or call **1-800-888-7504** to order direct and to receive a complete catalog. A shipping charge will be added to your order total.

Send all inquiries to:
John Muir Publications
P.O. Box 613
Santa Fe, NM 87504